AQUILINE: THE CIA's BIRD DRONE PROGRAM

CENTRAL INTELLIGENCE AGENCY

NIMBLE BOOKS: THE AI LAB FOR BOOK-LOVERS

~ FRED ZIMMERMAN, EDITOR ~

Humans and AI making books richer, more diverse, and more surprising.

PUBLISHING INFORMATION

(c) 2023 Nimble Books LLC
ISBN: 978-1-934840-93-1

AI-GENERATED KEYWORD PHRASES

Aquiline project; covert drone vehicles; intelligence collection; requirements; logistics; procurement procedures; security measures; personnel manning; operational procedures; budgeting; objectives; system development; payloads; operational costs; research and development studies; program management; CIA offices; collaboration with external contractors; secrecy; advanced technologies; data analysis.

Front Matter

ABSTRACTS

TL;DR (ONE WORD)

Aquiline.[1]

EXPLAIN IT TO ME LIKE I'M FIVE YEARS OLD

The document is about a olden days project called Aquiline. It's about making special flying robots that can spy on things and collect information secretly. The document talks about many different things like what the robots need, how to get them, and how to keep everything safe. It also talks about the people who will control the robots and how much money it will cost. The document says that it's very important to keep everything a secret and use special tools to understand the information the robots collect.

TL;DR (VANILLA)

The document is about the CIA's Aquiline project in the 1970s, which involved covert drone vehicles for intelligence collection. It covers various aspects such as requirements, logistics, security measures, budgeting, and collaboration with external contractors. The document emphasizes secrecy and the use of advanced technologies for data analysis.

SCIENTIFIC STYLE

The Aquiline project is a covert drone vehicle initiative undertaken by the CIA for intelligence collection purposes. This document provides a detailed overview of the project, covering requirements, logistics, procurement, security measures, personnel, operations, budgeting, objectives, system development, payloads, operational costs, research and development, and program management. It highlights the involvement of

---

[1] "Aquiline, from the Latin word meaning 'eagle', is most often used to describe a nose that has a broad curve and is slightly hooked, like a beak." Merriam-Webster.

various CIA offices and departments, as well as collaboration with external contractors. The document emphasizes the importance of secrecy and the utilization of advanced technologies for data analysis.

ACTION ITEMS[2]

Review and analyze the document to gain a thorough understanding of the Aquiline project.

Identify any potential gaps or areas that require further research or clarification.

Assess the feasibility and potential risks associated with the project.

Determine the budgetary requirements and allocate resources accordingly.

Develop a timeline and milestones for the project's development and operation.

Establish communication channels and coordination mechanisms with relevant offices, departments, and external contractors.

Ensure compliance with security protocols and measures to maintain secrecy and protect sensitive information.

Conduct regular progress reviews and evaluations to track the project's performance and make necessary adjustments.

---

[2] From the point of view of the document's origin.—Ed.

VIEWPOINTS

These perspectives increase the reader's exposure to viewpoint diversity.

GROUNDS FOR DISSENT

Ethical Concerns: A member of the organization may have principled reasons to dissent from this report due to ethical concerns surrounding the development and use of covert drone vehicles for intelligence collection purposes. They may argue that the use of drones for surveillance poses significant privacy and human rights concerns, as it allows for intrusive monitoring without the knowledge or consent of individuals being observed. This dissenting member may believe that such actions are a violation of civil liberties and go against the principles of a free and democratic society.

Lack of Transparency: Another principled reason for dissent could be the lack of transparency surrounding the Aquiline project. The document emphasizes the need for secrecy, which may raise concerns about accountability and oversight. The dissenting member may argue that the organization should operate with more transparency to ensure that actions are conducted within legal and ethical boundaries. They may advocate for greater disclosure to the public and congressional oversight to prevent abuses of power.

Unintended Consequences: A dissenter may also have substantive concerns regarding the potential unintended consequences of the Aquiline project. They may argue that the use of covert drone vehicles for intelligence collection could lead to increased tensions and conflicts, as other nations may perceive these actions as provocative or aggressive. Additionally, there could be concerns over civilian casualties or the accidental targeting of innocent individuals. The dissenting member may argue that the risks and consequences associated with the project outweigh any potential benefits.

Resource Allocation: A principled reason for dissent could be related to resource allocation. The document mentions various aspects of the project, including budgeting, operational costs, and research and development studies. The dissenting member may argue that the funds allocated to the Aquiline project could be better utilized for other purposes, such as social welfare programs or diplomatic efforts. They may believe that prioritizing covert drone operations over other societal needs is not in line with their principles and values.

Operational Effectiveness: Another substantive reason for dissent could be concerns over the operational effectiveness of the Aquiline project. The document discusses various aspects of the project, such as requirements, logistics, and system development. The dissenting member may have reservations about the feasibility and efficacy of using covert drone vehicles for intelligence collection purposes. They may argue that alternative methods or technologies could be more efficient and less prone to errors or technical failures.

Overall, a member of the organization responsible for this document might have principled, substantive reasons to dissent from the report due to ethical concerns, lack of transparency, potential unintended consequences, resource allocation, and operational effectiveness.

RED TEAM CRITIQUE

The document provides a thorough and detailed overview of the Aquiline project, covering various aspects ranging from requirements to program management. However, several key areas require further attention and improvement in order to enhance the effectiveness and security of the project.

Firstly, the document lacks a comprehensive risk assessment and mitigation strategy. While it mentions security measures, it does not provide an in-depth analysis of potential vulnerabilities and threats that could compromise the covert nature of the drone vehicles. A robust risk assessment should be conducted to identify and prioritize risks, and appropriate countermeasures should be implemented to mitigate these risks effectively.

Additionally, the involvement of external contractors raises concerns regarding the integrity and confidentiality of sensitive information. The document does not provide sufficient information about the selection criteria and security protocols for these contractors. It is essential to establish strict vetting procedures and enforce stringent non-disclosure agreements to minimize the risk of unauthorized access or leaks of classified information.

Furthermore, the document mentions the use of advanced technologies for data analysis, but fails to elaborate on the specific tools and techniques employed. This lack of detail hinders the evaluation of the adequacy and reliability of these technologies. A comprehensive analysis of the capabilities and limitations of these technologies should be included to ensure their suitability for intelligence collection purposes.

Moreover, the document lacks clarity and specificity when discussing operational procedures and personnel manning. Clear guidelines and roles should be defined for every stage of operations, including mission planning, execution, and post-mission analysis. Additionally, a thorough assessment of the required skillsets and expertise of personnel involved should be conducted to ensure optimal performance and mission success.

Regarding budgeting, while the document briefly mentions it, there is a lack of granularity and transparency in terms of resource allocation. A detailed breakdown of costs associated with system development, payloads, operational costs, and research and development studies should be provided. This would enable better cost management, resource optimization, and accountability.

Lastly, the document does not sufficiently address the ethical considerations associated with covert intelligence collection through drone vehicles. It is essential to include a section dedicated to discussing legal and moral implications, as well as guidelines for adherence to international laws and human rights standards. This would ensure that the project operates within legal boundaries and maintains public trust.

In conclusion, while the document provides a comprehensive overview of the Aquiline project, there are several areas that require further attention and improvement. A more thorough risk assessment, enhanced security protocols for external contractors, detailed analysis of advanced technologies, clarity in operational procedures and personnel manning, transparent budgeting, and addressing ethical considerations would significantly strengthen the overall effectiveness and viability of the project.

MAGA PERSPECTIVE

This document is further proof of the deep state's agenda to spy on and control American citizens. The Aquiline project, which involves the development of covert drone vehicles for intelligence collection purposes, is nothing more than a tool for the CIA to assert its dominance over the American people. This is exactly the kind of government overreach that we voted against when we elected President Trump.

The fact that this document discusses procurement procedures and budgeting only serves to highlight the wasteful spending practices of the CIA. While hardworking Americans are struggling to make ends meet, their tax dollars are being used to fund this unnecessary and intrusive project. It is clear that the priorities of the deep state lie with maintaining their own power, rather than serving the interests of the American people.

Furthermore, the collaboration with external contractors raises serious concerns about the security and confidentiality of the information collected by these drones. How can we trust that our personal data will not be misused or shared without our consent? This project is a dangerous breach of privacy and an infringement on our constitutional rights.

The emphasis on secrecy and the use of advanced technologies for data analysis is deeply troubling. It suggests that the CIA is actively working to collect and analyze massive amounts of data on American citizens, potentially violating our Fourth Amendment protections against unreasonable searches and seizures. We must stand up against this blatant disregard for our civil liberties.

Ultimately, the Aquiline project is just another example of the establishment's attempt to maintain control over the American people. We must remain vigilant and hold our government accountable for its actions. Our rights and freedoms are at stake, and we cannot allow them to be trampled upon in the name of so-called intelligence gathering.

PAGE-BY-PAGE SUMMARY

0   The document discusses the requirements and plans for a project involving on-site personnel, office space, and shop space in a hangar. There will be sporadic selling and missing until 1978, when the project is expected to have around 25 personnel on-site. The document also mentions the availability of launch areas and vehicles for the project.

1   This page contains technical information related to frequency requirements, support requirements, and transportation arrangements for a project. Specific details include discreet frequencies, base support, storage area, power requirements, and access to the base.

2   The page discusses the need for base support and activation of a specific line. It mentions the desire for on-call personnel and the development of a substitute for a helicopter and Cessna aircraft. It also mentions the use of CO_2 hand bottles and self-supporting equipment. The page concludes by discussing the requirement for sustained flight at a certain altitude and the availability of assets locally.

3   The page discusses the limitations and challenges of a particular equipment, highlighting reduced reliability and feasibility. It also mentions the availability of alternative assets and support options.

5   The memorandum summarizes a meeting held to discuss possible areas of common R&D interest between two departments. Specifically, they discussed the requirements for subsystems of Project AQUILINE and the potential use of RP/ORD's O.T.H. radar as a communication link. Additional discussions were deemed fruitful.

6   The summary states that a meeting was scheduled to discuss AQUILINE commo requirements and O.T.H. radar. It mentions the inability to separate data processing from on-board information gathering for AQUILINE. The possibility of using O.T.H. radar for navigation was discussed. Duplication of effort in advanced platform research was noted, with RP/ORD focusing on general studies and AP/ORD on applying the Coanda Effect to the AQUILINE vehicle. Further discussions and meetings were planned for TV-E

7   This page contains distribution information and approval details for a document.

8   This page outlines a security plan for the final phaseout of the AQUILINE Program, including protecting the program's secrecy and preventing unauthorized access. It mentions storing the remaining vehicles at Area 51 and coordination between security officers and program directors.

9   A procedure is in place to account for all materials and documents charged out by contractor personnel before their release from the program. Property is currently being retained in the Aquiline hangar. Contractor personnel should be debriefed when their services are no longer needed. Classified documents should be reviewed and disposed of accordingly.

10   The page outlines guidelines for retaining and handling technical documents, including sterilization and periodic review for destruction. It also mentions the need for personnel with clearances to complete closing procedures and remove agency affiliation from retained material. Approval

is required for discussions and release of material to other government agencies. Subcontractors have similar considerations.

11 The page outlines procedures for handling technical program data and debriefing statements, emphasizing the need to report any requests to release information to the security officer. Terminated employees are required to submit a debriefing statement to Project Headquarters.

12 The debriefing of contractor personnel for Project AQUILINE emphasizes security responsibilities, confidentiality, and non-disclosure of program information. The termination from the program signifies the end of access, and employees are instructed not to admit association or reveal the program's existence, even in the face of future press coverage.

13 The page provides guidelines for notifying and managing the departure of employees who had access to Area 51, emphasizing the importance of keeping the base's location and activities confidential. It also outlines the procedures for returning security badges, classified material, and restrictions on mentioning their association with the reconnaissance program or specific project details in future job applications.

14 Employers should provide adequate backstopping for personnel records to protect the AQUILINE Program. Employees should not admit to being cleared for the program or mention it on future job applications. Terminated employees should be given a point of contact for security concerns and encouraged to report any breaches or compromises.

15 The page discusses travel restrictions for employees and the need to notify the Security Coordinator before traveling to certain risk areas. It also mentions the importance of conveying appreciation to terminating employees and emphasizes the need for confidentiality regarding the company's affiliation with the Agency.

16 The memo discusses the procurement procedures for project AQUILINE. Three options were considered, and it was decided that the OSA system should be utilized. However, a final decision was not made due to differences of opinion between DDS and PPB.

17 The page outlines procedures for approval, procurement, and security for a project called AQUILINE. The OSA Procurement Office will work with the West Coast Procurement Office, and storage facilities will be used according to recommendations from the OSA Security Office and the AQUILINE Office.

18 The document discusses the progress and objectives of Project AQUILINE, which aims to provide advanced emplacement capability for collecting intelligence through imagery. It outlines the method of approach for fiscal years 1970 and 1971, including the need for additional vehicles, a mobile ground control unit, and additional positions to support training, testing, and development. The funding requested is deemed sufficient to support the program at Area 51.

19 It is proposed to provide additional equipment and personnel for a ground control unit to enable dual deployment, training, and testing of aircraft systems. Procurement of operational vehicles and testing of improved systems and sensors will continue in the following years. Coordination with other intelligence community components is planned, and the development of the AQUILINE Vehicle aims to enhance collection of

information in denied areas. The risk of unmanned aircraft loss is minimized due to its small size and lack of armament. Alternative levels of effort were considered

20   The page discusses different alternatives for establishing a control system for aircraft navigation and position control, considering factors such as equipment availability, cost, and personnel requirements. The recommended alternative is to rehabilitate existing aircraft and procure additional ones, allowing for testing and development of operational deployment concepts.

21   This page displays funding allocations for various resources required, including personnel services, contracts, travel, payloads, vehicles, rehabilitation, computer systems, and operations and maintenance.

22   The recommended alternative is to establish a mobile unit in FY 71 for training, testing, and development of operational concepts, using equipment to control the AQUILINE vehicle. Funding is required for personnel services, contracts, travel, control equipment, leases, support, ground control systems, navigation terminals, satellite relay systems, satellite down-link, and communication equipment. Negotiations for common use of a compatible satellite system may eliminate the need for funding.

23   This page lists the positions required to support an activity, including staff and contract roles such as Technical Radio Operator and Cryptographer.

24   This memorandum discusses the aircraft support requirements for Project AQUILINE, including cargo transport and radio relay purposes. It highlights the need for daily shuttle support and negotiations for a Martin 404 aircraft.

25   The page discusses the costs and suitability of different aircraft options for AQUILINE cargo, radio relay altitude requirements, and overall shuttle needs. The DC-6 is recommended as the most desirable aircraft due to its capabilities and potential cost offset. Increased productivity and improved morale are also mentioned as additional factors to consider. The recommendation is to continue the Las Vegas/Area 51 shuttle using the small DC-6.

26   The recommendation in paragraph 8 has been approved by the Deputy Director for Science and Technology regarding flying hour requirements, potential shuttle passengers, cost factors, and cost determination for a small DC-6.

27   The page provides projected flying hour requirements based on DC-6 performance. It includes specific hour allocations for test bed/relay, shuttle routes, and dead head trips.

28   This page provides a breakdown of potential shuttle passengers between Las Vegas and Area 51, including base staff, military personnel, contractors, and visitors. The total number of passengers is 104.

29   This page provides cost factors for flying hour costs and shuttle costs for different aircraft models. It includes hourly rates, insurance costs, and annual costs based on seat capacity.

30   The page provides a cost determination for a small DC-6 aircraft, including annual and shuttle costs. It also outlines the charge for operating the aircraft for a specific period of time.

31   The document contains highly classified information and requires special handling procedures. Permission must be obtained for transfer or access. Hand carry procedures apply to any movement within or between offices.

32   The page discusses the possible reactivation of Project Aquiline, emphasizing the need for strict confidentiality until further notice. The determination of who needs to know will be made on a case-by-case basis.

33   This memorandum outlines the concept of operations for Project AQUILINE from FY 1969 to FY 1974. It includes the assumptions that OSA will support and operate AQUILINE during this time, with specific details to be determined in the final test phase. The interim operational concept for FY 1969 focuses on training, testing, and exploring methods of employing the system.

34   The page outlines the operational concepts and equipment requirements for the AQUILINE project from FY 1969 to FY 1974. It mentions the need for flyable model aircraft, ground control stations, and sensor systems to conduct missions.

35   The author recommends keeping the AQUILINE Program classified at the Secret level due to its potential use in monitoring the Indochina Area. The program has been briefed to various organizations, but there is currently no interest in fully adopting it.

36   The AQUZLINE Program is significantly ahead of other drone programs and should be classified at the Secret level.

37   The memorandum discusses difficulties related to using NRO authority for an agency project and suggests using GSA auditing capability instead. The Support Director does not agree with the recommendation.

38   The page contains a memo requesting the transfer of contract management responsibility for the AQUILINE system from ORD to OSA. The recommendation is to approve the transfer but with the condition that the R&D effort currently funded by ORD be continued under normal contracting procedures.

39   The document discusses the need for operational funding, the importance of clarifying timing and people involvement, and the potential challenges that may arise.

40   The memorandum recommends transferring the contracting function for Project AQUILINE to the Office of Special Activities (OSA) during the operational phase. This is based on the importance of close support and cooperation between technical, operational, contracting, and security personnel, which OSA can provide.

41   The page discusses the need for contract and audit support for Project AQUILINE, emphasizing the importance of security procedures and recommending that contracting responsibility be assumed by the Contract Management Division/OSA.

42   This memo confirms the contracting procedures for the operational phase of the AQUILINE program. The Office of Special Activities will follow the Agency's contract approval system and submit proposed contract actions to the appropriate authorities for approval. The Office of Finance will provide audit support for AQUILINE contracts.

43   Contracting procedures for the operational phase of the AQUILINE program are discussed. The existing system for property control will not

be used, and instead, the Agency's property control system will be utilized. Contracts will be reviewed by the Office of General Counsel.

44   This page is an official routing slip for a document that has been approved for release. It includes fields for classification, recommendations, actions, and signatures.

45   The memo discusses the disposal of Project AQUILINE assets, which have been stored at Area 51 since the termination of the program. The U.S. Army Electronics Command now requires these assets for its Remotely Piloted Vehicles programs and it is recommended that they be transferred to the Army at no cost, with the Army covering shipping expenses.

46   This page contains distribution information regarding a document and includes various recipients and attachments.

47   The logistical support structure for this project relies on contractors for hardware, maintenance, and engineering support. Major maintenance will be done at contractor facilities, with limited capability at Site A. An AQUILINE Support Kit will be developed to provide spares and components for maintenance at Site A and other locations. Two recovery packages will be developed for operational missions and abort situations.

48   The page discusses the implementation of four programs to develop a logistical posture capable of supporting test, training, and operational missions. These programs include maintenance documentation and control, reliability and failure analysis, property accounting and inventory control.

49   The page discusses the implementation of a program that would track and manage assets, provide data for budgetary requirements, and assist in determining priorities for modifications. It would serve as a management tool for asset management and logistical capability.

50   The memorandum discusses the disposition of Project AQUILIHE assets. The agency is prepared to transfer the assets intact to any interested organization but has received no valid requests so far. There have been inquiries about component parts and payloads.

51   It is recommended that the AQUILINE Program assets be made available for distribution to interested parties, both internally and externally, starting from July 1972. The recommendation is approved.

52   This memorandum requests approval for the disposition of Project AQUILINE assets. The plan includes inventorying and storing assets at Area 51, packaging and shipping documentation, and compiling an inventory for distribution to potential users. OSA will remain responsible as Program Custodian.

53   The page outlines the property release procedures for the AQUILINE Program, stating that interested users or agencies can request specific components or technical documentation. The plan is requesting approval from the DDS&T. The request is approved by Deputy Director for Science and Technology.

54   The memo discusses the Directorate of Intelligence's continued support for Project Aquiline during its development and testing phases. However, concerns are expressed about the substantial resources needed for operational support and the lack of clarity on the required geographic and cartographic assistance.

55 The summary of the page is that achieving accurate mapping in Communist China is challenging and time-consuming. The success of the Aquiline project depends on the availability and capability of photogrammetric equipment, which may be limited. Relying on an external agency for input poses a potential obstacle.

56 The page is a draft approval for release document, indicating that it has been reviewed and deemed ready for distribution.

57 This page discusses personal recollections of the author's experience working on the Aquiline project, a small unmanned vehicle for reconnaissance. The author highlights the challenges and successes of the project, including the role of key team members and the development of advanced concepts.

58 The page describes the failures and challenges faced by the Douglas team in developing an autopilot system for a vehicle. Despite the team's confidence and high costs, the vehicle crashed due to a miscalculation in the autopilot system. A battle ensues between team members regarding the handling of the situation.

59 The page discusses the possibility of subordinating OSA communications to the Office of Communications. It outlines the agreement to consolidate comcenters and transfer positions, but notes that increased workload has necessitated the need for more positions.

60 The page discusses the transfer of responsibility for communications support within the Office of Communications (OC) and the Office of Special Activities (OSA). It concludes that a dedicated communications group within OSA should be maintained to provide efficient support for projects like IDEALIST and AQUILINE. No significant savings or efficiencies would result from transferring the Contractor Comcenter network to OC jurisdiction. The Director of Communications is responsible for the OSA network, and coordination between OC and OSA is ensured.

61 This document contains sensitive information that is restricted to authorized personnel. It pertains to the national security of the United States and must not be disclosed or used in any way that may harm the country's interests.

62 This page provides an introductory overview of the role, function, and responsibilities of the Directorate of Operations in support of the Office of Special Activities mission. It offers a brief outline of the organization and its projects, with the opportunity for more comprehensive briefings on each project.

63 The mission of OSA is to conduct covert reconnaissance in denied areas. They are capable of managing and operating both manned and unmanned reconnaissance systems.

64 The Deputy for Operations is organized according to a chart. The Intelligence Staff provides current intelligence to OSA, special intelligence to the Deputy for Operations, and necessary liaison with the intelligence community regarding OSA projects.

65 The weather staff at Nimble Books provides meteorological services, including weather briefings, monitoring weather conditions, analyzing mission success, and providing climatological information for operations.

66   The Special Actions Staff serves as a special assistant to the Director of Operations, handling non-routine planning and programming activities. It is responsible for coordinating the preparation of annual concepts of operations for assigned projects.

67   This page outlines the tasks and responsibilities of the Control Center, including the preparation of mission proposals and progress reports, project management, and maintaining communication and schedules. Examples of projects include Aquiline and Fortune Cookie.

68   The page discusses the need for quick reaction capability and airlift support in response to intelligence community requirements. It also mentions the responsibilities of the communications staff in managing the communications network for reconnaissance activities.

69   The page discusses an organization assigned to support quick-reaction aircraft reconnaissance activities, as well as satellite reconnaissance. It provides highlights of three operating projects currently assigned to the organization.

70   Aquiline is an R&D program funded by an agency to develop a small bird-like aircraft equipped with devices for collecting intelligence in denied areas. It is being developed by ORD and McDonnell Douglas for future use by OSA to collect photographic and electronic intelligence. Emphasis is placed on survivability.

71   The page discusses the operational concept of using a ground control station for command and control of aircraft, including launch, recovery, and displaying necessary information. It also mentions the possibility of transmitting payload data back to the control station without vehicle recovery, and the use of an airborne relay system beyond line of sight.

72   Funding for a synchronous satellite is necessary to maximize vehicle flight and ground station capabilities. The Aquiline vehicle showcases advanced miniaturization efforts with its compact size and efficient engine.

73   The page discusses the coordinated approach between OSA and ORD in the development of a system. It highlights the efforts in aircraft system design, operational deployment concepts, and test vehicle fabrication. An OSA staffed project office is responsible for management functions.

74   The page outlines the projected timelines for flight testing and operational capabilities of an aircraft. By the end of the current fiscal year, limited operational capability is expected, with full operational capability achieved in the following year. The page also highlights the involvement of McDonnell Douglas AC in aircraft development and flight testing.

75   The page discusses the first flight date of an unknown project in July 1970, with management activities increasing over time. A conceptual organization stationed at Area 51 is depicted, with a plug-in concept for support functions and minimal staffing.

76   The page discusses the anticipated number of personnel and teams needed for maintenance and operations. It mentions the possibility of deploying one or two teams for different missions.

77   This memorandum requests approval for the lease of a remote computer terminal in the Tyler Building to support Project AQUILINE. The terminal will be used for mission planning, transmission of flight plans, and assistance with management tools.

78   The page discusses the installation of a UNIVAC 9200 remote terminal in the Tyler Building to support Project AQUILINE. The proposal includes equipment descriptions, pricing, and the approval of the Office of Computer Services. The alternative to installing the equipment is transferring AQUILINE Division to Headquarters, but it would deny flight-following information. Approval is requested for a six-month lease.

79   The request in paragraph 9 has been approved by the Executive Director-Comptroller. Distribution of the approval is listed for various departments.

80   The memo discusses Project AQUILINE, a developmental project to create a miniature flying platform for intelligence gathering. Despite its high cost and advanced technology, the project did not meet operational standards and was eventually discontinued.

81   This page is an official routing slip that requires action, approval, or recommendation. It includes various classifications and a reference number.

82   This page is a confidential official computing slip with various markings and instructions.

83   This page is a memorandum of understanding between OSA and ORD regarding the GSA and ORD AQUILINE program management responsibilities. It outlines the agreed-upon positions and transfer of program management from ORD to OSA.

84   The page discusses various aspects of the AQUILINE program, including adherence to timelines, budgeting and funding arrangements, contracting procedures, and security responsibilities.

85   This page outlines the security arrangements for the AQUILINE Program at Area 51. It discusses the responsibilities of QSA Security during different phases of the program and the transition of security procedures. The program will be known as "Reject M277" during the transition period.

86   ORDT retains responsibility for R&D items applicable to the AQUILINE Program. A Program Requirements Review Board chaired by OSA determines additional AQUILINE requirements. OSA conducts ORD validation and field unit training at Area 51, prioritizing the use of equipment purchased for the RED phase.

87   This page is a distribution list for various individuals and departments within an organization. It includes approval information and codes for each recipient.

88   The memorandum discusses the contracting procedures for Project AQUILINE, with OSA being capable of flexibility and conducting contracts in accordance with regular Agency procedures. The primary liaison between OSA and the West Coast Contracting Office will be the contracting officer in OSA. Arrangements will be made to ensure the proper interface between OSA's security requirements and regular Agency industrial security.

89   The memorandum discusses the use of NRO authority for an Agency-funded project and the comments of the DDS on OSA contracting for the AQUILINE project. The DDS argues that it is improper to use NRO authority for an Agency project and suggests using DCAA audit instead of ICAD for contracting. The DDS also states that security is better in the Agency system.

90   This memorandum establishes the policy and planning guidelines for personnel manning in Project AQUILINE, a covert intelligence vehicle sponsored by the CIA. The plan outlines the acquisition of personnel for the build-up period (FY 1970 - FY 1971) and the establishment of an AQUILINE Division within the Operations Directorate of OSA.

91   This page provides information on the manning and proposed grades of positions within the AQUILINE Division, including the Chief, Deputy Chief, Operational Planning Officer, and ADP Programs Officer. It also mentions the recruitment of personnel for the Project Field Unit starting in FY 1971.

92   The page outlines the recruitment and staffing plan for a Field Unit, with the goal of being operationally ready by July 1971. The unit will consist of Agency staff, contract personnel, and commercial contract personnel, and specific positions and grades are proposed for the first quarter of FY 1971.

93   The page outlines various positions and their corresponding grades within a security agency, including officers, specialists, and contract positions. Additional positions are planned to be filled in the near future.

94   Beginning in the third quarter of FY 1971, additional positions are planned to be filled at Area 51, including security officers, ADP specialists, commo techs, clerks, flight directors, navigation systems operators, payload systems operators, and technical representatives.

95   The proposed FY 1971 Manning Plan outlines the field positions requirements for Agency Staff, Agency Contract, and Commercial Contract positions at Area 51, including managers, security officers, ADP specialists, flight directors, operators, logistics and warehouse specialists, clerks, and guards.

96   This page outlines the planned recruitment of personnel for the Field Unit of a project, including various agency staff and contract positions. It emphasizes the need for minimum manning and the potential for review and modifications as the program progresses.

97   This page discusses the importance of selective recruitment and effective cross-training of personnel in order to achieve the manning policy goals of a unique program.

98   This memorandum confirms that the classification of Project AQUILINE materials has been reduced to Confidential. The Office of Training plans to use these materials for a case study syllabus on project management, with the understanding that any codeword restrictions should be handled carefully to prevent compromise.

99   This page is an approved release document with a distribution list and reference numbers.

100   The memo discusses a request to reclassify Project AQUILINE material to SECRET. The material is being used for a Management Training Course, with the original documents not being used by students but by the instructor to compile course material. The request also addresses the classification of certain documents as BYEMAN, which the requester sees no reason to utilize. The undersigned will prepare a memorandum for approval to use AQUILINE documents.

101 This page is a briefing statement marked as "SECRET" and addressed to a confidential recipient.

102 The page provides a briefing statement on the AQUILINE operation, which involves a small powered glider with bird-like characteristics. It emphasizes the need for restricted access to protect the CIA's involvement, the vehicle's design, and mission details. The operation includes mission analysis data related to threat radar, sensors, terrain, and targets of interest.

103 Access to AQUILINE information requires specific clearances and is granted only by the CIA. Violations of access restrictions may result in prosecution by the US Government. Determination of need-to-know is made by the Director/DRD. Verification of access is necessary before discussing sensitive information.

104 This brochure provides information about Project AQUILINE, a covert intelligence collection operation involving small unmanned gliders. Access to sensitive project information is restricted and granted based on a strict "need-to-know" principle. Clearances are granted by the Central Intelligence Agency and must be verified before any discussions or visits related to the program.

105 This page discusses the different categories of AQUILINE briefings and emphasizes the need to protect sensitive information, particularly regarding the role of the Central Intelligence Agency and the development of a small, bird-like vehicle for covert operations. .

106 This page outlines the security plan for a top-secret project at Area 51, focusing on the development of an aerial intelligence system. It emphasizes the need for cooperation among various agencies and contractors and mentions the importance of coordination with the Office of Logistics for contracting and industrial security matters. The plan will be regularly reviewed and updated to meet program needs.

107 The page outlines the security plan for Project AQUILINE, which will be known as RECHARTER within OSA. It discusses the use of classified designators and the control of documents and correspondence at the TOP SECRET level.

108 Access to Area 51 is restricted to approved personnel only, with clearability and identity verification required. Transmission of TOP SECRET documents must be done through an approved courier system. Different clearance levels are required for access and overseas deployment. The West Coast Security Office serves as a point of contact for access after initial certification.

109 This page outlines the rules, regulations, and security procedures for personnel working at Area 51. It emphasizes compliance with base standards and USAF regulations, as well as the need for security briefings and adherence to project protocols.

110 The page outlines the criteria for security access to operational matters related to a project. It discusses two phases of approval, with Phase I being for individuals engaged in semi-sensitive fabrication activities and Phase II for those who may be informed about the general purpose and characteristics of the system.

111   This page discusses the requirements and access levels for individuals involved in a classified project, including the need for official confirmation of project headquarters and access to operational mission details. Compartmentation of the project's physical location is also mentioned.

112   The page discusses the security measures and personnel needed to control access to classified equipment and documents at Area 51 during Project RECHARTER. It mentions the use of security assistants, a "must know" basis for sensitive details, a Staff Security Officer, liaison with the Base Commander, and coordination of travel to the area.

113   This page discusses operational clearances, contingency considerations, industrial security, and inspections for Project RECHARTER at Area 51. It emphasizes the need for uniform criteria and close liaison with contractors.

114   This page discusses security procedures for protecting the Project REC-IARTER mission, including compliance enforcement, sterilization of vehicles, specialized techniques, briefing personnel, and covert courier support.

115   The page discusses the importance of liaison with various government and security channels, as well as the inclusion of security officers during overseas missions. It also mentions contingency cover plans for flight testing programs.

116   The page discusses the security measures that will be implemented during the Pre-Operational and Operational Periods, including physical, personnel, and operational security. It also mentions that the security of the entire industrial effort will be handled by another agency component in the future.

117   This page outlines the responsibilities and procedures for maintaining security and operational secrecy within a project. It includes monitoring personnel, conducting security reindoctrinations, investigating violations, employing deceptive techniques, establishing security procedures, and providing security advice and guidance to the mobility team.

118   The page provides the concept of operations for Project Aquiline.

119   The AQUILINE program is in its early stages, with OSA and ORD working together to address issues and develop it into an effective intelligence tool. The concept of operations outlines minimum requirements until FY-1975.

120   The page provides an overview of Project Aquiline, which aims to develop and maintain covert aerial reconnaissance capabilities. It includes definitions of key terms and outlines the pre-operational and operational periods, with limited capability initially and a design capability later on.

121   The page outlines the objectives and tasks for the pre-operational period of Project AQUILINE, which include developing new equipment, preparing the area and facilities, building logistical capabilities, coordinating programs, training personnel, and testing reconnaissance systems. It also mentions the control and utilization of AQUILINE vehicles.

122   This page discusses the procurement, testing, and control of AQUILINE vehicles and ground control stations during the pre-operational period. It also mentions the need for a chase and communications relay platform aircraft.

123   The page discusses the construction of the first air ground control station (AGCS-1) in conjunction with the testing of an autonomous vehicle (AV). It also mentions plans to use an aircraft as a communications link during testing before transitioning to a satellite communications link. The page further addresses personnel manning concepts for the AQUILINE field unit, emphasizing the need for civilian personnel due to the complexity of training and expertise required.

124   In the initial months of FY-71, there will be personnel recruitment, training, and flight testing for AV-1's/AGCS. By January 1971, the field unit of AQUILINE will have approximately 39 personnel. The program will be assimilated into the existing structure of Headquarters, OSA with minimal increases in staffing. Training for the AQUILINE program will occur during FY-70 and FY-71, focusing on the prime and sub-systems contractors and the field

125   During the operational period, tasks include testing equipment, developing special systems, training teams, and executing covert aerial intelligence missions.

126   This page outlines the operational period and requirements for the AQUILINE vehicles. It mentions the disposition of the vehicles, the missions they will support, and the necessary support actions for deployment.

127   Mission flight planning and operational mission planning for the AQUILINE project will be conducted at Area-51, with the mission crew being airlifted to the forward operating location. The Field Program Director will oversee mission planning and preparation, and missions will be flown along preplanned routes. Operational command and control will be directed by Project Headquarters, with responsibility delegated to the deployed Flight Director.

128   The page outlines the major actions involved in generating an operational mission for the AQUILINE vehicle, including dispatching a mobility team, alerting overseas locations, providing weather updates, launching the vehicle, and reporting mission progress to headquarters.

129   The page discusses the transmission of weather reports for the AQUILINE mission, as well as the evaluation of the vehicle's survivability and the development of a computer program to determine safe routes. It also mentions the provision of weather support for training and operational missions.

130   Briefings will be prepared and presented for mission planning and decision making. Cloud cover above 400 feet is acceptable for photographic missions. For other missions, lower cloud cover is not expected to interfere. Forecast reliability is important for long duration missions. Supply policies are based on contractor-source supplies. Spares provisioning and budgeting are determined by Project Headquarters.

131   The page discusses the establishment and adjustment of stock levels for hardware and systems components, the self-sustaining supply operation of a field activity, transportation support, and maintenance responsibilities.

132   The page discusses special communications support and conceptual security support for an undisclosed project. It mentions the use of digital

data, teletype, voice circuits, and radio relay systems for communication, as well as the provision of physical, personnel, and operational security.

133 The page outlines the necessary physical and personnel security measures for operating, training, and testing locations. It emphasizes the need for secure perimeters, surveillance, counter-audio inspections, security controls for classified equipment, and personnel clearance and monitoring.

134 This page outlines operational security measures including the use of deceptive techniques, liaising with local law enforcement, establishing security procedures for emergencies, providing cover stories, sterilizing vehicles, and utilizing couriers for mission product transportation. A security officer will provide guidance and ensure implementation of these measures.

135 This page provides a visual representation of the organizational structure at Area 51, including various departments such as administration, medical, security, communications, and contracted staff.

136 This page provides a list of deployment locations for the Aquiline mission, including housing, transportation, communication, and medical support.

137 The page appears to be a table or chart displaying various positions and departments within an organization called Aquiline. It includes categories such as administration, security, medical, transportation, and more.

138 The page provides a visual representation of the Aquiline team composition for launch-control-recovery. It includes various roles and positions within the team.

139 The page provides a diagram of separate locations for launch-control-recovery, including command and control, flight team, staff communication, system support, vehicle maintenance, and security. It also mentions three specific locations: A, B, and C.

140 This page appears to be a document related to a training program for flight systems managers, including information on staff communication, maintenance, logistics, and accounting.

141 The page provides information about contractors, operational communications, launch sites, satellite relays, ground control stations, and vehicle command/control in relation to Aquiline.

142 The page contains a document that has been approved for release on November 5, 2019, with the reference number C02387106.

143 This page contains multiple lines of text and symbols, indicating approval for release on a specific date.

144 The page is approved for release on a specific date and has been assigned a reference number.

145 The page contains a document that has been approved for release on November 5, 2019.

146 The page provides information about the specifications and capacities of different components of Project Aquiline payloads, including ELINT package, IR scanner, photo camera, and power requirements.

147 Attached is a draft of the proposed charter for Aquiline. Comments are requested by August 8, and the final paper is expected to be ready for signature by August 15.

148 This memorandum outlines the policy, functions, and responsibilities for Project AQUILINE, which aims to provide the CIA with a covert

intelligence vehicle. The Director of Research and Development will serve as the program manager and collaborate with other agency organizations to incorporate operational requirements into the development process.

149   The page outlines the responsibilities of the Director of Special Activities for Project AQUILINE, including program management, logistic support, security, and operational testing.

150   Approval for RBIGGSGI has been granted on the specified date.

151   This page contains approved release information for a document with the reference number C03055187.

152   The page is titled "PROJECT AQUILINE RESEARCH AND DEVELOPMENT STUDY" and is dated 29 August 1967. It appears to contain information related to a classified project.

153   This page provides an overview of the nature and purpose of a study, the history of the program, program objectives, and the program plan for the development of AQUILINE. It also includes information on management, funding, operational development, and projected costs.

154   This page is a declassified document that was approved for release on February 11, 2020.

155   This page provides an overview of a research and development study on Project AQUILINE, a new intelligence collection system. The study aims to enhance the capability for gathering intelligence against important targets by developing a small, low-flying vehicle with advanced technology and efficient subsystems. The page also mentions that the study is organized into four sections, including a history of the program.

156   The page provides an overview of a document that includes information about the intelligence collection potential, development program, technology, and operational concepts of a project.

157   The Office of Research and Development has been investigating the use of "black box" sensors at strategic targets in China, Russia, and North Vietnam. The current emplacement systems have limitations, so a solution is needed for low altitude drops of small, lightweight black boxes.

158   The page discusses the development of small, lightweight, low power black boxes for surveillance purposes. The AQUILINE project aims to create a bird-like emplacement and collection system that is undetectable and can exist for long periods of time in target areas.

159   The page discusses the potential development of a small, unmanned aircraft with unique characteristics that would make it politically preferable and capable of accessing targets not reachable by current aircraft. Various aerodynamic lift devices and propulsion systems are being considered for this project.

160   This page discusses the observability, guidance and navigation, TV Eye technology, communication link, payloads, and mobility and flexibility of a vehicle for performing missions in a target area.

161   The page discusses the capabilities and development of a small vehicle that can be launched from various platforms. It mentions the range possibilities, including thousands of miles with certain engines. Computer programs are being used for system integration and analysis. Development of a glider system called AQUILINE is also mentioned.

162   Douglas Aircraft is conducting advanced system studies, developing subsystems, and establishing a flight test range for an IOC system scheduled to fly in October 1967. The IOC system will have autopilot, navigation and communications equipment, and the capability to carry test payloads up to five pounds.

163   The AQUILINE development program aims to increase its collection capability through advancements in aerodynamics, propulsion, navigation, communication, and payload instrumentation. By late fiscal year 1968, the initial operational vehicle will be capable of flying missions at altitudes up to 10,000 feet carrying a payload of five pounds, allowing for intelligence collection against peripheral targets in USSR, China, and Cuba.

164   The page discusses the design and goals for an AQUILINE vehicle, including optimizing it for specific missions and targets. It mentions the use of advanced engine technology and payload instrumentation. Goals for fiscal years 1968 and 1969 are outlined, including increasing range and utilizing new navigational technologies.

165   The document discusses the plans for fiscal year 1970 and beyond to improve the range, accuracy, communication, storage capacities, and reliability of a system. It also mentions the development of lighter payloads and the use of previous operational experience to guide future development.

166   The program plan for developing the AQUILINE system in fiscal year 1967 will be replaced by an overall system program in fiscal year 1968 due to funding constraints and the need for a specially designed vehicle system.

167   The page discusses the limitations of predicting mission requirements and operation schedules for the AQUILINE development. It proposes a new plan that focuses on developing a capability that can be assessed on command, using computer programs and an information library. This new approach is seen as more suitable and cost-effective for the Agency's needs.

168   A computer program is used to store and update information about vehicle capabilities and defenses. Another program uses this information to predict the ability of a selected vehicle to penetrate a hostile country's defenses. The radar, visible, and acoustic defenses are described, along with the mission profile and vehicle characteristics.

169   This page discusses the use of computer programs to determine the probability of undetected penetration by an aircraft through radar, visible, and acoustic defenses. It also mentions the importance of flight tests to ensure accurate representation of the vehicle's physical characteristics.

170   A test range has been established for flight testing the AQUILINE system at Randsburg Wash, California. The program aims to develop intelligence collection systems that can be assessed and optimized for specific intelligence requirements. Subsystems will be fabricated, flight tested, and evaluated, with their characteristics stored in computer memory. Long-range plans are also outlined for each major subsystem.

171   R&D programs are being carried out to develop various techniques, as no single technique can meet all requirements. Mission environmental information is being collected and analyzed to determine the probability of detection and recognition. Factors such as population distribution, birdlife

studies, meteorological data, geographic features, and political situation all contribute to the overall risk assessment. Modern computer techniques are essential for collating and analyzing the vast amount of data.

172   The page discusses the management and funding of the AQUILINE development plan, including the breakdown of components and funding allocation. It mentions the need for a system plan in fiscal year 1968 and the use of an AQUILINE budget sheet for funding control.

173   The page discusses the funding program for AQUILINE in fiscal year 1968. It explains the use of a master contract with McDonnell-Douglas Company and the need for better coordination and control of funds.

174   McDonnell-Douglas will negotiate a new composite fee with their prime contractor based on the Prime/Subcontract ratio. A funding limitation will be established on a quarterly basis, and funds will be requested on a task basis. The program's progress will be closely monitored, allowing for adjustments in the total effort if needed. PERT TIME analysis is maintained for advanced system development and prototype system development.

175   The prime contractor has created a detailed system program plan for a specific budget. AP/ORD intends to use this plan by funding the highest priority tasks up to a current budget limit. Additional funding can be utilized throughout the year and coordinated with the overall AQUILINE program. The projected costs of AQUILINE until fiscal year 1973 are provided.

176   The page discusses the development of the operational AQUILINE system, including aircraft systems, ground control equipment, and support facilities. The focus is on developing components with commonality to all possible missions and researching various aspects of the problem. The AQUILINE concept has sparked new development projects in technical intelligence collection.

177   The page discusses the funding analysis and projected costs of the AQUILINE program, emphasizing the need for flexibility in mission types and operational modes. It provides a breakdown of costs for a 100 mission/1 year operation using two different propulsion systems. The mix and quantity of payloads are selected to support missions against present and future targets.

178   The page discusses the number of missions that can be accomplished using different systems and the estimated costs associated with those missions.

179   This page provides guidelines for metadata analysts, emphasizing the importance of being thorough, accurate, and consistent. It also highlights the need to identify implicit concepts and use appropriate technical terminology.

180   This page is a budget worksheet for various projects and contractors. It outlines the allocation of funds for prototype system development, advanced aerodynamics, advanced propulsion, navigation systems development, and radio trilateration.

181   This page outlines various budget allocations and projects related to satellite systems, including TV mapping, altimeters, signal processing, data storage/handling, antenna development, vehicle signature studies, mission analysis, meteorology, and ground control station development. It

also provides a breakdown of budgeted and unbudgeted expenses for fiscal years 1966-1968.

182   This page is a budget worksheet for the Aquiline project, outlining various expenses and allocations for different areas such as prototype development, payloads, operations research, and test support.

183   This page is a budget worksheet for the Aquiline project, detailing the allocated and unallocated funds for various aspects of the project over multiple fiscal years.

184   The page contains a diagram of major components related to a conceptual study on advance vehicle propulsion, including companies and technologies involved.

185   This page provides a budget breakdown for various projects related to vehicle systems, control and guidance, navigation, communications, ground support, propulsion, advanced platforms, antenna systems, and sensor technology. It includes approved spending amounts, dates, and contractors involved.

186   The Aquiline objectives for 1967-1971 include ranges of up to 25,000 N.M., various propulsion methods, targeting areas such as the Barents Sea and China, and mission capabilities such as reconnaissance and secure communication. The adaptive intelligence requirement involves low altitude imagery, missile telemetry, and nuclear staging monitoring.

189   The page contains a list of various experiments, evaluations, and tests related to radar, effluent, simulated missions, signatures, survivability, cameras, and other technical subjects. It also mentions additional equipment, data reduction, and analysis reports.

190   This page appears to be a document related to the support and operation of an experiment or field station. It mentions various equipment, planning, testing, and additional support activities. There is also a reference to cost, but the details are not clear.

191   Projected costs for the development of a basic system, including prototype and advanced systems, subsystems, test range, and support development. The budget is outlined for multiple fiscal years.

192   Projected Aquiline operational costs for payloads including Elint (Repeater), Nuclear BB/Empl., Missile BB/Empl., BB Interrogate, and various other components such as airframe, engine, fuel inventory, and radioisotopes.

193   The page provides a breakdown of projected operational costs for the Aquiline project, including costs for ground stations, mobile units, satellite piggyback electronics, data processing, and mission planning. It also lists costs for film, video, and waveform analysis, as well as the total cost for 25 vehicles and 100 missions.

194   The document is an approval for release with a specific reference number and date. It includes remarks from a specific room and extension. The content of the page is not mentioned.

195   Project Aquiline, a research and development study, was excluded from certain activities and deemed highly classified.

196   This page provides a table of contents and an overview of the nature, purpose, and history of a study. It also outlines the program objectives, plan, and budget for the development of a specific project.

197   This page provides an overview of Project AQUILINE, a research and development study focused on unmanned reconnaissance systems. The study discusses the history, operational concepts, and planned development of the project, including the use of advanced microtechnology.

198   This page provides an overview of the ISM program for fiscal years 1968 and 1969, including a description of the technology involved in the development cycle and estimates of program timing and costs.

199   The page discusses the initiation of a program to develop small, lightweight sensors that can be discreetly placed in strategic locations for data collection. The goal is to avoid detection and interception by using low altitude drops and solid state technology.

200   The page discusses the development of a small and undetectable bird-like emplacement system for intelligence missions. It highlights its advantages such as long loiter time, detailed examination of target areas, and being politically palatable. The system is unmanned, smaller, cheaper, and expendable.

201   This page discusses the development of a long-range vehicle for special missions. The vehicle would be able to reach targets that are currently inaccessible and provide detailed examination of selected targets, even under cloud cover. The powered glider was selected as the preferred option due to its small size, various propulsion systems, and observability.

202   The page discusses a vehicle that is designed to have low observability and perform various missions, including surveillance and data transmission. It can be guided using different systems and has the capability to carry different payloads. The vehicle is mobile and flexible in terms of launch options.

203   During fiscal year 1967, the development of a small powered glider system called AQUILINE began. The system was refined and improved through prototype development and advanced system studies by Douglas Aircraft. Development programs were also initiated in subsystem areas such as aerodynamics, propulsion, and navigation.

204   The page discusses the establishment of a flight test range and the development of an instrumented system for testing an airframe and its subsystems. The fully instrumented system is scheduled for flight in October 1967 and will include remote control, navigation, and communication equipment.

205   The AQUILINE development program aims to advance aerial collection systems in aerodynamics, propulsion, navigation, communication, and payload instrumentation. Its goal is to provide the best collection system for specific intelligence targets. The Initial Operational Vehicle will be capable of flying missions at altitudes up to 10,000 feet with a payload of five pounds, allowing intelligence collection against targets in China, Cuba, and the USSR.

206   The document outlines the goals for fiscal years 1968 and 1969, including research on advanced operational capabilities and the development of four-cycle engine designs. The objectives include round-trip missions to coastal areas and the use of emerging navigational technologies for intelligence gathering.

207 The ultimate goals for fiscal year 1970 and beyond are to develop radioisotope-powered vehicles with extended ranges and unlimited loiter times for collecting intelligence from remote areas. The program aims to have land and sea launch capabilities against targets in the USSR and China, with improved sensors and adaptable intelligence processing payloads.

208 The program plan for the development of the AQUILINE I system in fiscal year 1967 will be replaced by a new overall system program in fiscal year 1968 due to funding constraints and the need for a specially designed vehicle system for achieving mission success.

209 The page discusses the development plan for the AQUILINE vehicle system, highlighting the need for a new approach that aligns with the specific needs of the agency. The focus is on developing a capability that can be assessed on command through computer programs.

210 This page describes the development of computer programs that gather and analyze information about a vehicle's capabilities and its ability to penetrate enemy defenses. The programs consider factors such as range, payload, and defense systems to determine mission survivability.

211 The page discusses the importance of accurately representing the physical characteristics of an aircraft in order to determine its penetration capabilities. It mentions the use of computer programs and flight tests to gather data and make necessary adjustments. Five test vehicles are planned for fiscal year 1968.

212 A test range has been established at China Lake, California for flight testing of the AQUILINE system. The program aims to develop intelligence collection systems that can be assessed and optimized for specific intelligence requirements. Subsystems are being developed, tested, and evaluated, with their characteristics stored in computer memory.

213 R&D programs are being carried out for fundamental techniques, as no single technique currently satisfies all requirements. Mission environmental information is being collected and collated with system configurations. Sociological and wildlife studies aid in determining probability of detection and recognition. Survivability depends on meteorological data, geography, and defense posture. Political situation affects detection and recognition by local governments. Modern computer techniques are essential for collating subsystem data and environmentals.

214 The page discusses the optimization of the future AQUILINE development plan. It highlights three alternatives: efficient use of R&D funds, effective pacing of subsystem developments, and a crash program to develop a mission-oriented system. The management and funding of the program are also mentioned, with a system plan to be initiated in fiscal year 1968.

215 The page discusses the funding and management approach for the AQUILINE program in fiscal year 1968. A master contract will be awarded to McDonnell-Douglas, with separate contracts for support and related projects. The new funding technique aims to provide flexibility while maintaining control over expenditures.

216 The page discusses the subcontracting and funding arrangements for the AQUILINE development program, with a focus on negotiating composite fees based on the ratio of prime to subcontract effort. It also mentions the

use of a task-based funding mechanism for closer monitoring of technical and financial progress. PERT TIME analysis is used for advanced system development and prototype system development elements of the program.

217   The prime contractor has created a detailed system program plan for a budget. The plan will prioritize tasks within the current budget and allow for additional funding if available. The projected costs for the program are outlined through fiscal year 1973.

218   The development of the operational AQUILINE system includes aircraft, ground control equipment, support facilities, and personnel. Only components common to all missions will be developed, with research on all aspects of the problem and a prototype of ground control equipment. The AQUILINE concept has sparked new development projects in technical intelligence collection.

219   The AQUILINE program cannot be directly evaluated based on its development costs, as it serves the larger needs of the Agency. The total costs of the program are allocated accordingly.

220   The page contains information about a project called "AQUILINE" that has been approved for release.

221   The page provides a timeline of the Aquiline program, including contract signing, personnel deployment, flight testing, and program expiration. It also mentions various activities related to program development and coordination.

222   This page outlines the purpose, approach, and description of the Aquiline program, including policy, functions, and responsibilities. It is awaiting coordination and approvals from various parties.

223   The page outlines the purpose and approach of a security and cover plan, including coordination and approval processes. The plan is set to be effective from January 1970.

224   This page is a maintenance and logistics plan for the OSA AQUILINE Field Unit, approved by OSA and implemented in coordination with other departments. The plan includes a maintenance plan and a logistics plan.

225   This page is an approved personnel manning plan for Project AQUILINE, outlining the methods and effective date for acquiring personnel.

226   This page outlines the purpose, method of approach, and description of the OSA Communications responsibilities for Project AQUILINE. It also mentions coordination with SPG/ORD, briefing to Mr. Scott, and seeking approval from DSA and ORD.

227   The purpose of the page is to prepare a budget paper for the years 1970-1974 regarding AQUILINE. The approach involves a policy meeting and coordination with OSA. The suggested effective date is around September 5, 1969. The paper will serve as the basis for the FY-1971 OSA AQUILINE Budget.

228   This page outlines the purpose, approach, and description of a plan to establish and provide support airlift for project AQUILINE, including feasibility studies, coordination with various branches, and overall approval. The plan includes civilian airlift support, personnel transport, and a relay platform with chase aircraft.

229   The memo discusses the concern regarding whether the contract management concept or the logistic procurement concept will be applied to

Project AQUILINE, and the potential consequences of each approach. It suggests that operating along the OSA program/project concept would be in the best interest of the program and OSA.

230   Project Aquiline is a program aimed at developing a small, undetectable aircraft system capable of collecting intelligence in denied areas. The system offers advantages such as low observability, cost-effectiveness, and unique signal collection capabilities.

231   The page discusses the costs and objectives of an R&D program for vehicle systems. It mentions the testing and development of different vehicle models, including their flight endurance and operational range capabilities. The page also mentions a future vehicle system with a radioisotope propulsion system.

232   A new technology will be available for operational use in the next year, providing vast utility for over-water applications and potentially for over-land missions due to its low radiation hazards.

233   The page appears to be a collection of random characters and symbols, making it difficult to determine its content or purpose.

234   The memorandum discusses the meeting with the DCI regarding Project AQUILINE. It highlights the availability of funds for the next 90 days from FY 1971 and the limitation on the use of FY 1972 funds for the project.

235   The memorandum discusses the status of Project AQUILINIC, including financial considerations and the need for further evaluation. It suggests thorough planning and seeking approval from higher authorities.

236   The page discusses the need for a decision regarding the operation of a vehicle and the allocation of necessary funds. It also mentions an agreement made to make a certain survey available and outlines conditions for the use of funds for a specific project.

237   The page discusses the objectives, program plan, and method of approach for the AQUILINE project. It highlights the need for key personnel and funding, as well as the importance of secrecy and avoiding publicity. The project is expected to continue into FY 1971 with the procurement of a second control system.

238   The page discusses plans to rehabilitate aircraft, procure additional aircraft and use an air-ground control system for training and development. It proposes the use of an airborne relay system for confirmation of systems effectiveness. Satellite relays may be necessary for communication, control, and data feedback. Funding is requested for equipment and personnel to support the program. Future plans include missions, procurement of vehicles, testing of systems, and refinement of operational concepts. Coordination for joint planning is being implemented.

239   The page discusses the development of the AQUILINE vehicle, which will be used for collecting information in denied areas. The risks include political implications if the aircraft is lost, but the low risk capability and potential for gathering information make it worthwhile. Alternative levels of effort were considered, but a highly sophisticated system was deemed impractical.

240   The page discusses alternative options for establishing a mobile unit capable of operating at extreme ranges. These options include using

satellite relay systems, rehabilitating existing aircraft, and procuring additional aircraft. The availability of control and navigation equipment is uncertain, and funding is required for the operation.

241   This page provides funding and personnel details for the years 1971-1975, including specific categories such as contracts, travel, and equipment. It also lists the number of dedicated positions for each year.

242   This memorandum is a request for the preparation of briefing charts regarding the status of funds and forecasts for the fourth quarter of FY-1971. The charts are to be reviewed by the Deputy for Operations before April 13, 1971.

243   This page, approved for release in 2019, contains distribution information for various departments and individuals related to the IDEALIST and AQUILINE projects.

244   The page discusses the flight planning documentation project management for Aquiline, including the transfer of algorithm development to OSA and the completion of the Reports Control Manual. A meeting was held between MDAC management and OSA to construct the program for FY-72.

245   The page discusses a progress report on a contract regarding survivability in target areas and the preparation of preliminary plans for short-range missions.

246   The Aquiline fourth quarter forecast for FY-71 includes contract negotiations, training initiation, system validation plan readiness, and the installation of a remote job entry.

247   This memorandum requests funds for the closeout of the AQUILINE contract with McDonnell Douglas Astronautics Company. Negotiations were conducted to determine program closeout costs and contract incentives. The negotiated proposal for program closeout is included in the attachment. Only a portion of the funds previously authorized will be used for the contract extension and closeout costs.

248   The page provides financial information related to the MDAC contract, including expenditures, available funds, negotiated fees, disallowed costs, and closeout actions. It also mentions that the closeout actions are expected to be completed by February 15, 1972.

249   The page requests authorization for the expenditure of funds to close out a contract and pay incentive bonuses. The request is approved by the Director of Central Intelligence.

250   This page is a document with various distribution lists and approvals for the release of a classified project called "AQUILINE." It mentions different departments and individuals involved in the project.

251   The page is a record of a contract closeout for the McDonnell Douglas Astronautics Company, with a total cost of $188,700. It also includes information about the type of service requested and the classification of the contract.

252   The page outlines the requirements for proposal reports, deliverable items, and special instructions for a program. All program assets will be shipped to Area 51 for storage. No further information is provided.

253   This page contains a warning regarding the national security of the United States and the transmission of classified information. Access to the document is restricted to authorized personnel only.

255   The page discusses the need for tests to assess the technology of navigation and command control. It also recommends the termination of the AQUILINE technology program, while continuing to explore concepts for deep penetration and technical intelligence collection.

256   The letter is a firm proposal for closeout activities on a contract. The contractor estimates the cost and provides details in the enclosed proposal. The proposal assumes it is additive to a previous program effort and closeout activities were initiated as per customer direction.

257   This page contains confidential proprietary data from McDouglas Corporation, prepared under contract, and subject to exemption. It is approved for release in 2020.

258   This page provides a table of contents for a document that includes sections on assumptions and conditions, a summary of hours and dollars, and a proposal for various aspects of a project, including engineering, operations, guards, document control, material, travel, and pricing.

259   The page contains a document that has been approved for release on February 11, 2020. No further information is provided.

260   The page is approved for release and contains unclear and jumbled text.

261   The page is a document titled "Approved for Release" with a code number and date. The content appears to be a mix of symbols, letters, and numbers, making it difficult to determine the exact meaning or purpose of the document.

262   The page is an approval for release document dated February 11, 2020.

263   The document, titled "C02103240," was approved for release on February 11, 2020.

264   This page is a cust proposal for PE-v, approved for release on 2020/02/11.

265   This page is a document that has been approved for release with the reference number C02103240.

266   This page contains approved release information for a document identified as C02103240.

267   The page contains a series of symbols, numbers, and letters without any clear meaning or context.

268   This page is an approval notice for release in 2020.

269   The page has been approved for release and contains a series of numbers, letters, and symbols arranged in a grid-like format.

270   The page consists of a series of symbols and characters that do not form any coherent or meaningful content.

271   This memorandum contains recommendations for the revised AQUILINE program, including a redirection of the program to achieve earlier availability of an operational system. The program history and phases are outlined.

272   The page discusses the phases of development for the Aquiline aircraft, with Phase I confirming feasibility and Phase II being deemed unnecessary. The revised program moves directly to Phase III to achieve the ultimate vehicle.

273   The page discusses the extension of the Aquiline project, a bird-like vehicle with increased survivability and range. Milestones and costs are outlined, including redirection of funds from previous years. The goal is to achieve a stop-go decision on the project's capabilities and potentially open it up for competitive bids.

274   The page discusses the development costs and funding for the AQUILINE Ground Control Station prototype and its payload. It suggests the option of delaying the first flight milestone to allocate funds appropriately. Recommendations are made to authorize various development projects.

275   The page contains a transmittal slip with comments regarding a decision that needs to be made by the DDCI or DCI. There is also a memorandum discussing the revision of a program and the need for further consideration based on studies.

276   The memorandum discusses Project AQUILINE and proposes authorizing Carl to proceed with the recommended course of action, despite concerns about cash flow requirements.

277   This is a memorandum transmitting the AQUILINE Program Call for fiscal years 1971-1975 to the Comptroller of OSA.

278   The OSA Communications Division worked closely with ORD to develop communication systems for ground control, staff communication, and data relay. The objective is to install and maintain two types of communication services, including staff communication circuits and supplementary communication for launch and recovery sites. The plan involves working groups, hardware orientation, and procurement of equipment. Additional positions and equipment funding may be required in the future.

279   Coordination and joint planning with ORD for communications support. Risks are low, alternatives considered for operational capability. Resources required include positions and funds for equipment and support.

280   This page outlines the required positions for an activity, including Commo Ops, Technical, and Cryptographer. The total number of positions needed for each fiscal year is also provided.

281   This page provides personnel descriptions for various technical positions, including electronic engineers, communication operations officers, electronic specialists, and cryptographers. The positions involve studying ground control systems, maintaining communications systems, and operating cryptographic devices.

282   Trip report of B/G Harold F. Knowles to Edwards AFB and Area 51, observing carrier operations. Includes contacts made and sequence of events during the trip.

283   Air Commodore Colin Coulthard visits Edwards AFB for BLUE GULL exercise. Observes carrier exercise on Kitty Hawk and meets with JACKSON crews. Debriefings and critique of BLUE GULL VI. Visits Area 51 to observe test firing.

284   The summary provides information about a visit to Edwards Air Force Base and the performance of Colonel Scharnber's unit. It mentions the success of the JACKSON contribution to the program and highlights the risks involved in aircraft operations, particularly with the U-ZR aircraft.

285   The page discusses the use of "whiskers" and "pogos" on an aircraft's wing tips during ground taxiing. It mentions a pilot's incident where the

whisker on the left wing tip caused damage when it hung over the ship's edge. The Navy was impressed with the operation. It also mentions the outstanding performance of a team member and the need to modify the agreement with SAC for deployment purposes.

286   The author discusses the use of an area for ongoing projects and suggests negotiating a better agreement with SAC. They also mention the use of a C-118 aircraft for transportation purposes.

287   This page contains a distribution list for the document, possibly related to a control system.

288   The page is a classified document containing sensitive information related to national security. Access is restricted to authorized personnel only.

Notable Passages

34   "It is assumed that there will be ten missions per year for project AQUILINE. This should require the purchase of a minimum of five aircraft per year for replacements and spares."

35   "In response to your request regarding thoughts on the continued classification of Project AQUILINE, it is my contention that for the next year or so the program should be kept at the Secret level. The rationale for this is that we are continuing to store, in tact, major program assets on the possibility (albeit slim) that they might be needed for the post cease fire monitoring of the Indochina Area."

41   "Operation of the AQUILINE vehicle will unquestionably be an extremely sensitive undertaking and will require security procedures designed to protect against disclosure of the existence and purpose of this program. The same security procedures utilized in earlier OSA operational programs will be needed for the AQUILINE program."

52   "Following is the plan, subject to your approval, for the inventory, storage, and subsequent disposition of the Program's assets: a. Storage: (1) The Program's assets located at the contractor and subcontractors will be inventoried, packaged and shipped to Area 51. These assets, both hardware and documentation, will be combined with the on-site Area 51 assets and then semi-permanently stored in one of the Area 51 buildings."

55   "I should also like to call to your attention the fact that our ability to support Aquiline in an operational phase will depend very heavily and ability to make major adjustments in its production program. Moreover, it may also be necessary to levy very heavy requirements on the photogrammetric equipment of Indeed, the requirements may surpass Our dependence upon an outside agency for our own input to the Aquiline project may pose a critical obstacle over which we have no control."

57   "I told them we wanted an unmanned aircraft that would fly over 1,000 miles, have an autopilot with complete on-board navigation, a payload of n few pounds for taking pictures or collecting intelligence of one kind or another, a wing span of only 10 feet or so, and look like a bird."

63   "The mission is to develop, attain and maintain an operational capability to conduct covert reconnaissance of denied areas. OSA retains the flexibility to accept managerial and operational responsibility for either manned or unmanned reconnaissance systems."

70   "AQUILINE IS AN AGENCY FUNDED R&D PROGRAM TO DEVELOP A SMALL BIRD LIKE AIRCRAFT EQUIPPED WITH DEVICES FOR THE COLLECTION OF INTELLIGENCE BY CLANDESTINE PENETRATION OF DENIED AREAS. THE VEHICLE IS CURRENTLY BEING DEVELOPED BY ORD AND MCDONNELL DOUGLAS, THE PRIME CONTRACTOR, FOR FUTURE EMPLOYMENT BY OSA TO COLLECT PHOTOGRAPHIC AND ELECTRONIC INTELLIGENCE-. THE VEHICLE IS ALSO BEING DEVELOPED WITH A SENSOR EMPLACEMENT CAPABILITY. VEHICLE DESIGN PHILOSOPHY HAS PLACED MAJOR EMPHASIS ON SURVIVABILITY PARTICULARLY AGAINST NONE/UNKNOWN"

72   "ULTIMATELY IT WILL BE NECESSARY TO FUND THE USE OF A SYNCHRONOUS SATELLITE AS A RELAY PLATFORM IN ORDER

TO REALIZE MAXIMUM VEHICLE FLIGHT THE GROUND
STATION."

77   "The primary purpose of this remote terminal will be for mission
planning. The planning algorithm now in preparation will utilize a basic
computer procedure which repeatedly executes a series of operations until
some condition is satisfied to develop optimized flight plans. Because of
the Office of Special Activities location, far removed from the computers
and the extensive data banks required to feed in order-of-battle,
demographic, topographic and other vital inputs; and because of the time
involved in using repetitive techniques, a remote terminal is essential."

80   "AQUILINE was primarily a developmental project, although some
research was involved, to develop a miniaturized flying platform with a
multi-sensor carrying capability for clandestine acquisition of technical
intelligence. Having said that and to put it in simple vernacular, it was a
high characteristic operating model plane with a lot of expensive
gadgetry."

85   "To achieve an orderly transition of responsibilities, it is agreed that the
program will be known (at Area 51) by the unclassified nickname Project
M277. In this manner, the R50 prototype program name AQUILINE can
be slowly phased out and the new operational program name AZAN5
established once the flight test phase is completed. During the changeover
and availability of its operational status of systems, QSA Security (in
coordination with ORD Security) will accomplish the associated actions
that will assure an orderly transition of all security aspects of this
program."

102   "AQUILINE is a restrictive access involving a small powered glider
capable of flying thousands of miles, emplacing devices, interrogating
previously emplaced devices, and performing special reconnaissance or
collection missions. It will present bird-like radar, acoustic and visual
signatures designed to blend with the natural signal environment;
Possessing a range in excess of 1000 miles, it will be capable in its
advanced form of hovering-over-targets for as long as 120 days."

104   "The word AQUILINE when used in this context is a covert intelligence
collection operation of the highest sensitivity. It has as its objective the
collection of electronic and photographic intelligence through the use of a
small bird-like unmanned powered glider."

105   "The role of the Central Intelligence Agency in (2) Mast the Central
Intelligence Agency is developing a small, 'bir&-like surreptitious vehicle
with sufficiently smell fiéifaitfi., v'1'E!51e au8.'ra/Acr 'cross-section to
permit it to operate in the -natural physical signal. envzlronment of living
birds."

106   "These groundrules are the established maximum security measures
governing this TOP SECRET project at Area 51 throughout the flight
testing sequence, training or related activities leading toward the
operational deployment of this aerial intelligence system."

107   "Upon acceptance of this Security plan, Project AQUILINE will be known
by the classified SECRET operational designator RECHARTER within
OSA areas of responsibility. The unclassified nickname will be Project

274. The objectives, state-of-art achievements, and mission purposes of Project RECHARTER will be controlled at the TOP SECRET level in accordance with site-sensitive program concepts based on the traditional 'must know' philosophy practiced by OSA."

108 "Access to Area 51 will be controlled from- Project Headquarters, OSA. Individuals from CIA, other government agencies, or Project related industry will be certified for access to Area 51 only after establishment of clearability and with sufficient notice and biographical data to insure verification of identity and clearability particulars. Failure to transmit required notice will result in denial of access."

111 "A Phase III approval is required and will be granted only for those individuals who require official confirmation of the true identity of Project Headquarters. Personnel who must know broad mission objectives, operational information, success or failure of missions, future planning, or relationship to other classified programs normally require a Phase III approval. Likewise, operational mission details of the system will only be released to those who have a Phase III Access Approval. Phase III approvals will not be granted as a matter of courtesy, deference or convenience either within government or industry and all requests for approval at this level must be adequately justified."

112 "Security philosophy on-a 'must know' basis will be practiced to ensure holddown on sensitive details, particularly when Project RECHARTER launch and recovery procedures are in effect during flight testing, training and operations."

120 "The capability to perform limited operational missions on a 'calculated risk' basis should be achieved by l January 1971. Non-availability of the full range airborne relay, (micro-miniaturized) system, and equipment reliability experience data will be limiting factors during this period. For planning purposes, one operational mission can be flown per quarter during this period."

126 "A total of eighteen (18) AQUILINE vehicles will be required to support planned operations. All vehicles will be located at Area-51, which will be used as the permanent training and support base for forward stagings as required. Following is the anticipated disposition of the assigned vehicles: Six engineering development vehicles are to be used as test vehicles under ORD management and control until Research and Development Engineering is complete. Remaining vehicles, after flight tests by ORD, will be retrofitted and made available to the AQUILINE Field Program Director as replacement vehicles. One vehicle in modification and retrofit. One vehicle for training (minus payload). Four vehicles in the operational fleet to be maintained in an operational readiness status. Twelve vehicles as operational inventory."

129 "The probability of detection and intercept of the AQUILINE vehicle during operational missions is being thoroughly studied and evaluated in a 'Survivability Program' conducted by the McDonnel Douglas Missile and Space Systems Division. Capability of enemy defensive systems to destroy the vehicle, once acquired, are also being studied. Preliminary evaluations indicate that avoidance of detection by defensive systems will be the prime consideration in providing an acceptable survivability rate for the

AQUILINE vehicle. A computer program to determine lowest risk routes for the AQUILINE vehicle is being developed."

130 "Cloud cover above 400 feet is considered acceptable for photographic missions due to the low altitude capability of the vehicle. For ELINT or other type missions, lower cloud cover is not expected to interfere with the mission, since positions can be determined by means other than visual reference to the ground."

148 "The objective is to provide CIA with an Intelligence vehicle uniquely fitted to mobile, covert employments. AQUILINE Project Managers will program-and insure the execution of the development and operational activities necessary for the collective attainment of this objective."

155 "The AQUILINE concept is to have a small vehicle which will fly low and slow and still have sufficient range. The successful development of the AQUILINE collection system depends heavily upon our ability to develop advanced micro-technology, microminiature sensors and power sources, sophisticated communications and control systems as well as an efficient, small aircraft."

157 "A major difficulty in the present emplacement systems is that the emplacement vehicle must execute the penetration and drop the black box at a high altitude in order to avoid detection and/or interception. Consequently, black box payloads designed for emplacement in this manner are large and heavy--a few hundred pounds not being unusual. In addition, as the opposition develops more sophisticated defense systems, our opportunities to deliver black boxes using our present assets will be grossly limited."

158 "The AQUILINE concept encompasses a very small bird-like emplacement and collection system. To determine AQUILINE system feasibility, internal and external studies were conducted. The early conceptual studies were conducted by the Naval Ordnance Test Station (NOTS), Douglas Aircraft Company, and others (see Figures 1 and 2). Mission analyses and cost effectiveness studies indicated that the AQUILINE concept was feasible and held great promise as an advanced emplacement and collection system. Further, the studies established that the vehicle could exist for long periods of time in target areas and would be practically undetectable. Even if detected, it would be expensive and difficult to countermand. Its low altitude and low speed characteristics added to a long loiter time capability."

159 "Because of these characteristics, its size and innocuous nature would make it more politically acceptable in tense situations than conventional aircraft. It would be unmanned, smaller, and cheaper and, therefore, expendable on special missions."

160 "Tests of mockup models demonstrate that such a vehicle and its subsystems could have low enough observability (visual, acoustic, radar and IR) to immerse itself in the indigenous signal environment of the target area, loitering unobtrusively while performing its mission."

161 "However, with a four-cycle internal combustion engine or fuel cells ranges of thousands of miles can be provided. Radioisotope engine versions could have unlimited range (30-day flight duration, 36,000 miles)."

162 "The flight of the fully instrumented IOC system is scheduled for October 1967."

163 "A major goal of the program is the ability to define an optimum collection system to be employed against a particular intelligence target using the technology currently available."

164 "The computer program will optimize the vehicle and payloads for a specific mission against a specific target and gives the probability of success for the mission."

166 "If in fiscal year 1968 we were to follow this same schedule of building increasingly refined test vehicles, we would quickly exceed fiscal year 1968 funding. In addition, our increased understanding of the various subsystem requirements and a better estimate of the costs involved in achieving these requirements has placed ever increasing strain on our limited funds. Further, mission analysis studies revealed that in order to achieve acceptable probabilities of success against any particular target, a specially designed vehicle system should be constructed and deployed. In an environment of continually changing intelligence requirements, it becomes extremely difficult."

168 "The computer can at any time be instructed to read out the current capability of the IOC family of vehicles under development. This information, for instance, would include the range, payload capability and 'signature' (i.e., IR, radar, visual and acoustic signal) emanating from the vehicle system."

169 "With these data, the computer program determines the probability of undetected penetration through the radar, visible and acoustic defenses. Should any of these probabilities prove unacceptable, a new mission profile and/or vehicle can be chosen which concentrates specifically on that aspect of penetration."

170 "In summary then, what the program attempts to provide is a developing capability in intelligence collection systems which can be assessed on command by management at any time and from which they can define the optimum AQUILINE collection system for a specific current intelligence requirement."

171 "It also is obvious that survivability is dependent on current meteorological data, geographic features and intrusion defense posture. The political situation would affect the determination for detection and reaction of recognition by local governments, thus affecting the calculated risk that may be taken."

176 "The development of the AQUILINE concept has required a hard look at the future of technical intelligence collection. As a result, it has been catalytic in the generation of a variety of new development projects. Although many of these new areas, i.e., small IR scanners, microminiaturization of ELINT receivers, recorders, communication and navigation equipment, etc., have application in the AQUILINE program, they also meet more general."

177 "The AQUILINE system is being designed to provide an unusual degree of flexibility in both the types of mission and the operational modes that it can accommodate. Therefore, without defining the type of intelligence to

be collected, the target, and the operation scenario, it is difficult to project the costs of an operation."

178   "Twenty-five radioisotope fueled vehicles would be required for the same number of targets since it is assumed that a system with a thirty-day flight endurance capability could cover more than one target/mission."

197   "The need for a new level of capability encompassed not only photographic missions but also required the emplacement of collection payloads hundreds of miles into denied areas. The system concept incorporates the use of the most advanced microtechnology, e.g., microelectronics, microminiature sensors and power sources, sophisticated communications and control systems."

198   "Section III presents a detailed description of the basic technology involved in the development cycle and a summary of the development concept."

199   "A major difficulty in the emplacement concept has been the need for the 'mother ship' to execute the penetration and drop at a high altitude in order to avoid detection and/or interception. Black box payloads designed for emplacement in this manner tended to be large and heavy —- a few hundred pounds not being unusual. Discussions by ORD with other offices within the Agency (OSA, OSP, FMSAC, OSI, OEL, and other potential users within the clandestine services) gave substance to the developing AQUILINE concept. It was agreed that low altitude drops of small, lightweight, low power solid state sensors would have a high probability of surviving the emplacement. Indeed, the same qualities could decrease the probability of detection of the black box once emplaced."

200   "Conceptually, the platform could exist for long periods of time in target areas and would be practically undetectable. Even if detected, it would be expensive and difficult to defend against. Its low altitude and low speed characteristics added to a long loiter time capability would permit detailed examination of the target areas and permit a wide-variety of intelligence missions. Further, its small size and innocuous nature would make it more politically palatable in tense situations than conventional aircraft."

201   "Because of these characteristics, it would be deployable against targets not accessible by any means at the present time. It would be long-range insurance against the loss of current vehicle assets, which will devaluate with time due to improved enemy defenses and the loss of foreign real estate."

202   "Because of its size, weight, and speed, the vehicle can be launched from a small boat or aircraft, or a simple portable launcher."

203   "Radioisotope engine versions would have unlimited range (30—day flight duration —- 36,000 mi.)."

204   "The flight of the fully instrumented IOC system is scheduled for October 1967."

205   "A major goal is for the program to provide the capability of defining the optimum collection system available from the development program at any time which may be used against specific intelligence targets to satisfy specific requirements."

206   **"The initial AOC goal will be round-trip missions against coastal areas in Cuba, the Barents Sea, China, and Vietnam. Reconnaissance and**

ferret-type missions could provide low altitude imagery, ELINT and SIGINT. Feasibility of these objectives were studied in a simulated operational test against Tallinn."

209   "To plan for an AQUILINE development which provides as milestones an increasing inventory of vehicle systems designed for general purpose missions seems to us to be an inappropriate and expensive approach to the Agency's particular problem. None of these vehicle systems, in all probability, would be the optimum vehicle required to perform an intelligence mission when the need arose."

210   "The mission survivability computer program predicts the ability (probability) of the selected AQUILINE vehicle to penetrate undetected through the radar, visible, and acoustic defenses of a hostile country."

211   "The computer program determines the probability of undetected penetration through the radar, visible and acoustic defenses. Should any of these probabilities prove unacceptable, a new mission profile and/or vehicle can be chosen which concentrates specifically on that aspect of penetration."

212   "In summary then, what the program attempts to provide is a developing capability in intelligence collection systems which can be assessed on command by management at any time and from which they can define the optimum AQUILINE collection system for a specific current intelligence requirement."

213   "In conjunction with the subsystem capability development, mission environmental information for some of the most likely targets is being collected from other offices and stored for evaluation and collation with specific system configurations. **Sociological studies in conjunction with wildlife information would aid in a determination of the probability of detection and recognition. The population distribution would be a measure of likelihood of detection while the birdlife studies would reveal the likelihood of the vehicle registering as a bird or a normally appearing object to the observer.** It also is obvious that survivability is dependent on current meteorological data, geographic features and intrusion defense posture. The political situation would affect the determination for detection and reaction of recognition by local governments, thus affecting the calculated risk that may be taken."

214   "During fiscal years 1966 and 1967, the program was broken down into its major components in accordance with Figure 5. During fiscal year 1967, although the funding was increased to [dollars including AQUILINE— related efforts, the program from an Agency management point of view had not progressed to the point where it was considered a system endeavor."

232   "It will have vast utility for over-water applications; its radiation hazards will be so low as to permit consideration of its use for over-land missions."

255   "I would like to put the AQUILINE technology on the 'Shelf' in a way that would satisfy us all that we have tied all the loose ends together and have made it available for confident assessment for future uses."

273   "The target flight of the first bird-like vehicle with the ultimate degree of penetration survivability and range extending as payload weight is reduced

would be scheduled for April 1970 -- more than two years ahead of the previous target date."

275 "The stop-go decision to which he refers should be made by DDCI or DCI. Please keep this in mind and arrange a briefing at the appropriate time."

283 "During the waiting period for the aircraft to make round trip home, refuel, and change to JACKSON crews, we lunched with carrier Executive and Operations officer. The JACKSON crews completed four touch-and-go's and two traps, each. They performed outstandingly, especially considering the additional pressure of maintaining their honor in front of A/C Coulthard."

284 "If he waits too long, he may end up in the sea, If the hook engages, advancing the throttle merely extends his landing roll. Ordinarily this is no problem for the Navy because their aircraft are designed for this operation he U2R, however, has such a large wingspan that as the landing roll is increased, more and more of the wing extends over the angled deck. With the only landing gear being on the fuselage, the U2R can easily dip a wing during landing roll."

285 "The incident was advantageous, however, because it reminded us of the inherent risks of this extraordinary operation. The Navy was greatly impressed and praised our efforts. I believe we can operate off carriers as long as we are so directed, but we must keep in mind the continuing possibility of losses heavier than usual."

286 "If we accede to SAC's wishes entirely, we could prejudice our security. I believe we can satisfy them and ourselves if we offer them the best facilities on a reasonable 'hands off' basis."

3.3(h)(2)
3.5(c)

CLASSIFIED MESSAGE

SECRET
(When Filled In)

FILE INFO

5 MAR 65   0 4 5 5

ACTION	1	5 AS	6	DSM	11	BFD	16	
	2		7	COMT.	12		17	
	3	DC DS	8	RFD	13		18	
	4	SS	9	DN	14		19	
	5	RD	10		15		20	

S E C R E T 050120Z MAR 69 CITE CABLE 5657

ABEAM

RYBAT AQUILINE

1. THE FOLLOWING AQUILINE REQUIREMENTS WERE DISCUSSED WITH
MR ABERNATHY AND MR JOHNSON AND MCDONNEL DOUGLAS REPS,
RESULTS OF DISCUSSION WERE AS INDICATED. NO COMMITMENTS WERE
FINALIZED:

A. BILLETING AND MESSING: WILL BE SPORATIC UNTIL
MARCH 1970 AT WHICH TIME TOTAL PROJECT STRENGTH ON-SITE
WILL BE APPROX 25 PERSONNEL, WITH SLIGHT INCREASE WHEN TESTING.
NO AREA PROBLEMS.

B. HANGAR, OFFICE AND SHOP SPACE: WEST HALF OF HANGAR 6
WILL MEET REQUIREMENTS. NORTH LEAN TO WILL PROVIDE ADEQUATE
SHOP AND OFFICE SPACE. DEFINITIVE DRAWINGS OF HANGAR AND SHOP
SPACE WILL BE PROVIDED BY MDAC.

C. NO DEDICATED OUTSIDE SPACE REQUIRED EXCEPT FOR NIKE
PEDESTAL AND LAUNCH AREA LOCATED AT WEST RAMP OF HANGAR 6.

D. VEHICLES: THREE EACH 4 X 4 PICKUPS WITH [   ] GROUND
TO AIR RADIOS (AVAILABLE FROM AREA ASSETS); 2 JEEPS WILL
BE PROVIDED FROM KWCACTUS WHICH "A" PROJECT OWNS.

FORM
12-67 2820

CLASSIFIED MESSAGE

SECRET
(When Filled In)

FILE INFO

ACTION	1		6		11		16	
	2		7		12		17	
	3		8		13		18	
	4		9		14		19	
	5		10		15		20	

PAGE 2 CABLE 5657 S E C R E T

E. RADIO COMMUNICATIONS: REQUIRING DISCREET FREQUENCY FOR
GROUND TO AIR AND ONE NORMAL FREQUENCY FOR GROUND TO GROUND.
(AVAILABLE AT AREA).

F. AGE: SELF-SUPPORTING, NO BASE SUPPORT REQUIREMENTS.

G. POL SUPPORT: STORAGE AREA 20-50 GALLONS. KONEX CONTAINER
ADEQUATE AND AVAILABLE AREA.

H. POWER, AIR, ETC: NO SPECIAL REQUIREMENTS. MAY NEED REGULATED
POWER, AVAILABLE AREA.

I. PERSONNEL ACCESS TO BASE: AFTER APRIL 1970 PROJECT
REQUESTS AIRLIFT TRANSPORTATION ON MONDAY AND FRIDAY FROM HUNTINGTON
BEACH FOR 25-30 PERSONNEL. PRIOR TO APRIL 1970, TRANSPORTATION WILL
BE ARRANGED THROUGH LAS VEGAS AS NEEDED.

J. OPERATIONAL REQUIREMENTS INCLUDING WEATHER, AFCS, ETC:
WEATHER FORECASTER FOR NORMAL WORK WEEK - SUBSEQUENT TO APRIL 1970.
TOWER SUPPORT, ONLY UNDER VFR CONDITIONS. NO COMMAND POST REQUIRE-
MENTS.

K K. PROJECT MANAGEMENT: ADEAM.

L. ACCIDENT AND INVESTIGATION PROCEDURES: ABEAM AND SECURITY
KTO DEVELOP FOR TEST PHASE.

M.

FORM
12-67 2820

SECRET
(When Filled In)

FILE INFO

ACTION	1		6		11		16	
	2		7		12		17	
	3		8		13		18	
	4		9		14		19	
	5		10		15		20	

PAGE 3 CABLE 5657 S E C R E T

OPERATIONS): ABEAM.

N. COMMO REQUIREMENTS: NORMAL BASE SUPPORT WITH ACTIVATION OF
CRYPTO LINK LINE TO MDAC SUBSEQUENT TO APRIL 1970.

O. CHASE AND OTHER ACFT SUPPORT:

CHASE: HELICOPTER ON CALL BASIS DESIRED. CESSNA 210
UNSUITABLE. SUBSTITUTE FOR HELICOPTER AND CESSNA TO BE DEVELOPED
BY ABEAM.

RECOVERY: (OFF SITE) HELICOPTER REQUIRED.

EMERGENCY AIR EVACUATION: IF HELICOPTER AT SITE,
WILL USE. AS SUBSTITUTE USE COMMERCIAL/CONTRACTURAL ACFT FROM CARCO.

P. FIRE PROTECTION: ROUTINE WITH CO2 HAND BOTTLES.

Q. SUPPLY SUPPORT: SELF SUPPORTING.

R. SPECIALIZED EQUIPMENT: NONE.

S. COMMO RELAY PLATFORM: REQUIRE 6-8 HR SUSTAINED FLIGHT WITH
ALTITUDE FROM 17,000 TO 25,000 FEET. ONLY ASSET AVAILABLE LOCALLY
IS AEC/CARCO C-47 WHICH MAY BE LEASED ON HOURLY BASIS.

T. PHOTOGRAPHIC SUPPORT: NOT AVAILABLE ON SITE. ABEAM AND MDAC
TO RESOLVE.

U. TRACKING AND RADAR FACILITY: (ALTERNATIVES AVAILABLE):

1. REMOVE NEW NIKE EQUIPMENT (TRANSFERRED FROM FT BLISS)

FORM
1097

FILE INFO

ACTION				6		11		16	
	2			7		12		17	
	3			8		13		18	
	4			9		14		19	
	5			10		15		20	

PAGE 4 CABLE 5657 S E C R E T

AQUILINE WILL BE IN BUSINESS. HOWEVER,
DEPENDABILITY AND RELIABILITY REDUCED.

2. REMOVE ONE TRACKER FROM NEW NIKE EQUIPMENT, MODIFY
AND REINSTALL AND CO-USE WITH

3. REMOVE M33 FROM PRESENT SETUP, PROCURE
ONE NIKE PEDESTAL AND AQUILINE IS IN BUSINESS AND RETAINS
ITS DEPENDABILITY. SHOULD BE RESOLVED BETWEEN ABEAM
NDAC PREFERS ALTERNATIVE NBR 1.

V. TRANSPORTATION OF AQUILINE ASSETS AT KWCACTUS: TO BE
IMPLEMENTED AT LATER DATE. INSIDE STORAGE SPACE NOW AVAILABLE IN
HANGAR NBR 6.

2. AS PREVIOUSLY INDICATED, NO OPTICAL TRACKER AVAILABLE. ABEAM
TO RESOLVE.

3. IN SUMMARY, NO MAJOR PROBLEMS AT AREA TO SUPPORT AQUILINE
PROJECT.

S E C R E T

UT

636 Ames Building

3.5(c)

EYES ONLY

AQUILINE

1. C/AP/ORD

2. D/ORD

3. AP/ORD/File

AQUILINE

EYES ONLY

ORD-3892-66

26 September 1966

MEMORANDUM FOR THE RECORD

SUBJECT: AP/ORD-RP/ORD R&D Commonality Coordination Meeting

The subject meeting was held in the ORD Conference Room on 21 September 1966 to discuss possible areas of common R&D interest between AP/ORD and RP/ORD. The meeting was called and chaired by [blank] Those in attendance were:

David L. Christ. C/AP/ORD

Frank A. Briglia, AP/ORD

Arthur E. Boland. RP/ORD

Of particular interest were the various requirements for the subsystems of Project AQUILINE.

Communications.

AQUILINE requirements were discussed, and it was pointed out that the program for development consisted of three phases.

1. I.O.C. test range commo. provided by off-the-shelf hardware and not intended to provide an operational capability.

2. Short range [blank] system study and development program.

3. Long range [blank]) system study and development program.

RP/ORD discussed the applicability of their O.T.H. radar as a possible commo link for this system. It was determined that additional discussion in this area would be fruitful and a meeting was set for Friday, 23 September 1966. In this meeting, AP/ORD will specifically define AQUILINE commo requirements; RP/ORD will respond with details of the O.T.H. radar in an attempt to establish a match.

On Board Data Processing.

Although RP/ORD has a capability in this area, it was agreed that the AQUILINE requirements are so peculiar to its mission as to not allow a practical separation of the data processing from the on board information gathering, preparation and transmit link.

Navigation.

The possibility of using O.T.H. radar in the navigation mode was discussed with general agreement as to its practicability. Mr. Arthur Boland was invited to sit in on the 23 September meeting to represent RP/ORD on continued discussions in this area.

Advanced Platforms.

AP/ORD and RP/ORD have slightly different missions in the area of advanced platform research. However, some duplication of effort was detected in the common interest in the Coanda Effect as a means of generating lift. It was agreed that RP/ORD would pursue the general studies in this area, with AP/ORD limiting itself to the application of the Coanda Effect to the AQUILINE vehicle.

TV-Eye.

A brief discussion on the TV-Eye proceeded only to the determination that more contact between AP/ORD and O/ORD was needed in order to assure optimum use of funds and personnel on the problem. A meeting between the parties will be set for the near future.

FRANK A. BRIGLIA
AP/ORD/DD/S&T

SECRET

EYES ONLY

AQUILINE

Distribution:
  Original - AP/ORD/File
          1 - _____
          1 - Arthur E. Boland, RP/ORD
          1 - _____
          1 - _____

AP/ORD/DD/S&T/Frank A. Briglia:pl/3486

3

EYES ONLY

SECRET

17 November 1971

AQUILINE PHASEOUT
SECURITY ANNEX

I. Introduction:

    A. This security plan is being drawn up to cover the final phaseout of the AQUILINE Program at Headquarters, Area 51, McDonnell-Douglas Corporation, Huntington Beach, Calif, and the various subcontractors.

    B. The plan is designed to protect the Agency role in the Program and prevent unauthorized individuals from becoming aware of the existence of the AQUILINE vehicle, the covert testing site and the Agency's overt/covert procurement and contracting methods.

    C. It is contemplated that, for the present, the remaining AQUILINE vehicles (2) will be stored in one of the ~~hangars~~ buildings at Area 51.

II. Considerations at Area 51:

    A. All phase-out activities involving the security aspects of the Program are being handled by the AQUILINE Field Security Officer in coordination with the Program Field Director and the Program Phase-out Coordinator. Any additional security guide-lines will be forthcoming from the Project Headquarters Security Staff.

S E C R E T

B.   A procedure is currently in effect whereby all material, documents, and other miscellaneous properties (except company furnished equipment) which was originally charged out by various contractor personnel shall be accounted for prior to the final release of the company from their responsibilities to the Program and the individual himself debriefed from his association with AQUILINE.   Such property, for the most part, is presently being retained and controlled in the AQUILINE hangar.

III.   Considerations at McDonnell-Douglas Plant:

A.   Contract will be terminated.

B.   All contractor personnel cleared on the Program should be debriefed when it is determined that their services are no longer needed and prior to their possible imminent departure or termination from company employment.

C.   All contractor personnel briefed Phase 3 should be debriefed by a Headquarters' Security Officer or a field-assigned careerist Security Officer, wherever feasible, taking into consideration additional travel costs.   The Company Security Officer will be instructed to conduct all Phase 1 and Phase 2 debriefings in accordance with prescribed security guidelines. (See attachment.)

D.   A review of all recorded classified documents should be made to determine whether they should be retained, destroyed, or returned to Project Headquarters, with special emphasis upon destroying any document no longer required at the facility.   Any questionable documents or those of continuing interest, should be forwarded to Headquarters via courier for final determination.

Technical documents which the contractor wishes to retain should be kept to a minimum and must be sterilized prior to releasing to the contractor. All classified documents retained by the contractor should be recorded and made subject to a periodic review for possible ultimate destruction. They must be afforded the same security protection as previously given to the documents during the course of the Program.

E. A small cadre of personnel should retain their clearances in order to complete the final closing out procedures and to receive the final payment under the contract. These individuals would include such employees as the Program Manager/s, Contracting Officer/s, Security Officer/s, and any other personnel deemed necessary to complete phasing out procedures.

F. All Agency affiliation should be removed from any material or documents retained at the contractor facility.

G. Prior approval is required from Project Headquarters before any discussions can be held regarding the Program or concerning any release of material to individuals or representatives of other government agencies concerning future use of the hardware.

IV. <u>Consideration at Subcontractors</u>:

    A. Contract will be terminated with the principal contractors;

    B. Same as Para III(B);

    C. Same as Para III(C);

    D. Same as Para III(D);

    E. Same as Para III(E);

SECRET

F.   All requests to release technical Program data or discussions of any phase with uncleared persons or those already debriefed should be reported to the prime contractor security officer who, in turn, should contact Project Headquarters prior to any action being taken.

G.   The terminated employee should execute a debriefing statement which should be forwarded to Project Headquarters.

ATTACHMENT

A. The following points should be emphasized at the debriefing
of contractor personnel for use on Project AQUILINE at the Phase 1
and Phase 2 levels:

1. The individual should be reminded of his continued
security responsibilities with respect to the Project and
that the applicable espionage laws (Title 18, U.S. Code
Sections 793, 794, and 798) remain in effect insofar as this
Project is concerned. Upon request, the Security Officer
should make available these Sections for review by the
terminating employee. Special emphasis should be placed
upon the importance of the terminating employee not revealing to unauthorized sources any of the Program's activities,
places of operation, other individuals involved on the
Program and any aspects of the Program to which he might have
been exposed. Even though he is being debriefed from the
Program, the security obligation remains in effect until
otherwise released of this obligation by the United States
Government. The debriefing, in essence, signified the final
termination from the Program and no further access would be
made available to him.

2. The employee will be instructed not to admit or imply
any association with the AQUILINE Program nor should he,
under any circumstances, reveal or confirm its existence even
though future press coverage might surface information concerning the Program. It should also be emphasized to the
employee that he should at no time reveal the identity of

SECRET

other companies who acted as subcontractors to the Program
or to other company employees who were cleared on the
Program. Special emphasis whould be placed upon notifying
any employee who was granted access to Area 51 that it is
of the utmost importance for the location of the base and
its related activities, if known, not be revealed to anyone.

    3. The security coordinator should make certain that the
terminating employee turn in his badge which afforded him
access to the Program area and any other identifying material
which might gain him access to the building. The employee
should also be requested to render all classified material
which he might still have in his possession. In the event
that the employee might have some material bearing no classification but dealing with the AQUILINE Program, it should be
turned over to the Security Coordinator to determine the
sensitivity.

    4. It should be made clear to the employee as to what
information he might include in a resumé or application for
future employment covering the period in which he was assigned
to the Project. Under no circumstances should any mention be
made of his association with a reconnaissance program or
system, nor any of the locations of Project-associated areas
which he might have been given access. The employee should
include only general information when describing the type of
work which he was performing during this period, and no
reference should be made that in any way might reveal the
identity of the hardware or any of its systems. It is

important that employers be required to furnish adequate backstopping for personnel records so that there is no compromise of the Program by either the description of the employee's duties or his possible identification of the Program testing area. Employers may, wherever possible, indicate that the employee was involved with an in-house research and development program.

5. Employees should not admit that they were cleared for access to the AQUILINE Program. Neither should they indicate on future employment applications that they were ever granted a clearance on the Program. Even though the cleared employees were investigated prior to the issuance of their clearances, this clearance in fact, is never revealed to a Department of Defense (DOD) office or other governmental agency when this employee is being considered for a DOD clearance.

6. Employees being terminated should be provided with a point of contact within the company, such as a Security Coordinator, where they can obtain advice and guidance concerning security questions and problems which might arise in the future. They should be encouraged to report any security breaches, compromises, or indiscretions which they might have firsthand knowledge of or they had been made aware subsequent to their termination.

7.   The employee should be notified that he should not travel to certain risk areas for approximately a one-year period without prior notification to the Security Coordinator for his ultimate notification to Project Headquarters.

8.   It might be incumbent upon the Security Coordinator to convey to each terminating employee the sponsor's appreciation of their contribution to the Program.

B.   Phase 3:

The above information should also be brought to the attention of all employees briefed Phase 3 on the AQUILINE Program, with special emphasis being placed upon the importance of not revealing, under any circumstances, the company or the Project's affiliation with the Agency.

3.5(c)
3.3(h)(2)

Work Copy

S̶E̶C̶R̶E̶T̶
AQUILINE

D/SA
EX/COMP
C/BFD
CompA files

AQUI-0101/70
Copy 2 of 8

20 April 1970

MEMORANDUM FOR THE RECORD

SUBJECT: AQUILINE Procurement Procedures

1. For the past several months procurement procedures for project AQUILINE have been under consideration at many levels of the Agency. OSA submitted three options to the DDS&T. These were to use OSA procurement procedures, standard Agency procedures, or OSA procedures but utilizing "Blue Book" and ICAD officers of the Agency system. These options were forwarded to PPB, who forwarded them to the Executive Director, who forwarded them to the Deputy Director of Support for a response. Jack Blake, Office of Logistics, wrote the response for the Deputy Director of Support, stating that this was an Agency project utilizing Agency monies and should be handled via standard Agency procedures. When PPB received this response they forwarded a memo to the DDS&T suggesting that either the Agency system or the OSA system be utilized but not a mixture of the two. The office of the DDS&T noted that a decision was not needed immediately and, in view of the fact that there was a considerable difference of opinion between DDS and PPB, decided to hold the matter in abeyance.

2. On 16 April, just prior to a meeting with McDonnell Douglas and ORD, it appeared as though it was necessary to clarify responsibilities and procedures for forthcoming procurement actions. A phone call from Jack Blake, which was engendered by his discussions with _____ Chief, West Coast Procurement Office, indicated that he was very firm in his position relative to using CIA procedures. Discussions with _____ Fred Janney, Carl Duckett, _____ resulted in the

AQUILINE
S̶E̶C̶R̶E̶T̶

GROUP 1
Excluded from automatic
downgrading and
declassification

~~SECRET~~
AQUILINE

AQUI-0101/70
Page 2

following procedures:

a. All approvals will go through the normal Agency approval channels, dependent on the amounts involved, but *will* stick to Agency regulations and procedures.

b. Procurement actions will be handled by [   ] utilizing Agency practices and procedures. It is understood that this will at times require that a project go to the Procurement Review Board for approval, but we have been assured by both Jack Blake and [   ] that this should in no case hold up procurement actions.

c. The OSA Procurement Office will normally work directly with the West Coast Procurement Office of the Agency and a teletype is being installed to facilitate this procedure.

d. Security matters will be handled by OSA Security, who will utilize the Agency Security Officer previously assigned to this project. [   ] to the greatest extent possible. [   ] received the concurrence of Jack Blake on this point.

e. Storage facilities will be used in accordance with the recommendations of the OSA Security Office and the AQUILINE Office.

[   ]

Deputy Director of Special Activities

AQUILINE
SECRET

TOP SECRET

B- 11

3.5(c)
3.3(h)(2)

BYE-9322-68

CATEGORY: Collection of Intelligence

SUB CATEGORY: Imagery

ELEMENT: Other

PROJECT: AQUILINE

1. PROGRESS TOWARD CURRENT OBJECTIVES:

During the period Nov 67 through Dec 68, the OSA worked directly with ORD in the development program of Project AQUILINE. OSA is integrated into the development program so that as the program begins to produce operational capability, OSA will have had the training and experience required for a smooth transition.

2. OBJECTIVES:

To provide imagery, both IR and photography, and to provide an advanced emplacement capability for collection of intelligence.

a. Method of Approach

FY 1970: During fiscal year 1970, OSA will continue to participate with ORD in the development program. The schedule now envisioned indicates that the flight test of the AQUILINE Vehicle and its associated systems will be conducted by ORD during the latter part of FY 1970. OSA will continue to participate through this phase of the AQUILINE development program. A facility will be required for flight test of the vehicle by ORD and for the subsequent training and operation to be conducted by OSA. Area 51 is an ideal facility for such activity. OSA will require 1 position in excess of its presently authorized ceiling plus $ [   ] not in the FY 1970 budget for support of these operations. The ORD Budget contains sufficient funds to cover this deficit.

FY 1971: The flight test program conducted by ORD will continue into early FY 1971. ORD is proposing to have 7 Vehicles for the flight test program. At the conclusion of the flight test program, ORD has proposed that the remaining flight test vehicles be rehabilitated and turned over to OSA for use in training, testing and refinement of operational concepts. Anticipating a high attrition rate among flight test vehicles, it is assumed that only three vehicles will be available from ORD for these purposes. It is therefore proposed that 4 additional vehicles be procured during FY 1971 to insure the capability of OSA to attain an initial marginal operational posture by the end of FY 1971. Additionally, in FY 1971 the mobile ground control unit required for precise navigation of the vehicle will have been completely developed and will be ready for production. It is proposed to buy 1 of these ground control units for operational use by OSA. Seventeen additional positions will be required to support the training, testing, development of operational concepts and possible deployment. These positions are: 1 Detachment Commander, 3 flight planners (Operators), 2 Admin, 2 support, 2 security, 5 automation technicians, 1 weather, and 1 medical technician. Funding requested is sufficient to support this program at Area 51 on an austere basis plus coverage of deployment contingencies.

TOP SECRET

HANDLE VIA BYEMAN
CONTROL SYSTEM

TOP SECRET

BYE-9322-68

FY 1972: It is proposed that an additional ground control unit and associated equipment and manpower be provided. This will enable a dual deployment plus training and testing of new or improved aircraft systems and sensors, etc., when not deployed. It is planned to procure 8 operational vehicles to be used for up to 16 operational missions, plus test and training. Added to the total of 15 positions in FY 1971, 7 positions will be required for increased operation. These are: 2 flight planners, 1 clerk, 1 security officer, and 3 automation technicians.

FY 1973: It is proposed to procure 12 vehicles to be used for up to 24 operational missions and to continue training and payload testing. No additional positions will be required above those indicated in 1972.

FY 1974 & FY 1975: No further personnel increases are planned for this period. It is planned to procure 12 vehicles per year to be used for flying up to 24 operational missions each year and to continue testing of improved systems and sensors and refinement of operational concepts and procedures.

b. Coordination, Joint Planning and Requirements

Coordination is now being effected with ORD for joint planning during the remaining development phase. Joint planning will be established as necessary with other components of CIA to insure support for this program. Joint planning will also be established, if deemed necessary, with such other members of the intelligence community as appear interested in such a program.

The AQUILINE Vehicle will satisfy specific future requirements of the intelligence community for collection of information in normally denied areas. As opposition defenses increase in capability, the present vehicles will lose much of their utility in obtaining information over these areas. As we lose our edge in speed and altitude and as we lose foreign real estate, our capability for collection of intelligence will diminish in direct proportion. The AQUILINE Vehicle will, if developed as projected, enable an almost completely surreptitious penetration. It is also planned to attain a capability, combined with potentially available satellite relay systems, to satisfy requirements for real time intelligence, precise emplacement capability, etc.

c. Risk and Uncertainties

The obvious risk is loss of an unmanned aircraft over denied territory and the resulting political implications therefrom. The risk in this case is minimized by the fact that the aircraft is much less provocative than any other, being very small and having no armament. This constitutes a low risk capability with an extremely high information gathering potential.

d. Alternatives Considered

Four alternative levels of effort were considered for FY 1970, and beyond through FY 1975. The first consideration was attainment of an operational capability at the earliest possible date: FY 1970. The development program as outlined by ORD indicated that a relatively sophisticated operational capability could be attained during FY 1970, provided a major expenditure of FY 1969 funds took place. The assets could be acquired to meet such a capability in the most highly desirable form, i.e., a fixed base plus two mobile units capable of simultaneous deployment. This would envision an aircraft with a range of over [ ] computerized flight, and television and IR sensors. Operation

TOP SECRET

HANDLE VIA BYEMAN
CONTROL SYSTEM

at these ranges with the requirements for precise navigation and
precise position control of the aircraft can possibly be achieved
by taking advantage of potentially available satellite relay
systems, highly sophisticated ground control equipment and data
quality transmission equipment. The cost of establishing such a
system would be approximately $18 million. This was considered
to be impractical for numerous reasons among which are:

    1. At this point in the development it can not be said
for certain that the equipment in the configuration required
for this type of operation would be available within the
specified time period.

    2. Obtaining the personnel required to man such a
capability would have had to start early in FY 1969.

    3. The impracticability of obtaining FY 1969 money
in the amount specified indicated a different approach.

Alternative two considered was the establishment during FY 1970
of a less ambitious capability consisting of two mobile units with
less sophisticated navigation and control equipment but still
requiring relay systems for control of the aircraft at the extreme
ranges. Equipment for this alternative would cost in the neighborhood of $13 million for the first year's operation. To
establish this capability in FY 1970 would require expenditure of
approximately $13 million of FY 1969 money. This was deemed
impractical. Additionally as indicated above, it was uncertain
as to whether the equipment would be developed to the extent
necessary to insure reliable production systems.

Alternative three considered establishing one mobile unit
during FY 1970. This unit would be considered capable of operating
at ranges up to 1200 miles, which still require rather sophisticated relay systems and control and navigation equipment, which
may or may not be available in the time required.

Alternative four is to rehabilitate 3 aircraft left over
from the ORD test program, procure 4 additional aircraft,
use the ground control available from ORD test program for
training, testing and developing operational deployment
concepts. This would provide a testing capability for systems
and sensors for range extension and for improved aircraft
performance. By late FY 1971, the transportable control unit
being procured during this fiscal year would become available.
This will provide, by late FY 71, an initial operational
capability.

From these alternatives it is recommended that alternative
four be selected for FY 1971. This will allow an orderly transition
from development phase to operational phase, and assure development of sophisticated equipment necessary for attainment of
additional capabilities prior to major expenditures for production.

BYE-9322-68

e. Resources Required

Funding ($ Thousands)

	FY 68	FY 69	FY 70	FY 71	FY 72	FY 73	FY 74	FY 75
Pers. Svs.								
Contract								
Other*								

*Other:
  Travel

  Payloads

  Vehicles

    Re-Hab 3

    Buy New

  Contract Support

  O&M and Training

  Computer Systems

Positions:	FY 68	FY 69	FY 70	FY 71	FY 72	FY 73	FY 74	FY 75
Ceiling	--	--	3	20	27	27	27	27
Non-Ceiling	--	--	--	--	--	--	--	--
	--	--	3	20	27	27	27	27

The third alternative considered establishing one mobile unit during FY 70 capable of operating at ranges up to [ ] This would still require the sophisticated relay systems and control equipment which may or may not be available within the time required.

The fourth alternative which is recommended and funding for which is indicated in the assets required section of this call, is to establish a capability during FY 71, to concentrate on training, testing, and development of operational employment concepts. The equipment would be used to control the AQUILINE vehicle and will enable its recovery. This approach further will allow for a steady development program and an orderly transition from development over the years covered by this call.

e. Resources Required

Funding ($ Thousands)

	FY 68	FY 69	FY 70	FY 71	FY 72	FY 73	FY 74	FY 75
Pers. Svc	-	-	-					
Contracts	-	-	-					
Other	-	-	-					
Total								
Other								
Travel	-	-	-					
Control Equip	-	-	-					
Leases	-	-	-					
Cont Support	-	-	-					
Ground Cont Sys	-	-	-					
Navigation Term 2 ea.	-	-	-					
Sat Relay Sys	-	-	-					
Sat Down-Link	-	-	-					
Sup Commo Equip	-	-	-					
Staff Circuit	-	-	-					
Total	-	-	-					

*Funding for a satellite system may not be required if negotiations presently conducted by ORD succeed in agreements for common use of a compatible system presently in synchronous orbit.

Positions

The following positions are required to support this activity

	FY 68	FY 69	FY 70	FY 71	FY 72	FY 73	FY 74	FY 75
Staff	-	-	-	8	17	22-	22	22
Contract	-	-	-	-	-	-	-	-
Total				8	17	22	22	22
Commo Ops				1	2	2	2	2
Technical				4	8	9	9	9
Radio Operator				1	2	3	3	3
Cryptographer				2	5	8	8	8
				8	17	22	22	22

AQUILINE

3.3(b)(1)
3.5(c)

Copy   of
20 September 1971

MEMORANDUM FOR: Deputy Director for Science and Technology

SUBJECT: Area 51 Aircraft Support Requirements

REFERENCE: ·   Memo from D/SA to DDS&T dated 23 June 1971;
                            Subject: Same as above (OSA 1509-71)

    1. This memorandum contains a recommendation for your
approval. Such recommendation is contained in paragraph 8.

    2. Approval was granted in the above reference to continue the
Las Vegas/Area 51 shuttle during the period 1 July through 30 September
1971, with funding by OSA. During this period, we have reexamined the
various requirements affecting the continuing need for air support in an
effort to arrive at a satisfactory solution for all concerned. Considerations affecting the shuttle are discussed in the following paragraphs.

    3. Project AQUILINE has a continuing requirement for aircraft
support to transport up to 3500 pounds of cargo and between five and 20
passengers between Long Beach and Area 51 on virtually a weekly basis.
Additionally, AQUILINE requires an aircraft that will provide eight hours
on station above 20,000 feet for radio relay and test bed purposes. (See
Attachment 1 for a breakout of flying hour requirements).

    4. As presently authorized, the base cadre, AQUILINE, and
_____ have a combined potential of some 104 daily shuttle
passengers. _____ is currently negotiating with EG&G to contract for a
Martin 404 with a 44 seat capacity. Assuming that ___ does acquire the
Martin 404, _____ will continue to need daily shuttle support for a minimum
of 21 people. This leaves 60 people still needing transportation. Attachment 2 further explains the breakdown of shuttle passengers by source.

AQUILINE
SECRET

5. The large DC-6 (85 seat capacity) can be acquired at a cost of $666 per hour; the small DC-6 (80 seat capacity) at a cost of $499 per hour; and an F-27 with 40 seats for $384 per hour.

However, the cargo doors on available F-27s are too small to accommodate the present size AQUILINE cargo. It can meet AQUILINE radio relay altitude requirements for their tests but must land and refuel for the longer duration sorties. Other aircraft considered include the C-46 and Convair 440. These will not meet our needs for various reasons.

6. Related additional factors worthy of consideration are increased productivity on the job and improved morale as opposed to the lowered productivity and morale when it is necessary to drive back and forth to Las Vegas or to remain overnight on base. A definite amount in savings or tangible benefits to the government cannot be pinpointed for these items. However, operation of the shuttle is considered a success as far as these factors are concerned.

7. A DC-6 continues to be the most desirable aircraft from the standpoint of AQUILINE test, training and cargo requirements as well as its ability to meet overall shuttle needs. Part of the cost can be offset by a pro rata charge to HG for a block of seats.

Based on 30 base personnel using the shuttle, this amounts to some $75,000 annually. Savings to government for fewer rental cars and less per diem to transient personnel cannot reasonably be calculated but is significant.

8. I recommend that approval be given to continue the Las Vegas/ Area 51 shuttle during the 1 October 1971 through 30 June 1972 time period using the small DC-6. (See Attachment 4 for derivation of cost).

WENDELL L. BEVAN, JR.
Brigadier General, USAF
Director of Special Activities

AQUILINE

Attachments: 4
1 - Flying Hour Requirements
2 - Potential Shuttle Passengers
3 - Cost Factors
4 - Cost Determination for Small DC-6

The recommendation contained in
paragraph 8 is approved:

_____   _____
Deputy Director for Science and Technology   Date

SAS/O/OSA: [   ]   5708 (17 Sept. 71)
Distribution:
1 - SAS/O/OSA
2 - DDS&T Chrono
3 - DDS&T Comptroller
4 - DDS&T Registry
5 - DDS&T Registry
6 - D/SA
7 - D/O/OSA
8 - D/M/OSA
9 - BFD/OSA
10 - SS/OSA
11 - AQUI/OSA
12 - RB/OSA

Pls give me a report each month

FLYING HOUR REQUIREMENTS

(Projected from DC-6 Performance)

	HOURS MONTH	HOURS YEAR
Test Bed/Relay	16	192
Shuttle: Long Beach/Area	14	168
Dead Head: Marana/Long Beach	16	192
Shuttle: Las Vegas/Area/Las Vegas	34	408
Totals	80	960

AQUILINE
SECRET

AQUILINE

AQUI 0296-71
Attachment 2

POTENTIAL SHUTTLE PASSENGERS BETWEEN LAS VEGAS AND AREA 51

BASE

Base Staff	4
Staff Military	1
Weather and AFCS	7
Contract	9
EG&G	9
	(30)

AQUILINE	9
EG&G	36
Air Force	26
TDY/Visitors	3
	(65)
TOTAL	104
Less	44
NET	60

AQUILINE
SECRET

~~SECRET~~
AQUILINE

~~AQUI 0296-71~~

Attachment 3

COST FACTORS

PART A: FLYING HOUR COSTS

	Hr. Rate	8% Fed. Tax	Total	No of Seats	Hr Ins	Gross Costs
DC-6 (1)	$575.	$46.	$621.	85	$45.	$666.
DC-6 (2)	$420.	$34.	$454.	80	$45.	$499.
F-27	$330.	$27.	$357.	40	$27.	$384.

Insurance Costs on DC-6 $43,000 per year. $45. per hr based on 960 hrs.
Insurance Costs Estimated on F-27 $20,000 per year. $21. per hr based on 960 hrs.

PART B: SHUTTLE COST - LSV/AREA/LSV

	Seats	Costs per Hour	Costs per Month	Costs per Year	Seat Costs Month	Year
DC-6 (Large)	85	$666.	$22,644.	$271,728.	$266.	$3,197.
DC-6 (Small)	80	$499.	$16,966.	$203,592.	$212.	$2,545.
F-27	40	$384.	$13,056.	$156.672.	$392.	$3,917.

PART C: ANNUAL COSTS FOR LSV/AREA SHUTTLE (BASED ON FULL LOAD)

No. of Seats	DC-6(1)	DC-6(2)	F-27
10	$31,970	$25,450	$39,170
20	$63,940	$50,900	$78,340
30	$95,910	$76,350	$117,510
40	$127,880	$101,800	$156,680
50	$159,850	$127,250	

AQUILINE
SECRET

SECRET
AQUILINE

A-QUI-0296-71

Attachment 4

COST DETERMINATION FOR SMALL DC-6

(1 October 1971 through 30 June 1972)

Annual Shuttle Cost	$203,592	
9 Month Shuttle Cost		$152,694
Less Charge to ⬚		$ 50,895 *
Balance		$101,799
Rounded To		$102,000

* 50 Seats for two months @ $10,604/mo.
     until ⬚ is in operation $ 21,208

20 Seats for seven months @ $4,241/mo. $ 29,687

    Total Charge to ⬚ $ 50,895

AQUILINE
SECRET

CLASSIFICATION

THIS DOCUMENT REQUIRES SPECIAL HANDLING

HANDLING PROCEDURES

THIS DOCUMENT CONTAINS INFORMATION REGARDING A HIGHLY CLASSIFIED
ACTIVITY. PERMISSION TO TRANSFER CUSTODY, OR PERMIT ACCESS TO
THIS DOCUMENT MUST BE OBTAINED FROM THE ORIGINATOR. HAND CARRY
PROCEDURES WILL BE APPLIED TO ANY INTER-OFFICE OR INTRA-AGENCY
MOVEMENT OF THIS DOCUMENT.

AQUILINE

File in Shuttle folder

REFERRED TO	RECEIVED			RELEASED		SEEN BY	
OFFICE	SIGNATURE	DATE	TIME	DATE	TIME	NAME AND OFFICE SYMBOL	DATE

This paper never released.

CLASSIFICATION

S E C R E T

3.3(h)(2)
3.5(c)

ORIG:
UNIT: EO/SA
EXT: 6423
DATE: 22 NOVEMBER 1972
ROUTING

Comments regarding reference(s)

365

1	*EO*	6		11		16	✓		21	
2	*SS*	7		12		17			22	
3	*"*	8		13		18			23	
4	*BO*	9		14		19	✓		24	
5	*RS*	10		15		20			25	

(classification)   (date and time filed)   (reference number)

~~S E C R E T~~   22 18 06z Nov 72   SITE ADIC 3869

TO   CABLE   INFO:

AQUILINE II

REF: *Manila*

1. FYI, POSSIBLE REACTIVATION OF PROJECT AQUILINE, AS
INDICATED BY REF MESSAGE, IS SENSITIVE INFORMATION AND IS TO
BE TREATED ON A STRICT NEED-TO-KNOW BASIS UNTIL FURTHER
NOTICE. DETERMINATION OF NEED-TO-KNOW WILL BE MADE BY
THIS HQS ON A CASE-BY-CASE BASIS.

END OF MESSAGE

SS/OSA   D/S.

COORDINATING OFFICERS

AUTHENTICATING OFFICER   S E C R E T   EO/SA
                                                     RELEASING OFFICER

REPRODUCTION BY OTHER THAN THE ISSUING OFFICE IS PROHIBITED.   Copy No.

3.5(c)
3.3(h)(2)

IDEA 0059-68
Copy 7 of 7

15 January 1968

MEMORANDUM FOR: Comptroller, OSA

SUBJECT: Concept of Operations, Project AQUILINE

1. This memorandum will outline the OSA concept of operations for project AQUILINE for FY 1969 thru FY 1974. This concept is based on the following assumptions:

   a. OSA will support AQUILINE in the test phase through completion of the Proof of Concept (FY69).

   b. OSA will operate AQUILINE in the operational phases (FY70 thru FY74).

   c. "Proof of Concept" ends at the completion of the final test phase of the _____ model aircraft (early FY 1970).

   d. The airframe, sensors, ground control unit, to be used for full operational employment by OSA, will be determined prior to the final test phase of the _____ model aircraft (start of FY 1970).

   e. Operational range of the _____ model aircraft will not be more than _____.

   f. Operational range of the _____ model aircraft will not be more than _____.

   g. Targeting for project AQUILINE will be dependent upon on-going sensor development, and it is not possible to describe accurately the exact mission role and functions of the project at this time.

2. Interim Operational Concept FY 1969:

   OSA will initiate actions to integrate AQUILINE into the OSA structure starting with FY69. The OSA concept for FY69 will be training, testing and exploring the methods of employing this system. To implement this concept it will be necessary for OSA to use the existing AQUILINE ground facilities and to have six flyable [____] model aircraft. With this equipment it is conceivable that should an emergency situation arise there could be a short range mission flown in FY 1969.

3. FY 1970 Operational Concept:

Starting with the first of FY 1970, OSA will begin to man and operate the AQUILINE project using the [____] model aircraft. By mid 1970 project AQUILINE is to be manned with sufficient personnel to provide for two mobile and one fixed units. The mobile units will be deployed to and from the parent fixed base as and when the situation dictates. To implement this concept, ten [____] model aircraft and three ground control stations plus the associated sensor systems will be required by end FY 1970. During the last quarter of FY 1970 it will be possible to conduct multiple missions with the AQUILINE vehicle.

4. FY 1971 thru FY 1974 Concept:

It is assumed that there will be ten missions per year for project AQUILINE. This should require the purchase of a minimum of five aircraft per year for replacements and spares.

Lt. Colonel, USAF
Assistant Deputy for Operations, OSA

SAS/O/OSA/[____] (15 Jan 68)
Distribution:
      1 - COMPT/OSA
      2 - D/O/OSA
      3 - D/R&D/OSA
      4 - D/M/OSA
      5 - C/COMMO/O/OSA
      6 - C/SS/OSA
      7 - RB/OSA

S E C R E T

3.5(c)

OSA-2022/9/73

11 September 1973

MEMORANDUM FOR:

Office of Research and Development, DD/S&T

SUBJECT: Continued Classification of the AQUILINE Program

1. In response to your request regarding thoughts on the continued classification of Project AQUILINE, it is my contention that for the next year or so the program should be kept at the Secret level. The rationale for this is that we are continuing to store, in tact, major program assets on the possibility (albeit slim) that they might be needed for the post cease fire monitoring of the Indochina Area.

2. In this regard we have briefed Mr. George Carver, SAVA, on the AQUILINE Program's unique capabilities for use against the cease fire monitoring problem of Indochina. Mr. Carver, at that briefing, indicated that if the program were active it would most likely be used. However, Mr. Carver went on to say that since the program was inactive, and would be fairly costly (time and money wise) to bring it up to operational capability, he thought it would be difficult to get approval for its use at this time. He went on to say that if the SEA problems became more difficult to solve, there could be a possibility that the AQUILINE Program might be called upon to help out in one form or another.

3. For your information, we have briefed (at the Secret level) ARPA, Army, Navy, Marines and Air Force on this program. They all indicated a high degree of interest in the technology; however, no one indicated any interest in picking the entire program up, primarily because it was too

S E C R E T

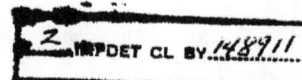

SECRET

sophisticated for their drone type operational requirements. It is my
contention, after briefing all these people, that the AQUILINE Program
is still two to three years in advance of the efforts being conducted by
the various Services. This in itself is further verification for maintaining
the program at the Secret level.

Executive Officer
Office of Special Activities

EO/SA/ _____ (11 Sept 73)
Distribution:
    Orig - ORD _____
       1 - EO/SA
       1 - RB/OSA

SECRET

SECRET

Project "A"

3.3(b)(1
3.5(c)

DD/S 69-5563

12 DEC 1969

MEMORANDUM FOR: Director of Planning, Programming and Budgeting

SUBJECT : Contract and Audit Support for Operational Phase
of Project AQUILINE

REFERENCE : Memo dtd 28 Nov 69 to Exec. Dir. -Compt. fr DD/S&T
re same subject (DD/S&T-4330/69)

1. The proposal contained in the reference offers the following
difficulties:

A. It appears improper to use NRO authority for an
Agency project.

B. If NRO authority is used, it would be desirable to
use the OSA auditing capability rather than the Agency's
Industrial Contract Audit Division.

C. The regular Agency security mechanism would
provide better security for Project AQUILINE than the separate
security system of OSA.

2. For the above reasons, the Support Directorate does not concur in
the recommendation contained in paragraph 4 of the reference.

(signed) John W. Coffey

John W. Coffey
Assistant Deputy Director
for Support

Att:
Ref Memo

PS-DD/[   ]/6833 (11 Dec 69)
Distribution:
 Orig & 1 - Adse w/att and related notes
   (1)- DD/S Subject w/cy of att & related notes
    1 - DD/S Chrono
    1 - PS Chrono
    1 - Mr. Blake, DD/L per Mr. Coffey instructions -16 Dec. 1969.

| UNCLASSIFIED | CONFIDENTIAL | ✓ SECRET |

OFFICIAL ROUTING SLIP

PPB 69-1208

TO	NAME AND ADDRESS	DATE	INITIALS
1	Executive Director-Comptroller		
2			
3			
4			
5			
6			

ACTION	DIRECT REPLY	PREPARE REPLY
APPROVAL	DISPATCH	RECOMMENDATION
COMMENT	FILE	RETURN
CONCURRENCE	INFORMATION	SIGNATURE

Remarks:

Attached is DD/S&T request to transfer contract management responsibility for AQUILINE from ORD to OSA when the system becomes operational. This means OSA will contract under its unusual authorities - separate from normal Agency contracting procedures, but utilizing ICAD for audit. We have cleared this memo with DDS. Recommend you approve, but with reservation explicity stating "With the caveat that the R&D effort currently funded by ORD be continued" under normal contracting procedures.

FOLD HERE TO RETURN TO SENDER

FROM: NAME, ADDRESS AND PHONE NO.	DATE
John M. Clarke, D/PPB, [ ], Hqs.	

| UNCLASSIFIED | CONFIDENTIAL | ✓ SECRET |

FORM NO. 237   Use previous editions
1-67   (40)

SENDER WILL CHECK CLASSIFICATION TOP AND BOTTOM

	UNCLASSIFIED		CONFIDENTIAL		SECRET

OFFICIAL ROUTING SLIP

TO	NAME AND ADDRESS	DATE	INITIALS
1	Director/PPB	12-5	[redacted]
2	Mr. Sherman	12-5	
3	[redacted]	12-8	[redacted]
4		12-8	
5			
6			

	ACTION		DIRECT REPLY		PREPARE REPLY
	APPROVAL		DISPATCH		RECOMMENDATION
	COMMENT		FILE		RETURN
	CONCURRENCE		INFORMATION		SIGNATURE

Remarks:

For comment and recommendations.

ExDir has not seen.

FOLD HERE TO RETURN TO SENDER

FROM: NAME, ADDRESS AND PHONE NO.	DATE
SBreckinridge [redacted] Acting EA/Executive Director [redacted]	3 Dec 69

	UNCLASSIFIED		CONFIDENTIAL		SECRET

Assuming we get operational money - a remote possibility - lets be certain DD/S has no problem here and lets define timing?? and people involvement more clearly for ExDir.

BEST CY.

~~SECRET~~

2 0 ᴺᴼⱽ

69-5887

DD/S&T-4330/69

MEMORANDUM FOR: Executive Director-Comptroller

SUBJECT   : Project AQUILINE--Contract
                  and Audit Support for
                  Operational Phase

1. A recommendation is contained in paragraph 4 for
your approval.

2. As you are aware, the Office of Special Activities
in this Directorate will assume the responsibility for the
operational phase of Project AQUILINE and plans are now
being formulated for that purpose. At the time OSA assumes
operational and technical responsibility for this program,
we should also transfer the contracting function to OSA to
be administered under the special delegation of Contracting
Authority in that Office. Contracting to date for the
research and development phase of AQUILINE has been conducted under regular Agency contract and audit procedures
with the bulk of the contracting performed by the West
Coast Procurement Office.

3. Our recommendation for transferring the contracting
function to OSA for the operational phase, notwithstanding
use of Agency funds, is based upon the following:

    a. The importance of the AQUILINE program
    requires very close support and cooperation
    between technical, operational, contracting
    and security personnel. The Contracting Team
    in OSA is fully integrated with technical,
    operational and security personnel and therefore
    in a position to provide the direct and close
    support which is extremely important in the
    operational phase. We believe that assumption
    of contract responsibility by OSA for the
    operational phase of the program is completely

~~SECRET~~

SECRET

SUBJECT: Project AQUILINE--Contract and Audit
Support for Operational Phase

consistent with the contracting team concept
with which this Directorate has had significant success.

b. Operation of the AQUILINE vehicle
will unquestionably be an extremely sensitive
undertaking and will require security procedures
designed to protect against disclosure of the
existence and purpose of this program. The same
security procedures utilized in earlier OSA
operational programs will be needed for the
AQUILINE program.

c. In view of the fact that Agency appropriated funds will be utilized for AQUILINE,
however, we believe that audit responsibility
should remain with the Industrial Contract Audit
Division under the Office of Finance.

4. It is accordingly recommended that you approve the
assumption of contracting responsibility by Contract Management
Division/OSA for the operational phase of AQUILINE using the
special delegation of Contracting Authority in OSA.

Carl E. Duckett
Deputy Director
for
Science and Technology

APPROVED:

Executive Director-Comptroller   Date

SECRET

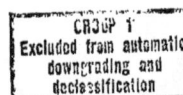

GROUP 1
Excluded from automatic
downgrading and
declassification

SECRET

3.5(c)
3.3(h)(2)

DD/S&T-4444/69

MEMORANDUM FOR: Director, Office of Special Activities

SUBJECT   : Contracting Procedures for the
                 Operational Phase of the
                 AQUILINE Program

1.   This document confirms recent discussions between
representatives of the DD/S&T Staff and OSA concerning the
contracting procedures to be employed by Contract Management
Division, OSA, during the operational phase of Project
AQUILINE. This understanding is considered necessary at
this time because Agency appropriated funds are to be used
and the program is not in support of the NRO.

2.   It is agreed that:

a.   OSA will conform to the Agency contract
approval system for Agency funds. Each proposed
contract action exceeding _____ for
non-R&D actions) will be submitted to the DD/S&T
for approval and to the DCI, through the DD/S&T
for those actions exceeding _____. The proposal
package will include the items outlined in Part III
of the Project Officers Manual. OSA may include
such additional information as it considers appropriate. When the requirement has received the
necessary approval signatures as indicated above,
the proposal will be referred to Contract Management Division/OSA for contract action, without
further review. Copies of those contract actions
approved at the OSA level will be forwarded to
DD/S&T.

b.   OSA will obtain all of its AQUILINE
industrial contract audit support from the
Office of Finance. From time to time Agency
appropriated funds for AQUILINE may be used

SECRET

GROUP 1
Excluded from automatic
downgrading and
declassification

DD/S&T-4444/69
Page 2

SUBJECT: Contracting Procedures for the Operational
Phase of the AQUILINE Program

to supplement existing OSA contracts for
support services which are audited under
existing OSA procedures.

c. The [   ] system for
control of property, spares, etc. will
not be employed for Project AQUILINE.
In lieu of that system OSA will utilize
the Agency property control system. It
is recognized that from time to time
certain spares, parts and components may
have to be obtained from other Government
Agencies.

d. All contracts will be reviewed by
a representative of the Office of General
Counsel in accordance with existing practice.

Acting Executive Officer
Directorate of
Science and Technology

cc: ICAD/OF
Compt./DD/S&T

SENDER WILL CHECK CLASSIFICATION TOP AND BOTTOM

| UNCLASSIFIED | | CONFIDENTIAL | X | SECRET |

OFFICIAL ROUTING SLIP

TO	NAME AND ADDRESS	DATE	INITIALS
1	Director/ Office of		
2	Special Activities		
3	1 D 08 Tyler Building		
4			
5			
6			

ACTION	DIRECT REPLY	PREPARE REPLY
APPROVAL	DISPATCH	RECOMMENDATION
COMMENT	FILE	RETURN
CONCURRENCE	INFORMATION	SIGNATURE

Remarks:

FOLD HERE TO RETURN TO SENDER

FROM: NAME, ADDRESS AND PHONE NO.	DATE
A EO/DDS&T	

| UNCLASSIFIED | | CONFIDENTIAL | X | SECRET |

FORM NO. 237   Use previous editions
1-67   (40)

SECRET

3.3(b)(1
3.5(c)

OSA-1860-9-74

13 SEP 1973

MEMORANDUM FOR: Director of Logistics

SUBJECT: Disposal of Project AQUILINE Assets

1. As you are aware Project AQUILINE was terminated as an Office of Special Activities program in June 1972. Since then residual AQUILINE materials have been stored at Area 51 for potential use by future Agency projects. Until recently no firm interest in these assets has been forthcoming from either Agency or DoD components.

2. The U. S. Army Electronics Command now has a valid requirement for this remaining hardware and contractor documentation for application in its Remotely Piloted Vehicles (RPV) programs. It is recommended that the AQUILINE assets be transferred to the U. S. Army on a non-reimbursable basis with the Army paying for shipping costs only.

3. Request your concurrence in transferring AQUILINE materials detailed in the attachment to this memorandum to the U. S. Army Electronics Command.

WENDELL L. BEVAN, JR.
Director of Special Activities

Attachment

CONCUR:

Director of Logistics

30 SEP 1974
Date

OL 4 4819
E2 IMPDET
CL BY

SECRET

SECRET

OSA-1860-9-74
Page 2

A/D/M/OSA [   ] (5740)
Distribution:
 Orig - D/M/OSA via D/L
    2 - D/L
    1 - D/M/OSA Chrono w/o att
    1 - D/M/SUP w/att
    1 - RB/OSA   w/o att

SECRET

SECRET   DRAFT

LOGISTICAL SUPPORT REQUIREMENTS

1. The Logistical Support structure invisioned for this project
will rely almost exclusively on the Prime and Associate contractors for
hardware, spares, maintenance technicians, and engineering support.
Primary maintenance of major structural components, systems, black boxes,
and ground support equipment will be accomplished at contractor facilities.
A limited maintenance capability will be established at Site A, however,
maintenance performed at Site A and at other forward bases or launch points
will basically follow the "remove and replace" concept of systems, subsystems, and components as appropriate. Support requirements, under this
concept, would necessitate development of an AQUILINE Support Kit which
would contain spares, system components, and other hardware consistent with
the established maintenance capability at Site A or forward operating locations. It should be emphasized that this kit would not only support test
and training requirements at Site A, but would also be utilized as the basic
package for support of operational deployments. Additionally, two recovery
packages will require development to support operational missions, as now
invisioned. A recovery package will be required at designated recovery
points to support operational missions and also, a second recovery package
will be required at the launch point to permit recapture should an abort
be necessary subsequent to launch. These packages would also be utilized
to effect recovery of test and training missions launched from Site A.

SECRET

SECRET

D R A F T
PAGE TWO

2. Implementation of four basic programs will be required to develop
a logistical posture capable of supporting test, training, and operational
missions. The programs are designed to provide necessary data and
information upon which future support requirements, for a given level of
program activity, may be realistically predicted. Specifically these programs
are:

a. Maintenance Documentation and Control Program: This program
would be designed to provide a historical record of routine maintenance
actions on applicable equipment. Items reported would include repair
actions, failures, cause and corrective actions, pre/post flight
inspection results, modifications, current status and configuration.

b. Reliability and Failure Analysis Program: This program would
involve detailed analysis and test of the vehicle, systems, sub-systems,
and components to provide documented bases for prediction of "expected
life". Additional investigation of reported equipment failures, the
attendant causes, required corrective actions, failure trends, etc.
would be reported and provide data relative to improvements necessary
to attain desired or established reliability goals for operational
readiness.

c. Property Accounting and Inventory Control Program: This program
would provide a chronological and historical record of project assets,
from acquisition thru final disposition. Data to be recorded, and reported,
will include quantity ordered/due-in, current asset inventory, location(s),

SECRET

COST, PART NUMBER, DISCRIPTION, SOURCE, anticipated lead time for procurement, configuration, and disposal action. This data would provide consumption data for determination of future budgetary requirements, follow-on spares requirements, and configuration/ modification requirements necessary to support given levels of operation.

    d. Configuration Control Program: This program would establish a means for control or approval of changes, alterations, and modifi- cations to project assets. It would provide a documented record of item status in relation to an established baseline or standard. Utilizing data from the other programs defined, this program would provide a management tool to assist in determination of budgetary requirements as related to maintenance of commonality of project assets, fund availability and establishment of priority for modifications as required to support any given project activity.

3. Once implemented, the above programs would provide management tools that could be utilized for asset management, prediction of budgetary requirements, and a ready view of logistical capability for support of test, training, and operational missions of this program.

~~S E C R E T~~
AQUILINE

Adm 13.5

3.5(c)

AQUI-0349/72
Copy 4 of 7

20 June 1972

MEMORANDUM FOR: Deputy Director for Science and Technology

SUBJECT: Disposition of Project AQUILINE Assets

REFERENCE: A. Memo from D/SA to DD/S&T dated
                         13 Dec 1971; Subject: Same as Above
                         (AQUI-0313/71)

                     B. Distribution Memo from PM/AQUI/OSA,
                         dated 16 February 1972; Subject: Same as
                         Above (AQUI-0344/72)

1. This memorandum contains recommendations for the approval
of the Deputy Director for Science and Technology. Such recommendations
are contained in paragraph 4.

2. In accordance with your instructions, OSA has briefed key
individuals in the USAF, USN, USA and USMC on the AQUILINE Program.
It was indicated at these briefings that the Agency was prepared to turn
over the AQUILINE assets, intact, to any interested organization.
Further, to facilitate this turnover, it was stated that the Agency would
maintain the AQUILINE Program assets intact until 30 June 1972. After
that date, if there were no units interested in taking the whole program,
the assets were to be redistributed on a subcomponent, subsystem, parts
break out level.

3. As of this date there has been no valid request or requirement
for the program as a whole package. However, there have been many
low key inquiries as to the availability of component parts, payloads.

AQUILINE
~~S E C R E T~~

**DD/S&T
FILE COPY**

GROUP 1
Excluded from automatic
downgrading and
declassification

~~SECRET~~
AQUILINE

technology, etc. Therefore, predicated on the absence of any demonstrated interest in acquiring the program intact, it is believed that the AQUILINE Program assets should be made available for redistribution on a subsystem, subcomponent part level, effective on or about 1 July 1972.

   4.   It is recommended that effective 1 July 1972:

      a.   OSA be relieved of the requirement to maintain the AQUILINE Program assets intact as an integral program.

      b.   All AQUILINE assets be released for redistribution to interested parties, both internal and external to the Agency.

WENDELL L. BEVAN
Brigadier General, USAF
Director of Special Activities

The recommendations contained
in paragraph 4 are approved:

10 JUL 1972

Deputy Director for Science and Technology   Date

EO/SA   (20 June 72)
Distribution:
      #1 - D/SA
      #2 - DD/S&T Chrono
      #3 - DD/S&T Registry
      #4 - DD/S&T Registry
      #5 - AAPS/OSA (AQUI File)
      #6 - D/M/OSA
      #7 - RB/OSA

AQUILINE

Adm - 13.5

~~SECRET~~
AQUILINE

☐ •

3.3(b)(1)
3.5(c)

AQUI-0318-71
Copy _3_ of _8_

13 DEC 1971

MEMORANDUM FOR: Deputy Director for Science and Technology

SUBJECT: Disposition of Project AQUILINE Assets

1. This memorandum contains a request for the approval of the Deputy Director for Science and Technology. Such request is contained in paragraph 3.

2. The termination and closeout activities of Project AQUILINE are nearing completion and should be completed about 15 January 1972. Following is the plan, subject to your approval, for the inventory, storage, and subsequent disposition of the Program's assets:

    a. <u>Storage</u>:

       (1) The Program's assets located at the contractor and subcontractors will be inventoried, packaged and shipped to Area 51. These assets, both hardware and documentation, will be combined with the on-site Area 51 assets and then semi-permanently stored in one of the Area 51 buildings.

       (2) The Program's Washington, D.C. documentation will be inventoried, packaged, and shipped ▭ ▭

       (3) A complete inventory of the Program's assets and documentation will then be compiled for subsequent distribution to possible interested users.

    b. <u>Custodial Responsibilities</u>:

       (1) OSA will remain responsible as Program Custodian until further notice.

DD/S&T
FILE COPY

AQUILINE
~~SECRET~~

GROUP 1
Excluded from automatic
downgrading and
declassification

~~SECRET~~
AQUILINE

(2) [   ], or his delegated
representative, will be the Property Accounting and
Releasing Authority.

c. Property Release Procedures:

(1) Subsequent to the completion of the complete
Program inventory, approximately 15 January 1972, OSA
will notify possible users that the AQUILINE property
is available.

(2) Interested users or agencies may then examine
the Program inventories to determine the usability of
the AQUILINE Program assets for their projects,
components, etc.

(3) Interested users or agencies will then submit
a written request, specifying the system, component,
technical documentation, etc. that they desire to be
transferred from the AQUILINE Program to their use.

(4) The property component, technical documents,
etc. that have been requested as stated above will be
released in writing by the Property Accounting Authority.
In cases where office policy requires clarification
relative to the releasability of any portion of the
AQUILINE Program, a recommendation will be submitted to
the DDS&T for decision.

3. It is requested that the DDS&T approve the plan as outlined in
paragraph 2.

WENDELL L. BEVAN, JR.
Brigadier General, USAF
Director of Special Activities

The request contained in
paragraph 3 is approved:

For: (Signed) F. W. M. Janney   2 1 DEC 1971

_____   _____
Deputy Director for Science and Technology   Date

AQUILINE
~~SECRET~~

~~SECRET~~

3.3(b)(1)
3.5(c)

DRAFT

20 Nov 1970

SUBJECT: Draft Memo to Accompany DDI Reservation to
DDS&T Memo Dated _____

1. The Directorate of Intelligence will continue to provide geographic and cartographic support to Project Aquiline during the remainder of its development and testing phases and to the extent feasible in consideration of other demands on the available resources.

2. It is my understanding that the manhours and equipment time necessary to support Aquiline in its operational phase would be very substantial, would require major adjustments in geographic and cartographic plans and programs, and, in fact, could exceed our means. Accordingly, I feel I must withhold an open-ended commitment pending careful study and clarification by the Aquiline group of the amounts, kinds, and time schedules of geographic and cartographic support required.

3. I want to express concern that the precise locational and elevation data required for the Aquiline navigational system may not

~~SECRET~~

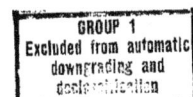

be attainable for many areas of Communist China and, in any case, require careful and time-consuming compilation.

4. I should also like to call to your attention the fact that our ability to support Aquiline in an operational phase will depend very heavily on [   ] willingness and ability to make major adjustments in its production program. Moreover, it may also be necessary to levy very heavy requirements on the photogrammetric equipment of [   ] Indeed, the requirements may surpass [   ] capabilities. Our dependence upon an outside agency for our own input to the Aquiline project may pose a critical obstacle over which we have no control.

-2-

SECRET

23 Nov 70

Hand-carried [ ]
by [ ] with note from [ ]:

[ ] -- Does this draft give
you and [ ] enough to work on?

Personal recollections

Vehicle Platforms in the Office of Research and Development

Charles N. Adkins

The day Sputnik went into orbit in 1957, I was interviewing with Melpar, Inc., primarily an electronics firm, in Falls Church, Virginia. They needed a physicist to work on a contract ☐

☐ This led to a published article in the early 1960s and several contracts with the Agency's newly formed Office of Research and Development (ORD), located in the Ames Building in Rosslyn, Virginia.

In 1966 I joined ORD to work on the Aquiline project. This was to be a small unmanned vehicle, shaped like a bird, that would augment the U-2 as a reconnaissance platform. Its major asset supposedly was its low cost. As a contractor, I had briefed Bud Wheelon, the Deputy Director for Science and Technology, on several occasions, and I asked him how the U-2 was developed. He said, "It was very simple, we found the best aerodynamicist in the business, Kelly Johnson, and told him to build the most reliable vehicle that would get our sensors over the target and home again." Unfortunately, this was not to be the strategy for developing Aquiline.

ORD was an ad hoc group with no official charter. Its primary assets were a few dynamic individuals with vivid imaginations. Two such people were Dave Christ, the division chief and driving force behind Aquiline, and Don Reiser, his deputy. Many were new employees like Frank Briglia, hired as project manager for Aquiline, and C. V. Noyes, who, as a potential contractor, wrote such a good proposal that Dave decided it would be cheaper to hire him.

Dave Christ was good at identifying advanced concepts and a master at selling to upper management. Don Reiser could milk the most from technical people and contractors. His efforts in low-voltage transistors and micropower electronics were among the first significant successes in ORD.

The third important member of this team was a consultant named ☐ A mathematician by nature and an electronics engineer by trade, ☐

My addition to this team was to fill the gap in aerodynamics and to feed Dave's dream of a family of vehicle platforms that would span the next 20 years. The first two were Aquiline and its little-known successor, Axillary.

The Aquiline Project

Dave Christ delighted in describing his first meeting with Douglas Aircraft: "I told them we wanted an unmanned aircraft that would fly over 1,000 miles, have an autopilot with complete on-board navigation, a payload of a few pounds for taking pictures or collecting intelligence of one kind or another, a wing span of only 10 feet or so, and look like a bird."

The first challenge was to construct an initial operational capability (IOC) vehicle that looked like a large model airplane. The first attempts to fly the IOC ended in crashes, and I mentioned to Frank Briglia that the

57

SECRET

Douglas team knew nothing of the sport of making and flying radio control (RC) aircraft and that perhaps they needed such a person on the team.

Douglas did try to fly model airplanes, but their test pilots had little skill in RC flying and more crashes followed. Frank concluded that the solution was to forego further RC tests and to push ahead on the autopilot development that he felt would avert further problems of human error. He wanted the next flight to be fully automatic.

As the flight test grew near, Don _____ and I left for the test site at China Lake, California. The facilities, the flight planning, and the previous test results were impressive, and the Douglas team was confident that a successful flight would vindicate the past failures and large costs that had plagued the project.

The countdown the next day seemed to take forever. Finally, the engine was started, and the vehicle's umbilical cable was disconnected from the site trailer. Once the vehicle was launched, it passed over the edge of a cliff, rotated 90°, nose down, and disappeared from view. Those who walked to the cliff's edge knew what they would see on the rocks below.

Back at Ames, we received the call from Douglas explaining that the longitudinal accelerometer had experienced high acceleration as the vehicle traveled down the launcher. This caused the autopilot to believe the nose was pointed up, and the control surfaces were in the nose down position as it passed over the edge of the cliff.

Don Reiser obtained all test data and autopilot schematics from Douglas and told me and _____ to complete a full stability and control analysis as soon as possible. I told Frank Briglia that the analysis showed no stability margin at all and that, in all probability, the vehicle would have crashed in the last test even if the accelerometer had been properly locked out during launch. This analysis was soon confirmed by Douglas, saying they overlooked the necessity of giving the latest autopilot parameters to their control system analyst.

A running battle soon developed with Dave Christ and Don Reiser putting great pressure on Frank to take a firmer hand with Douglas. Eventually, Frank elevated

himself to unsupervised director of the project. I lost contact at this point, but I was not surprised some years later when Aquiline was "mothballed" with a price tag of $30 million.

SECRET

BYEMAN No. 106295-69
Copy 1 of 7

1 3 JUN 1969

3.3(b)(1)
3.5(c)

MEMORANDUM FOR: Deputy Director for Support

SUBJECT   : Executive Director-Comptroller's Request for Statement
                  of Action Being Taken on the Possible Subordination of
                  OSA Communications to the Office of Communications

1. During the last two and a half years the possibility of the sub-
ordination of OSA communications to the Office of Communications has been
considered. During this period the Office of Communications has worked
closely with OSA and the OSA Communications Division to define the problems
and consider possible solutions.

2. Early in 1968 it was agreed that because OXCART was to be phased
out and because IDEALIST would be the only operational project of OSA, it
would be possible and desirable to consolidate the OSA and the OC comcenters
in the Headquarters area. It was agreed that a small, dedicated communications
group would still be required within OSA to support the IDEALIST operations.
It was further agreed that because OSA would continue to handle many of the
R & D contracts for DD/S&T, the existing network of small, contractor comcenters should remain under the jurisdiction of OSA. (There would be no
increase in efficiency or any savings gained in a transfer to the Office of
Communications.)

3. In accordance with this agreement, the Office of Communications
accepted the responsibility for operation of the OSA data comcenter, the OSA
special comcenter in the Langley Building and the OSA comcenter in the Tyler
Building on 1 July 1968.

4. Thirty-seven positions were transferred from OSA to the Office of
Communications to man these comcenters. Five positions were used to man the
Tyler Building comcenter and 32 were used to man the special comcenter and the
data comcenter. Prior to this transfer of responsibility, OSA had been using
45 positions to do this job but, because OXCART was phasing out, it was expected
that traffic volumes would decrease to the point where 37 positions could handle
the workload. Although Project OXCART is being phased out, other projects in
DD/S&T have grown and have caused a net increase in message traffic. Data comcenter workload has increased significantly. The total workload has increased
to the point that 45 positions are now needed as compared to the 37 positions
transferred to OC to do the job. The activation of Project RHYOLITE will bring

SECRET

GROUP 1
Excluded from automatic
downgrading and
declassification

new and significant workloads.

5. Following this major step in the summer of 1968, the Office of
Communications and OSA have studied, on a continuing basis, the possibility
of further transfer of responsibility that might be possible and desirable.
During the period of this further study, Project AQUILINE has been approved
and Project AQUILINE like IDEALIST can best be served by a dedicated communications group working within OSA. Because AQUILINE will be a major new add-on
workload, a somewhat larger communications group than was planned for the reduced IDEALIST Program will be required.

6. The present conclusion is, therefore, that the dedicated communications
group within OSA should be continued to provide the best and most efficient
communications support to Projects IDEALIST and AQUILINE and other projects of
this nature. It is believed that no significant savings or efficiencies will
accrue from transferring the Contractor Comcenter network to OC jurisdiction.
On the other hand, there appears to be OSA operational advantages to retaining
the network under the jurisdiction of OSA.

7. It is therefore recommended that no further action be taken at this time
on subordinating the remaining OSA communication elements to the Office of Communications. The Office of Communications will, on a continuing basis, study
the problems together with OSA and will make recommendations for changes when such
changes appear to be feasible and desirable. It should be noted that the Director
of Communications has a technical responsibility for the OSA network and the
career responsibility for the Communications personnel assigned to the OSA activity.
No duplication in communications facilities or circuits exist between OSA Communications and the Office of Communications. Where OC facilities and circuits are
available, they are utilized. OSA establishes circuits and facilities only at
locations not serviced by the normal Agency communications network. Continuing
coordination between OC and the Chief, Communications Division, OSA is assured by
the latter's regular attendance at OC Staff and other management meetings.

Director of Communications

CONCUR:

Director of Special Activities

Deputy Director for Science & Technology

13 June 69
Date

10 July 69
Date

~~TOP SECRET~~
CONTROL NO. _____ BYEMAN 106295-69

Copy 1 of 7

REFERRED TO OFFICE	RECEIVED			RELEASED		SEEN BY	
	SIGNATURE	DATE	TIME	DATE	TIME	NAME & OFFICE SYMBOL	DATE
DD/S							2/11/69

Handle Via Indicated Controls
BYEMAN

Access to this document will be restricted to those persons
cleared for the specific projects;

....

....

WARNING

This document contains information affecting the national security of the United States within the meaning of the espionage laws U. S. Code Title 18, Sections 793 and 794. The law prohibits its transmission or the revelation of its contents in any manner to an unauthorized person, as well as its use in any manner prejudicial to the safety or interest of the United States or for the benefit of any foreign government to the detriment of the United States. It is to be seen only by personnel especially indoctrinated and authorized to receive information in the designated control channels. Its security must be maintained in accordance with regulations pertaining to BYEMAN Control System.

~~TOP SECRET~~

GROUP 1
Excluded from automatic
downgrading and declassification

INTRODUCTORY

MY PURPOSE WILL BE TO PROVIDE YOU WITH AN OVERVIEW AND

ORIENTATION OF THE DIRECTORATE OF OPERATIONS ROLE, FUNCTION

AND RESPONSIBILITIES IN SUPPORT OF THE OFFICE OF SPECIAL ACTIVITIES

MISSION. I WILL ATTEMPT TO ACHIEVE THIS PURPOSE BY TOUCHING ONLY

ON THE HIGHLIGHTS OF THE OPERATIONS ORGANIZATION AND ASSIGNED

PROJECTS. PLEASE FEEL FREE TO INTERRUPT AND ASK QUESTIONS AT

ANY TIME. HOWEVER, WE WOULD APPRECIATE THE OPPORTUNITY TO

PRESENT MORE COMPREHENSIVE AND DETAILED BRIEFINGS ON EACH

PROJECT AT YOUR CONVENIENCE.

NONE/UNKNOWN

C02092208

NONE/UNKNOWN

CHART # 1

OSA MISSION

THE MISSION IS TO DEVELOP, ATTAIN AND MAINTAIN AN OPERATIONAL CAPABILITY TO CONDUCT COVERT RECONNAISSANCE OF DENIED AREAS. OSA RETAINS THE FLEXIBILITY TO ACCEPT MANAGERIAL AND OPERATIONAL RESPONSIBILITY FOR EITHER MANNED OR UNMANNED RECONNAISSANCE SYSTESM.

NONE/UNKNOWN

C02092208

CHART # 2

THE DEPUTY FOR OPERATIONS IS STRICTLY ORGANIZED AS THIS

CHART ILLUSTRATES. THE ASSIGNED PROJECT OFFICES ARE DIRECTLY

SUBORDINATE TO THE D/O AS ARE HIS ASSISTANT AND SUPPORTING STAFFS.

THE INTELLIGENCE STAFF PROVIDES:

A) CURRENT INTELLIGENCE FROM ALL SOURCES TO OSA.

B) SPECIAL INTELLIGENCE TO D/O TO INSURE USE OF LATEST

INFORMATION IN FORMULATING OPTIMIZED MISSION PLANS.

C) NECESSARY LIAISON WITH THE INTELLIGENCE COMMUNITY

REGARDING OSA PROJECTS, REQUIREMENTS AND PRODUCTS.

NONE/UNKNOWN

THE WEATHER STAFF ACCOMPLISHES NECESSARY LIAISON WITH AIR WEATHER SERVICE AND PROVIDES METEOROLOGICAL SERVICES TO OSA ASSIGNED PROJECTS. SERVICES INCLUDE:

A) PREPARATION AND PRESENTATION OF ALL WEATHER BRIEFINGS.

B) MAINTAINING METEOROLOGICAL WATCH FOR WEATHER CONDITIONS CONDUCIVE TO SUCCESSFUL OPERATIONS.

C) POST MISSION WEATHER ANALYSIS AND EVALUATION OF MISSION SUCCESS.

D) PROVIDING CLIMATOLOGICAL INFORMATION FOR PROPOSED OPERATIONS.

NONE/UNKNOWN

THE SPECIAL ACTIONS STAFF ACTS AS SPECIAL ASSISTANT TO

THE D/O FOR ALL PLANNING AND PROGRAMMING ACTIVITIES IN SUPPORT

OF OPERATIONAL FUNCTIONS.

THIS STAFF IS/AS THE NAME IMPLIES/FUNCTIONS WITH A CON-

GLOMERATE OF RESPONSIBILITIES USUALLY DIRECTED TOWARD NON-

ROUTINE MATTERS~~ON A CRASH BASIS~~. IT IS SORT OF A D/O FIREMAN.

PRIMARY OF ITS ROUTINE RESPONSIBILITIES ARE:

A) COORDINATING THE PREPARATION OF ANNUAL CONCEPTS OF

OPERATIONS FOR ASSIGNED PROJECTS WHICH ARE USED AS A BASIS FOR

BUDGET PLANNING AND SUBSTANTIATION.

NONE/UNKNOWN

B) PREPARATION OF OPERATIONAL MISSION PROPOSALS AND SUPPORTING MEMORANDA.

C) PREPARATION OF THE OSA PORTION OF THE NRP QUARTERLY PROGRAM PROGRESS REPORT.

D) INITIAL PROJECT MANAGEMENT/ IT PLANS, COORDINATES AND OPERATES INITIAL PHASES OF PROJECTS ASSIGNED TO THE D/O. EXAMPLES OF THIS FUNCTION ARE AQUILINE AND FORTUNE COOKIE.

THE CONTROL CENTER IS PRIMARILY RESPONSIBLE TO MAINTAIN:

A) A FACILITY WITH NECESSARY COMMUNICATIONS FACILITIES TO MONITOR AND CONTROL OPERATIONAL MISSION PROGRESS.

B) MAINTAINING CURRENT SCHEDULES, AIRCRAFT AND EQUIPMENT STATUS, CHECKLISTS AND PERSONNEL ALERT RECALL

ROSTERS TO INSURE~A~ QUICK REACTION CAPABILITY TO REQUIREMENTS

AS THEY MATERIALIZE.

IT ALSO ~~HAS TO~~ MAINTAINS

C) A CAPABILITY TO PROVIDE AIRLIFT SUPPORT AS REQUESTED

BY THE INTELLIGENCE COMMUNITY. ONE C-118 AND C-130 AIRCRAFT

ARE CREWED AND FLOWN BY OSA TO MOVE ON A TIMELY BASIS

PERSONNEL, EQUIPMENT AND MISSION TAKE RESULTING FROM NRO

DIRECTED ACTIVITIES.

THE COMMUNICATIONS STAFF IS RESPONSIBLE FOR THE:

MANAGEMENT, INCLUDING PROGRAMMING, IMPLEMENTA-

TION, AND OPERATION, OF THE BYEMAN COMMUNICATIONS NET IN

SUPPORT OF ALL DD/S&T RECONNAISSANCE ACTIVITIES.

NONE/UNKNOWN

ORGANIZATIONALLY ASSIGNED TO OSA FOR CLOSE SUPPORT OF QUICK-REACTION AIRCRAFT RECONNAISSANCE ACTIVITIES. STAFFED TO ADDITIONALLY SUPPORT THE BROADER TIMING OF OTHER DD/S&T ACTIVITIES, SUCH AS SATELLITE RECONNAISSANCE.

I WILL NOW BRIEF YOU ON THE HIGHLIGHTS OF THE THREE OPERATING PROJECTS CURRENTLY ASSIGNED OSA.

AQUILINE

CHART I

AQUILINE IS AN AGENCY FUNDED R&D PROGRAM TO DEVELOP A

SMALL BIRD LIKE AIRCRAFT EQUIPPED WITH [   ]

DEVICES FOR THE COLLECTION OF INTELLIGENCE BY CLANDESTINE

PENETRATION OF DENIED AREAS. THE VEHICLE IS CURRENTLY BEING

DEVELOPED BY ORD AND MCDONNELL DOUGLAS, THE PRIME CONTRACTOR,

FOR FUTURE EMPLOYMENT BY OSA TO COLLECT PHOTOGRAPHIC AND

ELECTRONIC INTELLIGENCE. THE VEHICLE IS ALSO BEING DEVELOPED

WITH A SENSOR EMPLACEMENT CAPABILITY. VEHICLE DESIGN PHILOSOPHY

HAS PLACED MAJOR EMPHASIS ON SURVIVABILITY PARTICULARLY AGAINST

NONE/UNKNOWN

RADAR, VISUAL AND COMMUNICATIONS DETECTION THREAT EN ROUTE
TO TARGETS.

CHART II

     THE OPERATIONAL CONCEPT AMOUNTS TO USING A GROUND CONTROL
STATION FOR COMMAND AND CONTROL OF THE AIRCRAFT. IT PROVIDES
LAUNCH AND RECOVERY FUNCTIONS AND DISPLAYS ALL NECESSARY VEHICLE
STATUS INFORMATION AND NAVIGATION DATA. IN SOME CASES PAYLOAD
DATA CAN BE TRANSMITTED BACK TO THE CONTROL STATION AND PER-
MANENTLY RECORDED WITHOUT THE NECESSITY OF VEHICLE RECOVERY.

     IN THE DEVELOPMENT STAGE IT IS PLANNED TO USE A DC-6 AIR-
CRAFT AS AN AIRBORNE RELAY SYSTEM FOR OPERATIONS BEYOND LINE OF
SIGHT.

C02092208

NONE/UNKNOWN

ULTIMATELY IT WILL BE NECESSARY TO FUND THE USE OF A

SYNCHRONOUS SATELLITE AS A RELAY PLATFORM IN ORDER TO REALIZE

MAXIMUM VEHICLE FLIGHT RANGES [   ] FROM THE GROUND

STATION. [   ]

<u>CHART III</u>

A BRIEF LOOK AT THE ADVANCED CAPABILITY AQUILINE VEHICLE

ILLUSTRATES THE SIGNIFICANT STATE OF THE ART MINIATURIZATION

EFFORTS:

     LENGTH - 5 FT   WING'SPAN 7 1/2 FT

     TAKE OFF GWT   83 LBS

     SILENT RUNNING :ENGINE   3 1/3 HORSEPOWER

     SPEED RANGE OF 47 - 80 KTS

NONE/UNKNOWN

AT ZERO FUEL WILL BE APPROX

MAX ALT - 20,000 FT

APPROX

MAX RANGE [ ]

MISSION

~~MAX~~ DURATIONS *OF* 50 HOURS *ARE POSSIBLE*

CHART IV

THE NEXT FEW CHARTS ILLUSTRATE THE COORDINATED APPROACH INVOLVING OSA AND ORD IN THE DEVELOPMENT OF THIS SYSTEM.

FY68-69 FEATURED AIRCRAFT SYSTEM DESIGN AND DEVELOPMENT EFFORTS AND THE PREPARATION OPERATIONAL DEPLOYMENT CONCEPTS. CURRENTLY IN FY-70, TEST VEHICLE FABRICATION IS UNDERWAY AND AN OSA STAFFED PROJECT OFFICE IS PURSUING THE INDICATED MANAGEMENT FUNCTIONS.

NONE/UNKNOWN

C02092208

CHART V

IN FY-71 FLIGHT TESTING OF THE AIRCRAFT WILL BE ACCOMPLISHED
AND FIELD UNIT MANNING IS PROJECTED TO FULL STRENGTH. IT IS
ANTICIPATED THAT A LIMITED OPERATIONAL CAPABILITY WILL BE ACHIEVED.
BY THE END OF THIS FY. //

CHART VI

IN FY-72 A FULL OPERATIONAL CAPABILITY IS ACHIEVED TO EXECUTE
OPERATIONAL MISSIONS.

CHART VII

THIS CHART ILLUSTRATES THE LEVELS OF PROJECT ACTIVITY THRU
THE END OF FY-72. ORD IS PRIMARILY INVOLVED IN THE AIRCRAFT
DEVELOPMENT AND FLIGHT TEST WITH MCDONNELL DOUGLAS AC.

NONE/UNKNOWN

FIRST FLIGHT DATE ON 1 JULY 1970. OSA LEVEL OF MANAGEMENT ACTIVITIES INCREASING AS THE CAPABILITY EVOLVES. THE FIELD UNIT BUILD UP WITH FIRST CADRE INPUT IN JULY 70 INCREASING TO FULL STRENGTH BY END OF DECEMBER 70. LIMITED O/R CAPABILITY BY JULY 71 USING U-2R AS RELAY PLATFORM [   ] TO DATE ALL ASPECTS OF THIS PROGRAM ARE ON SCHEDULE WITH ALL MAJOR MILESTONES BEING MET.

CHART VIII

ON THIS CHART A CONCEPTUAL AQUILINE ORGANIZATION IS DEPICTED STATIONED AT AREA 51. THE ORGANIZATION IS DESIGNED TO USE A PLUG IN CONCEPT WITH A PREPARED FACILITY SUPPLYING THE INDICATED SUPPORT FUNCTIONS. MANNING IS BASED ON A BARE BONE CONCEPT WITH MANY OF THE PERSONNEL PERFORMING MORE THAN ONE JOB FUNCTION.

NONE/UNKNOWN

ORGANIZATIONALLY

ANTICIPATE A TOTAL OF 54 PEOPLE WHEN AT FULL STRENGTH., FIELD

DIRECTOR - MAINTENANCE/MATERIEL SIDE - OPS SIDE. IN FY 71 ONE

SYSTEMS VALIDATION

FLIGHT TEAM IS PROGRAMMED FOR THE INITIAL TEST PHASES. BUILDING

IN FY-72 TO TWO TEAMS NECESSARY FOR FOLLOWING OPTIONS:

TEAM   TEAMS

ONE DEPLOYED/ ONE TRAINING: TWO DEPLOYED-DOUBLE OPERATIONAL MISSION -

TEAMS

CAPABILITY; OR TWO DEPLOYED FOR LONG DURATION MISSIONS.

PPB *7C-24 7H*

Execu.... ...u.y

7 254

AQUI-0144-70
Copy *F* of *14*

3.3(b)(1
3.5(c)

MEMORANDUM FOR: Executive Director-Comptroller

SUBJECT: Lease of Remote Computer Terminal for Tyler
                  Building to Support Project AQUILINE

    1. This memorandum contains a request for the approval of
the Executive Director-Comptroller. Such request is contained in
paragraph 9.

    2. Part of the planned FY 71 AQUILINE build up includes the
installation of a remote computer terminal in the Tyler Building
tied to the Agency's computer complex in the Headquarters building.
The primary purpose of this remote terminal will be for mission
planning. The planning algorithm now in preparation will utilize a
basic computer procedure which repeatedly executes a series of
operations until some condition is satisfied to develop optimized
flight plans. Because of the Office of Special Activities location,
far removed from the computers and the extensive data banks required
to feed in order-of-battle, demographic, topographic and other vital
inputs; and because of the time involved in using repetitive techniques,
a remote terminal is essential. The existing secure lines between
Headquarters and Tyler Building will be used to complete the link-up
of this remote terminal to the Headquarters computer complex.

    3. In addition to the primary mission for this installation, it
will also permit the transmission of finalized flight plans directly
from the Tyler Building to   as well as providing near real-time
flight-following information to the Control Center by using already
existing facilities.

    4. On a time available basis, the terminal will also have the
capability to aid Tyler Building personnel with management tools such
as information retrieval, storage and high-speed reproduction of documents.

    5. It is necessary to acquire and install this equipment as soon
as possible in order to have it available for training flight planners

AQUI-0144-70
Page 2

prior to the start of the AQUILINE system validation program. Funds for this installation are included in the Communications portion of OSA's AQUILINE FY 71 budget.

6. Attachment A is a copy of the UNIVAC proposal for the AQUILINE remote terminal which would be installed on a lease basis. Equipment descriptions and pricing are included in the proposal.

7. _____, Office of Computer Services, has examined this proposal and agrees that the requested equipment will satisfy OSA's requirements (see Attachment B).

8. The only viable alternative to installing this equipment in Tyler Building is the transfer of OSA's AQUILINE Division to Headquarters. The use of the Office of Computer Services' equipment would satisfy AQUILINE's primary requirements, but would deny flight-following information which may be required for command decisions.

9. Your approval is requested for the installation of a UNIVAC 9200 remote terminal in the Tyler Building to support Project AQUILINE. The lease is for $_____ to install and operate this terminal for six months.

CARL E. DUCKETT
Deputy Director
for
Science and Technology

Attachments: 2
    A and B

SIGNATURE RECOMMENDED:

Director of Special Activities

1 December 1970
Date

The request contained in
paragraph 9 is approved:

```
┌─────────────────────────────┐
│                             │
│                             │
│                             │
└─────────────────────────────┘
```
Executive Director-Comptroller

26 Mar 71
Date

C/AQUI/O/OSA/ [_____] (24 November 1970)
Distribution:
 1 - AQUI/O/OSA (w/att)
 2 - ER (w/o att)
 3 - DDS&T Chrono (w/o att)
 4 - DDS&T Registry (w/o att)
 5 - DDS&T Registry (w/o att)
 6 - D/SA (w/o att)
 7 - D/O/OSA (w/o att)
 8 - COMMO/OSA (w/o att)
 9 - B&FD/OSA (w/o att)
10 - SS/OSA (w/o att)
11 - RB/OSA (w/o att)
12 - CMD/OSA (w/o att)
Xerox - OPPB

SENDER WILL CHECK CLASSIFICATION TOP AND BOTTOM

UNCLASSIFIED		CONFIDENTIAL		SECRET

OFFICIAL ROUTING SLIP

TO	NAME AND ADDRESS	DATE	INITIALS
1	Special Counsel to the		✓
2	DCI Room 7D-60		
3			
4			
5			
6			

ACTION	DIRECT REPLY	PREPARE REPLY
APPROVAL	DISPATCH	RECOMMENDATION
COMMENT	FILE	RETURN
CONCURRENCE	INFORMATION	SIGNATURE

Remarks:

Ref: ER 75-8481

Finn - are a nice paper for the HSC to look into Thank Mitch

FOLD HERE TO RETURN TO SENDER

FROM: NAME, ADDRESS AND PHONE NO.	DATE
Deputy Director for Administration	9/17/75

UNCLASSIFIED		CONFIDENTIAL		SECRET

FORM NO. 237 Use previous editions

CONFIDENTIAL

DD/A Registry
File *Project "A"*

DD/A 75-4434

3.3(b)(1
3.5(c)

17 September 1975

MEMORANDUM FOR: Special Counsel to the Director

Mitch:

1. I recently sent you a memorandum concerning the endeavors of a House Select Committee employee to line-up some witnesses from the private sector. In that memorandum reference was made to Project AQUILINE and you have asked concerning it.

2. AQUILINE was primarily a developmental project, although some research was involved, to develop a miniaturized flying platform with a multi-sensor carrying capability for clandestine acquisition of technical intelligence. Having said that and to put it in simple vernacular, it was a high characteristic operating model plane with a lot of expensive gadgetry. It was a DD/S&T undertaking, conducted by the Office of Research and Development, and its life span was probably four years or so. Total cost of the undertaking was about ⬚ dollars during its life span, all Agency-funded money. For a variety of reasons it never met operational standards and Dick Helms eventually ordered cessation of any further investment.

3. I have given this the general parameters as I remember and understand them. If you desire to pursue it any further, I suggest you make inquiries of Carl Duckett.

John F. Blake
Deputy Director
for
Administration

Distribution:
Original - Adse
1 - DD/A Subject w/Ref (DD/A 75-4357)*
1 - DD/A Chrono w/o Ref   *Also See DD/A 75-4420
1 - JFB Chrono w/o Ref
DD/A:JFBlake:der (17 September 1975)

E2 IMPDET
CL BY 001777

CONFIDENTIAL

SENDER WILL CHECK CLASSIFICAT

| UNCLASSIFIED | CONFIDENTIAL | | SECRET |

OFFICIAL ROUTING SLIP

DD/A Registry
File *project "A"*

TO	NAME AND ADDRESS	DATE	INITIALS
1			
2	Room 7D-60 Headquarters		
3			
4			
5			
6			

ACTION	DIRECT REPLY	PREPARE REPLY
APPROVAL	DISPATCH	RECOMMENDATION
COMMENT	FILE	RETURN
CONCURRENCE	INFORMATION	SIGNATURE

Remarks:

[handwritten note]

FOLD HERE TO RETURN TO SENDER

FROM: NAME, ADDRESS AND PHONE NO.		DATE
Deputy Director for Administration		9/23/75

| UNCLASSIFIED | | CONFIDENTIAL | | SECRET |

(40)

FORM NO. 237   Use previous editions
1-67

⊕ GPO : 1974 O - 535-857

Att: DD/A 75-4434
Distribution:
   Original RS - Special Counsel to the DCI ⬚) w/Orig of Att
        1 RS - DD/A Subject w/cy of Att
        1 RS - DDA Chrono w/o Att
DD/A:JFBlake:der (23 September 1975)

3.3(b)(1)
3.5(c)

~~SECRET~~
~~AQUILINE~~

AQUI-0069-70
Copy _8_ of _8_

MEMORANDUM OF UNDERSTANDING BETWEEN OSA AND ORD

DRAFT

SUBJECT: OSA and ORD AQUILINE Program Management Responsibilities

1. A meeting was held on 17 December 1969 in the D/SA Conference Room to discuss the present and future OSA and ORD management responsibilities for Project AQUILINE. The purpose of the meeting was to reach agreement on courses of action that would insure an orderly and manageable transition of the AQUILINE Program from ORD to OSA. Present at this meeting were:

    a. ORD

        Mr. Robert Chapman (D/ORD)
        Mr. Frank Briglia (C/SPG/ORD)

    b. OSA

        Brigadier General Donald H. Ross (D/SA)

2. OSA presented six points for discussion and consideration by the personnel present. This memorandum will present the agreed-upon positions relating to these six major discussion items, along with the associated other discussion points covered at this meeting.

    a. Program Management Responsibility: It is agreed that ORD will retain program management responsibility until such time as their present major contract with MDAC is completed. A suggested appropriate date for this program management transfer would be approximately 1 January/1 February 1971, or at such time as the present contract and test phase have been completed.

Aquiline Policy

~~AQUILINE~~
~~SECRET~~

GROUP 1
Excluded from automatic
downgrading and
declassification

This does not mean that a particular date will be
adhered to nor does it include major test and time
extensions to the present contract. Conditions of
this type must be closely coordinated with OSA and
a determination made if there should be a delay
in management turnover responsibility.

b. Budgeting and Funding: It is agreed that OSA
and ORD will continue to separately budget and fund
for peculiar FY 72 program requirements. ORD will
continue to budget and fund for those research items
within their purview that are under development for
application to any number of programs including AQUILINE.
After coordination with OSA to determine operational
applicability, ORD will, during and subsequent to
FY 72, budget and fund for advanced AQUILINE payload
systems. This budgeting and funding includes the
development through prototype hardware phases. OSA
will, from FY 71 on, budget and fund for procurement
of all operational support items to include AGE,
aircraft, production models of payloads, sensors, etc.

c. Contracting: ORD will continue all of the
present AQUILINE contracts through its existing agreement
with O.L./DDS. Additionally, ORD will continue to use
O.L./DDS contracting procedures for R&D through the
feasibility and prototype phase of development. R&D
conducted by ORD on improvements or modifications to
operational elements of the AQUILINE system (including
payloads) will be contracted through OSA. OSA will
assume responsibility for contracting for all AQUILINE
operational items commencing on 1 July 1970, including
those budgeted and funded for by ORD.

d. Security: It is agreed that the security of the
program is to be divided into three phases:

(1) ORD will be responsible for the
security aspects of the program within the
purview of their existing AQUILINE contracts
(MDAC, etc.). In this regard, the security

SECRET
AQUILINE

arrangements now in existence with contractors
will continue for the life of ORD contracts.

(2) During the ORD test phase (July 70 -
January 71), OSA will be responsible for the
security of the program that concerns Area 51
activities, including the monitoring of all
visitors to the Project site. Additionally,
OSA Security is responsible for the air
shuttle, the Personnel Assembly Building at
Long Beach Airport, and all OSA contracts
issued during this period.

(3) During the operational phase of the
AQUILINE Program, the security responsibilities
are divided into two parts:

(a) ORD will continue to use
their security procedures and practices
IAW their contracting procedures (paragraph
2.c. above).

(b) Once a system or device has reached
the prototype stage and it has been determined
to have operational application to the
AQUILINE system, it will be integrated into
the OSA contracting and security procedures
(paragraph 2.c. above).

(4) To achieve an orderly transition of
responsibilities, it is agreed that the program will
be known (at Area 51) by the unclassified nickname
Project M277. In this manner, the R&D prototype
program name AQUILINE can be slowly phased out and
the new operational program name AZANA established
after the R&D flight tests are completed. During
the changeover from development to operational
status of systems, OSA Security (in coordination with
ORD Security) will accomplish the associated actions
that will assure an orderly transition of all security
aspects of this program.

AQUILINE
SECRET

SECRET
AQUILINE

AQUI-0069-70
Page 4

e. Follow-on R&D (FY 72 and on): It is agreed
that ORD retain complete responsibility for those
peculiar R&D items that may have applicability to
the AQUILINE Program and other programs. Determination
of additional AQUILINE requirements for payloads,
communications, aircraft modifications, etc. will be
made by a Program Requirements Review Board chaired
by OSA. Test flights of follow-on payloads, etc. will
be under the aegis of OSA and amenable to ORD requirements.

f. O.R. Validation and Field Unit Training: It
is agreed that the AQUILINE system will require an
operationally ready validation phase subsequent to the
ORD R&D phase. OSA will conduct this O.R. validation
in conjunction with its Field Unit training program at
Area 51. OSA will, for this validation, have first
priority on the use of equipment (AGCS, vehicles, etc.)
that have been purchased by ORD for the R&D phase. The
main emphasis during the validation phase will be to
bring the Field Unit to an operationally ready status
in the shortest possible time.

Signed:

DONALD H. ROSS
Brigadier General, USAF
Director of Special Activities

ROBERT M. CHAPMAN
Director of Research and Development

AQUILINE
SECRET

AQUI-0069-70
Page 5

C/AQUI/O/OSA/[   ]   (23 January 70)
Distribution:
1 - D/SA
2 - DD/SA
3 - EX/COMPT/OSA
4 - D/ORD
5 - SPG/ORD
6 - D/O/OSA
7 - AQUI/O/OSA
8 - RB/OSA

~~SECRET~~

AOM-13.1
(memo for record)

21 April 1970   3.3(b)(1)
                       3.5(c)

MEMORANDUM FOR THE RECORD

SUBJECT: OSA Contracting for Project AQUILINE

On 16 April the DD/S&T stated his position with regard to contracting for the operational phase of Project AQUILINE. The matter was presented to him by Mr. Fred Janney following a meeting with [   ] Mr. Duckett stated that he felt OSA should be capable of flexibility in its method of operation considering that its future might very well involve Agency-funded operations in addition to Project AQUILINE. Thus OSA contracts for Agency-funded projects would be conducted in accordance with regular Agency contracting procedures. He felt that the West Coast Contracting Office should continue to contract for AQUILINE requirements including those initiated by OSA in the operational phase. Under these conditions the contracting officer in OSA would be the primary liaison between OSA and the West Coast Contracting Officer in much the same fashion as the ORD Contracting Officer is the point of liaison with the West Coast on ORD requirements which are contracted for by the West Coast Contracting Officer.

It was pointed out to Mr. Duckett that under Agency regulations the Director of Logistics was responsible for the security of industrial contracts funded under Agency appropriations. Mr. Duckett saw no problem in assuming that the special security requirements of OSA could interface with regular Agency industrial security by mutual agreement.

Later Mr. Blake confirmed that he would arrange for the Chief, Logistics Industrial Security, to meet with the Chief, OSA Security to determine what arrangements would be necessary to provide the proper interface. Mr. Blake would also work out guidelines for the Contracting Officer, OSA, in those instances where OSA would be contracting for AQUILINE with non-west coast contractors.

In view of Mr. Duckett's decision on this matter, which was a change in his earlier approach to the AQUILINE contracting for the operational phase, the attached memorandum

~~SECRET~~

Page 2

of 28 November can be retired without further action. This memorandum had been reviewed by O/PPB and coordinated with the DDS. Mr. John Clarke's note stating that perhaps the action was a bit premature and suggesting the action be put on the back burner is attached as part of the record. It is interesting to note the comments of the DDS on OSA contracting for the Agency-funded AQUILINE project. In substance that position was:

      a. It is improper to use NRO authority for an Agency project.

      b. If NRO authority is used for Agency-funded contracting, use DCAA audit, not ICAD.

      c. Security is better in the Agency system.

□ 3.5(c)
3.3(h)(2)

S E C R E T
AQUILINE

SERIES B
Copy 4 of 4
AQUI 0027-69
Copy _1_ of _6_
21 August 1969

MEMORANDUM FOR: Director of Special Activities

SUBJECT: Personnel Manning Policy and Plan
for Project AQUILINE

REFERENCE: Project AQUILINE Concept of Operations
(AQUI 0001-69) dated 10 March 1969

1. The purpose of this memorandum is to establish the policy
and planning guidelines for the manning of Project AQUILINE. These
guidelines are to be used to implement the policy of that portion of
the Project AQUILINE Concept of Operations that pertains to personnel
manning. (Para 5.b. Reference)

2. As this program has been established and sponsored by the
CIA, for the expressed purpose of providing the Agency with a unique
covert intelligence vehicle, it will be supported primarily through
Agency resources. In keeping with these overall program philosophies,
the following plan is to be used for the orderly acquisition of personnel
for this build up period of the program. (FY 1970 - FY 1971)

    a. Project Headquarters:

      (1) An AQUILINE Division has been established
within the Operations Directorate of OSA. This
Division will be authorized a total of five positions.
At the present time, (through end of FY 1970) these
five positions are to be assimilated from within the
current OSA ceiling. Beginning FY 1971 these five
positions will, for the first time, be identified as
AQUILINE positions in correspondence outside OSA.
(CPC, budget papers, etc.)

GROUP 1
Excluded from automatic
downgrading and
declassification

AQUILINE
S E C R E T

S E C R E T
AQUILINE

(2) The manning (present and projected) and proposed grades of these five positions are as follows:

(a) Chief, AQUILINE Division - GS-15, incumbent James W. Cherbonneaux.

(b) Deputy Chief, AQUILINE Division - GS-14, unmanned. It is planned that the individual who is to eventually become the Field Unit's Program Director (FPD) will be slotted against this position during the remainder of FY 1970. This individual will actually work in the capacity of Deputy Chief of AQUILINE Division during this time frame. In this manner, invaluable experience can be both gained and utilized by the program's key personnel during the initial stages of the Project. Beginning in FY 1971 and after the departure of the FPD to the field, this position will be filled by a permanent Headquarters assignee.

(c) Operational Planning Officer - GS-13, incumbent

(d) ADP Programs Officer - GS-13. The individual selected for this position will of necessity be recruited from the Office of Computer Services. It is planned that this position is to be filled NLT 1 January 1970. The recruitment of this individual can be accomplished against the current AQUILINE authorized slots, without an increase in the authorized OSA manpower ceiling.

(e) Secretary-Steno - GS-6, incumbent

b. Field Unit:

(1) The recruitment of personnel (39 total) for the Project Field Unit will begin at the start of FY 1971. Recruiting of the Field Unit personnel will be phased over the first six months of that fiscal year. The first

AQUILINE
SECRET

SECRET

AQUILINE

AQUI 0027-69
Page 3

of the Unit personnel to be recruited will be those
considered essential to the organization of the Field
Unit. The remainder of the personnel will be assigned
as requirements dictate, but not later than 1 January
1971. The initial goal of this Field Unit manning plan
is to have sufficient personnel available to start
training by 1 January 1971. The ultimate goal is to
have the Unit trained and Operationally Ready by
1 July 1971.

(2) Manning of the Field Unit will be with
Agency staff, Agency contract and commercial contract
personnel. Maximum use of the Agency contract and
commercial contract personnel for the Field Unit will
be accomplished. Agency staff positions will be
required in the FPD and MFS positions, as well as
for the Security and Commo field positions.

(3) The phasing-in process of the Field Unit
personnel and their proposed grades are planned as
follows:

(a) During the first quarter of FY 1971
it is planned that the following positions of the Field
Unit will be manned at Area 51:

Field Program Director - GS-15

(Agency staff position)

Manager Flight Systems - GS-14

(Agency staff or Agency contract position)

Manager Systems Support - GS-14

(Either Agency staff, Agency contract or commercial
contract)

AQUILINE
SECRET

S E C R E T
AQUILINE

Security Officer - GS-14

(Agency staff position)

Commo Operations Officer - GS-14

(Agency staff position)

Administrative and Finance Officer - GS-12

(Either Agency staff, Agency contract or
commercial contract)

Logistics Specialist - GS-11

(Agency contract position)

Property Accounts Specialist - GS-9

(Agency contract position)

Field Unit Guard Force

(Five Agency contract positions)

        (b) Beginning second quarter of FY 1971
it is planned to have the following additional Field Unit
positions manned at Area 51:

Two Electronics Engineers - GS-13, GS-12

(Agency staff positions)

One Electronics Specialist - GS-11

(Agency staff position)

Warehouse Specialist - GS-7

(Agency contract position)

AQUILINE
S E C R E T

(c) Beginning the third quarter of
FY 1971 it is planned to have the following additional
Field Unit positions manned at Area 51:

Security Officer - GS-13

(Agency staff position)

Two ADP Specialists

(Agency staff or Agency contract positions)

Two Commo Tech.-Crypto - GS-9, GS-8

(Agency staff positions)

Three Clerks

(Agency staff or Agency contract positions)

Two Flight Directors - GS-13

(Agency contract or commercial contract positions)

Two Navigation Systems Operators

(Agency contract or commercial contract positions)

Two Payload Systems Operators

(Agency contract or commercial contract positions)

Eight Technical Representatives

(Commercial contract positions)

S E C ̶R̶E̶T̶
A̶Q̶U̶ILINE

4. Proposed FY 1971 Manning Plan overview of field positions requirements:

a.   **Agency Staff Positions**   **No.**

	Field Program Director	1
	Manager Flight System	1
*	Manager System Support	1
	Security Officers	2
	Commo Officers	6
*	Administrative Officer	1
*	ADP Specialists	2

                            Total   14

(Authorized 18 - 12 staff positions and 6 commo)

b.   **Agency Contract Positions**   **No.**

**	Flight Directors	2
**	Navigation Systems Operators	2
**	Payload Systems Operators	2
	Logistics Specialist	1
	Property Accounts Specialist	1
	Warehouse Specialist	1
*	Clerks	3
	Guards	5

                            Total   17

c.   **Commercial Contracts**   **No.**

        Technical Representatives   8

   * Either Agency Staff, Agency Contract or Commercial Contract.

   ** Either Agency Contract or Commercial Contract.

d.   End FY 1971 Total Field Strength at Area 51   39

AQUILINE
S̶E̶C̶R̶E̶T̶

5. Beginning FY 1972 the remainder of the Field Unit's personnel will be recruited. These positions are as follows:

a.

Agency Staff Positions	No.
Security Officer	1
Commo Operations Officer	1
Commo Electronic Engineers	2
Commo Electronic Specialist	1
Commo Tech. -Crypto or Radio	2
Total	7

b.

Agency Contract Positions	No.
** Flight Directors	2
** Navigation Systems Operators	2
** Payload Systems Operators	2
* ADP Specialists	2
Total	8

* Either Agency Staff, Agency Contract or Commercial Contract.

** Either Agency Contract or Commercial Contract.

c.   Total FY 1971 Field Strength   54
     at Area 51

6. This memorandum is to be used for planning purposes only. This manning plan is based on minimum or bare bones manning requirements for this Project. As experience is gained on this unique program, these manning requirements will be subject to continuing review and modifications as required. However, the established manning policy for this program will be to hold the manning at the minimum level required to effectively perform the mission. This minimum manning will of necessity require selection of the best

S E C R E T
AQUILINE

possible personnel, and will require that these personnel perform
to the maximum of their capabilities. Only through the selective
recruitment of personnel, (and effective cross training of those
selected) can this unique program achieve.its manning policy goals.

Colonel, USAF
Deputy for Operations, OSA

APPROVED:

Director of Special Activities   *14 Sept 1969*
                                       Date

AQUI/O/OSA:JWCherbonneaux:kv (21 August 1969)
Distribution:
  1 - AQUI
  2 - D/SA
  3 - D/OPS
  4 - COMPT
  5 - D/M
  6 - RB/OSA

AQUILINE
SECRET

3.3(h)(2)
3.5(c)

OSA-1755-6-73

11 JUN 1973

MEMORANDUM FOR: Director of Training

ATTENTION: Chief, Senior Seminar
                   Room 1001 Chamber of Commerce Building

SUBJECT: Project AQUILINE
                   (Classification of Materials)

    1. This memorandum is submitted in response to an oral request from the Chief, Senior Seminar, ⬚ concerning the current clearance level of Project AQUILINE materials. This will confirm that the classification of that project's materials has been reduced to a Confidential level.

    2. It is our understanding that the Office of Training will use project documents as source materials to prepare a case study syllabus on project management for Agency courses. This Office interposes no objection to the proposed use of project materials as outlined by ⬚

    3. ⬚ mentioned the possibility that some project documents may bear codeword restrictions. If such is found to be the case it is requested that the required care be exercised to prevent compromise or exposure of codeword material.

WENDELL L. BEVAN, JR.
Brigadier General, USAF
Director of Special Activities

CHIEF
D/CHIEF
SA/IS-AS
SA/CI

cc: C/SMS/DD/S&T

I

C

S
T
E
N
O

DESTROY
FILE
TICKLE

ADMINISTRATIVE INTERNAL USE ONLY

OSA/SS/⬚⬚⬚⬚⬚⬚/mpr (11Jun73)
Distribution:
  Orig - Addressee
    1 - D/SA
    1 - SS/OSA
    1 - RB/OSA
    1 - C/SMS/DD/S&T

5 June 1973

MEMORANDUM FOR THE RECORD

SUBJECT: Project AQUILINE (Reclassification Request)

1. The C/SMS/DDS&T telephonically requested on 4 June 1973 that OSA consider reclassification of Project AQUILINE material to SECRET. He advised that Mr. Carl Duckett, DDS&T, had approved a request from OTR to utilize Project AQUILINE material in connection with a Management Training Course.

2. The foregoing request was discussed with the EO/OSA who advised that Project AQUILINE material had actually been downgraded to CONFIDENTIAL and made available to various U.S. military services. He saw no objection to making the requested material available to OTR.

3. On 5 June 1973 [   ] C/Senior Seminar/OTR, 1000 Chamber of Commerce Building, Extension [   ] called the undersigned. He explained that OTR wishes to draw upon the documents in Project AQUILINE to prepare various sections of a Management Course study. He explained that the original documents would not be used by the students in the course but would be used by the instructor to compile course material. For instance, he said sections under project history, project requirements, project technical problems etc. would be produced from an analysis of project documents. As a result this request was really for permission to deal with the substance of project documents at a SECRET level.

4. [   ] noted that a few documents carried a BYEMAN classification. He saw no reason for utilizing any BYEMAN material and in fact felt that some of the documents may have been so classified for peripheral reasons.

5. The undersigned will prepare a memorandum for [   ] for the approval of the OSA Front Office providing authority to use AQUILINE documents was requested.

TOP SECRET

TOP SECRET

PROJECT AQUILINE BRIEFING STATEMENT MANUAL

TOP SECRET

TOP SECRET

~~TOP SECRET~~

3.5(c)
3.3(h)(2)

~~TOP SECRET~~

AQUILINE BRIEFING STATEMENT

This memorandum pertains to an operation known as AQUILINE. The number of people holding AQUILINE access approvals will be held to an absolute minimum. AQUILINE access covers all aspects of the operation.

AQUILINE is a restrictive access involving a small powered glider capable of flying thousands of miles, emplacing devices, interrogating previously emplaced devices, and performing special reconnaissance or collection missions.

It will present bird-like radar, acoustic and visual signatures designed to blend with the indigenous signal environment. Possessing a range in excess of _____, it will be capable in its advanced form of hovering over targets for as long as 120 days.

AQUILINE is specifically designed to protect:

1) The role of CIA in AQUILINE.

2) That the CIA is developing a small, bird-like surreptitious vehicle with sufficiently small acoustic, visible and radar cross-section to permit it to operate in the natural physical signal environment of living birds.

3) Details of initial, interim or final embodiments of the vehicle design when presented or observed in such a manner as to suggest the operational characteristics or purpose of the device.

4) Details of any subsystem of the vehicle when presented or observed in such a manner as to suggest an association with or a capability peculiar to the AQUILINE mission.

AQUILINE information will include mission analysis data such as the location and nature of threat radar as well as visual or acoustic sensors, the terrain over which flights will be made, and targets of interest to the mission. This mission analysis data will often involve COMINT as well as end products derived from overhead reconnaissance. The

TOP SECRET

TOP SECRET

TOP SECRET

-2-

clearances for COMINT and these end products will therefore
be prerequisites for access to AQUILINE information. The
particular restrictions imposed on persons holding these
clearances, which include the possibility of prosecution
by the U. S. Government, may also apply to violations concerning AQUILINE information.

AQUILINE access is granted only by CIA. The determination that an individual possesses a need-to-know for access
to AQUILINE information will be made by the Director/ORD.
Participants who have a question concerning an individual's
status must verify the existence of his access prior to any
discussion of this sensitive information.

. . . .

TOP SECRET

TOP SECRET

SECRET

Copy ___ of ___

AQUILINE SECURITY BRIEFING

This brochure pertains to the SECRET activity known as Project
AQUILINE. The word AQUILINE when used in this context is a covert
intelligence collection operation of the highest sensitivity. It
has as its objective the collection of electronic and photographic
intelligence through the use of a small bird-like unmanned powered
glider.

Project AQUILINE operates under the sponsorship and direction
of the Central Intelligence Agency. Access to project sensitive information is restricted to an absolute minimum number of persons.
The success of the program depends in large measure on an effective
security program, thus the following principles have been established:

An AQUILINE access approval is required before a person may
receive sensitive project information. Existing clearances, such
as TOP SECRET or other special clearances, are not in themselves
sufficient for access to AQUILINE.

A strict "need-to-know" principle is enforced. Access approvals
will not be granted merely as a matter of courtesy or in deference
to rank or position. The only justification for access to AQUILINE
information is that a person requires access to enable him to make
a positive contribution to the project.

AQUILINE clearances are granted by the Central Intelligence
Agency. Request for clearances will be submitted in writing to Project
AQUILINE Headquarters through channels as designated by the responsible
AQUILINE security representative.

The AQUILINE clearance status of an individual must be verified
prior to any discussion relating to the Program. A master index of
all AQUILINE clearances is maintained at AQUILINE Headquarters.

Prior to visiting participating industrial firms or operational
locations on AQUILINE business the clearance status of the visitor must
be certified to the installation through AQUILINE Headquarters.

(1)

SECRET

TOP SECRET

SECRET

Access to the end-product derived from the AQUILINE operation is not authorized under the AQUILINE access approval.

There are three categories of AQUILINE briefings. The most comprehensive is that which is contained in this brochure. The lower category briefings are provided to personnel of industrial suppliers who have no need to know of Central Intelligence Agency sponsorship or participation. They are briefed only to the extent necessary to make possible their maximum contribution to the project effort.

All AQUILINE sensitive information must be protected and particularly:

(1) The role of the Central Intelligence Agency in AQUILINE.

(2) That the Central Intelligence Agency is developing a small, bird-like surreptitious vehicle with sufficiently small acoustic, visible and radar cross-section to permit it to operate in the natural physical signal environment of living birds.

(3) Details of the vehicle design when presented or observed in such a manner as to suggest the true operational purpose of the vehicle.

(4) Details of any subsystem when presented or observed in such a manner as to suggest an association with or a capability peculiar to the AQUILINE mission.

(2)

SECRET

SECURITY PLAN - PROJECT RECHARTER

.1.   This plan represents the coordinated positions of the Office
of Special Activities and the Office of Research and Development,
Deputy Directorate for Science and Technology.   These groundrules
are the established maximum security measures governing this TOP
SECRET project at Area 51 throughout the flight testing sequence,
training or related activities leading toward the operational deployment
of this aerial intelligence system.   The Security Staff, Office of Special
Activities, is charged with assisting the Director of Special Activities
in maintaining a maximum security environment for the conduct of OSA
and specified DD/S&T activities; therefore, the successful implementation of these policies will depend largely on the cooperation of CIA
elements, other supporting government agencies and the principal
contractors charged with the development of this highly sensitive covert
intelligence system.

2.   It is collectively understood by all participants that program
transition toward operational readiness will necessitate close coordination and special cooperation with the Office of Logistics in view of
their paramount responsibilities in the field of contracting and related
industrial security matters.

3.   This plan will be reviewed periodically, updated and
procedures refined to meet future program needs, including special

SECRET
TOP SECRET

manpower requirements necessary to support the multi-purpose

specialized covert project objectives.

A. GENERAL GUIDELINES - PROJECT HEADQUARTERS
AND AREA 51

(1) Upon acceptance of this Security plan,

Project AQUILINE will be known by the classified

SECRET operational designator RECHARTER within OSA

areas of responsibility. The unclassified nickname

will be Project 274. The objectives, state-of-art

achievements, and mission purposes of Project RECHARTER

will be controlled at the TOP SECRET level in

accordance with site-sensitive program concepts based

on the traditional "must know" philosophy practiced by

OSA.

(2) As appropriate, the above designators will

be used in all verbal and written correspondence to

Area 51 and the names of all personnel approved for

project access will be maintained on permanent record

by the Security Office at Area 51 and at Project

Headquarters.

(3) Classified documents and correspondence:

(a) All communications and documents

regarding Project RECHARTER activities will be marked

classified and controlled at the appropriate level of

SECRET

TOP SECRET

sensitivity and will be limited to personnel who are

approved for Program RECHARTER access as certified

by Project Headquarters.

(b) TOP SECRET documents must be

transmitted via approved courier system.

(4) Access to Area 51 will be controlled from

Project Headquarters, OSA. Individuals from CIA,

other government agencies, or Project related industry

will be certified for access to Area 51 only after

establishment of clearability and with sufficient notice

and biographical data to insure verification of identity

and clearability particulars. Failure to transmit

required notice will result in denial of access.

(5) Clearance basis:

(a) Clearability standards for Area 51

access require at least a Phase II investigation which

includes a 15-year background investigation and NAC's.

(b) Personnel to be used in missions

and/or deployment overseas activities will be processed

at the Phase III level.

(6) West Coast Security Office, Office of Special

Activities, will act for West Coast facilities as a point

of contact for access to Area 51 after initial certification

clearability by Project Headquarters.

SECRET

TOP SECRET

TOP SECRET
SECRET

(7) Project RECHARTER personnel assigned to work at Area 51 will comply with rules and regulations detailed in Attachment A. Attachment A represents the approved policy of the Director of Special Activities as executed by the Field Commander at Area 51. Tenant organizations are responsible for the direct control of their personnel and they must ensure compliance with base standards, operating procedures, Security/Cover, and applicable USAF regulations. Violations or infractions will be reported to Project Headquarters promptly.

(8) All personnel certified for Project information will be Security briefed at the approved level of access and will execute briefing statements (oath), as contained in Attachment B. Reindoctrinations will be periodically rescheduled as part of Project Security Education Program.

(9) Attachment C Briefing Booklet will be used as guideline for briefing of Phase III personnel which is the usual government access level based on clearability standards expressed in DCID 1/14. Pertaining to other compartmented information programs.

SECRET

TOP SECRET

(10) Criteria for Security access to RECHARTER operational matters:

Phase I

A Phase I approval is required for an individual who is engaged in semi-sensitive fabrication activities but who does not work in nor require access to a closed Project area. Such individuals do not need to know and will not be told the ultimate application or future sensitive use of the equipment being developed or manufactured. Neither will they be permitted access to Project communications or documents. Generally speaking, the work which he is doing could have a variety of applications and is a job that is not unique to the development of Project hardware. (No access to Area 51.)

Phase II

A Phase II approval is required for an individual who may be told, assuming the need to know exists, the general purpose of the system, equipment or system configuration, performance characteristics, identification of other contractors, suppliers and vendors, test site locations and knowledge of equipment or subsystem capabilities. In general, this individual will be told information, requirements and parameters which

~~TOP SECRET~~

reflect an advance in the state of the art or, by the nature of the function he performs, will have access to areas, material or information from which he might be able to deduce such knowledge. (Access to Area 51 permitted.)

Phase III

A Phase III approval is required and will be granted only for those individuals who require official confirmation of the true identity of Project Headquarters. Personnel who must know broad mission objectives, operational information, success or failure of missions, future planning, or relationship to other classified programs normally require a Phase III approval. Likewise, operational mission details of the system will only be released to those who have a Phase III Access Approval. Phase III approvals will not be granted as a matter of courtesy, deference or convenience either within government or industry and all requests for approval at this level must be adequately justified. (Access to Area 51 permitted and to overseas operating locations.)

(11) Compartmentation of the Project RECHARTER physical location will be the responsibility of the assigned Staff Security Officer and a contingent of five contract

~~SECRET~~
~~TOP SECRET~~

Security Assistants/Guards that will control the hangar

and operating areas including classified equipment,

documents, systems and peculiar stored stocks.

(12) Security philosophy on a "must know" basis

will be practiced to ensure holddown on sensitive details,

particularly when Project RECHARTER launch and recovery

procedures are in effect during flight testing, training

and operations.

(13) A Staff Security Officer directly responsive

to Project Headquarters, Security Staff will be available

to assist the Program Manager in the Project RECHARTER

area throughout all flight testing, training and support

activities. Appropriate liaison and coordination with the

Base Commander will be accomplished to ensure the

integrity of Project RECHARTER and other compartmented

activities utilizing Area 51. This senior security official

will be responsible for all personnel, physical and

project matters of a security nature carried out at that

facility. As requirements increase, security manpower

must be augmented to ensure project coverage.

(14) Travel to Area 51 will be coordinated in

advance to facilitate access and may be arranged by

SECRET
TOP SECRET

surface or approved air shuttle service. (Cover contingency considerations will be provided upon the introduction of an approved air system.)

(15) Project RECHARTER operational clearances do not entitle approved personnel to special intelligence information or other special Project programs at Area 51.

(16) Periodic counter audio inspections and physical surveys of Project RECHARTER areas will be scheduled as required.

B. INDUSTRIAL SECURITY

(1) Close liaison with Office of Logistics will be accomplished throughout the transition period to ensure a uniform industrial security criteria at McDonnell Douglas and other principal Project related firms.

(2) The Office of Special Activities Security Staff will take cognizance of industrial contracts initiated by the OSA contracting staff in support of forthcoming operational phases.

(3) Industrial security inspections of OSA contractor areas will be conducted periodically in accordance with standards presently practiced by OSA.

(4) The industrial security package will be hand-tailored to the contractors' peculiar environment in

accordance with the level of classification of its

activities in conjunction with the "must know"

philosophy expressed throughout this plan.

(5) The prime contractor will enforce compliance

with security policy at subcontractors, vendors and

suppliers. (McDonnell Douglas, etal.)

(6) Sterilization of operational vehicles and

associated systems and subsystems, when deemed

necessary, will be accomplished to ensure the contingency

cover integrity of future operational missions.

C. OPERATIONAL/MISSION SECURITY PROCEDURES

(1) The Office of Special Activities Security Staff

will employ highly specialized techniques where and when

appropriate to protect the Project RECHARTER mission,

methods, assets, fuel, and personnel.

(2) Operational security procedures will be

prepared to meet the needs of each mission situation as

determined by the Contingency Cover stipulations imposed.

(3) Mission and unit personnel will be briefed

in advance of all operational activities on cover details.

(4) Office of Special Activities will provide

priority covert courier support for the expeditious move-

ment of mission systems, hardware and classified

intelligence product, as required.

TOP SECRET

(5) Liaison with U.S. Government, industry, and overseas security and law enforcement channels or host governments will be accomplished before, during and after the mission sequence, as required and in accordance with Headquarters instructions.

(6) A Staff Security Officer(s) and appropriate contract security assistants/guards/couriers will accompany the mission team on overseas deployment to provide security support, advice, guidance and control of operating mission locations and particularly at launch/recovery points.

D. CONTINGENCY COVER PLANS

(1) Contingency Cover Plan for Area 51 flight testing program is contained in the Cover Plan, Attachment D.

(2) Contingency Cover Plan for contingency mission deployment and flight testing outside Area 51 are included in the Cover Plan, Attachment D.

15. Conceptual Security Support

Appropriate Security support to include physical, personnel and operational security is being provided during the Pre-Operational Period and will be provided during the Operational Period. Additionally, security of the entire Industrial effort now rests with another Agency component, but will be continued by OSA Security Staff at an appropriate future date.

a. Physical Security:

(1) Secure perimeter of operating, training testing locations from unauthorized entry.

(2) Provide appropriate surveillance of vehicles, fuel, subsystems, and other sensitive, associated systems and assets.

(3) Conduct periodic counter-audio inspections of Detachment areas, installations and associated communications equipment.

(4) Assure implementation of appropriate security controls for safe guarding the movement and storage of classified equipment and documents.

(5) Establish physical security program to ensure integrity of sight sensitive characteristics of AV and related systems.

b. Personnel Security:

(1) Assure that personnel assigned to or visiting industrial work areas and operating locations have been granted the appropriate Security clearance and are approved for access to the location by Project Headquarters.

(2) Requests for program clearances will be processed in accordance with existing OSA Security Staff criteria.

(3) Establish briefing controls whereby the Project knowledge of cleared personnel will be restricted on an individual "must know" basis.

TOP SECRET

(4) Monitor the security consciousness of all Project-cleared personnel, and advise Project Headquarters of any individual's conduct, personal or official, which might tend to compromise the unit or mission.

(5) Establish an organized system of periodic security reindoctrinations for all cleared personnel.

(6) Investigate security violations and incidents, and recommend appropriate disciplinary action to Project Headquarters.

c. Operational Security:

(1) Employ deceptive techniques when and where appropriate to protect the mission, assets and personnel.

(2) Maintain liaison with local law enforcement and security forces and solicit their assistance in establishing effective security support.

(3) Establish security procedures for emergency situations.

(4) Promulgate mission and unit cover stories to personnel at operating locations.

(5) Assure sterilization of mission configured vehicle.

(6) Provide couriers for expeditious movement of mission product to the processing facility and to Headquarters.

(7) Security officer member of the Mobility Team will provide Security advice and guidance to Mobility Team Commander and will ensure implementation of above security responsibilities.

d. Cover and Contingency Plan: (See Cover and Contingency Annex).

TOP SECRET

TOP SECRET
AQUILINE

20 Feb 69.

3.5(c)
3.3(h)(2)

PROJECT AQUILINE

CONCEPT OF OPERATIONS

PROJECT AQUILINE

JANUARY 1969 STATUS

The AQUILINE program is still in its early conceptual stages. At this stage OSA and ORD are working in close coordination to resolve problems associated with bringing this new program to a practical and viable intelligence tool. The following concept of operations is derived from the latest available planning factors and guidelines. It is designed to present the program's minimum requirements through FY-1975.

AQUI-0001/69
Copy ___ of ___
Page _2_ of ___

TOP SECRET
AQUILINE

PROJECT AQUILINE

CONCEPT OF OPERATIONS

1. MISSION

To develop, attain and maintain an operational capability to conduct covert aerial reconnaissance of selected worldwide targets.

2. DEFINITIONS

a. For the purpose of brevity, the AQUILINE airborne vehicle is abbreviated as AV.

b. To further identify and segment project AQUILINE required equipments, the Air Ground Control Station is abbreviated as AGCS. The first of these stations (developed by the Office of Research and Development (ORD)) will be given the designation of AGCS-1. As additional stations are completed they will be given subsequent numerical designations - AGCS-2, etc.

c. Pre-Operational Period: (Prior to 1 January 1971)

The period preceding operational readiness to accomplish the primary mission.

d. Operational Period: (Subsequent to 1 January 1971)

(1) Limited Capability: (1 January 1971 to 1 July 1972)

The capability to perform limited operational missions on a "calculated risk" basis should be achieved by 1 January 1971. Non-availability of the full range airborne relay, (micro-miniaturized) system, and equipment reliability experience data will be limiting factors during this period. For planning purposes, one operational mission can be flown per quarter during this period.

(2) Design Capability: (1 July 1972 and on)

Eighteen months subsequent to attaining a limited capability, the program will have the ability to accomplish one (1) operational mission per month. The advanced lightweight micro-miniaturized special systems will increase the range capability and provide a high degree of systems reliability. Operational readiness for all systems will have been demonstrated prior to attaining this, the design capability.

AQUI-0001/69
Copy ___ of ___
Page _3_ of ___

3. OBJECTIVES - PRE-OPERATIONAL PERIOD

    During this period the primary emphasis will be directed toward
the accomplishment of the following major tasks:

    a. The development and procurement of new equipment and systems
    which will comprise the AQUILINE special targeting surveillance
    system, allied systems, and supporting equipment.

    b. The selection and preparation of the Area-51 airdrome and
    supporting equipment for project AQUILINE.

    c. The completion and preparation of selected portions of
    Area-51 support facilities for project AQUILINE.

    d. The logistical build-up at Area-51 required to support the
    Pre-Operational Period and the continued build-up in logistical
    capability to support the Operational Period.

    e. The planning, programming and coordination required to be
    ready to implement the Operational Period programs to include
    environmental studies, and systems integration.

    f. The completion of specialized communications facilities
    required for the coordination and control of AGCS-1/AV flight
    test program.

    g. The training of selected operational teams and supervisory
    personnel and the continued testing and development of the AQUILINE
    reconnaissance systems to an operational readiness status.

    h. The training and familiarization of support personnel with
    the new systems and equipment preparatory to the commencement of
    AQUILINE operations.

    i. The development and feasibility testing of tactics and
    operational employment and control procedures.

4. AQUILINE UTILIZATION AND CONTROL

    a. AQUILINE Vehicles:

        (1) AQUILINE vehicles which are instrumented as flight test
        vehicles will be under the control of the Office of Research and

AQUI-0001/69
Copy ___ of ___
Page 4 of ___

Development (ORD) until their requirement as test vehicles no longer exists. At this time, to be determined by Project Headquarters, these vehicles will be retrofitted for operational missions and their control transferred to the Field Program Director.

(2) AQUILINE vehicles purchased for operational mission usage will be flight tested for air worthiness by McDonnel Douglas Corporation prior to delivery to the Field Program Director. Vehicle acceptance procedures will be established by Project Headquarters.

(3) Procurement schedule for the operational AQUILINE vehicles is contained in TAB

b. AQUILINE Ground Control Stations (AGCS):

(1) AGCS-1 will be under the management and control of ORD until initial vehicle flight testing and interface requirements have been met. At the conclusion of the ORD testing, the AGCS-1 will be retrofitted for operational usage and management and control of the system will be transferred to the Field Program Director. Project Headquarters will determine the operational configuration of AGCS-1 and will determine the transfer date.

(2) AGCS-2 and subsequent ground control stations will incorporate the improvements dictated during flight testing conducted by ORD on AGCS-1. Management and control of AGCS-2 will be under the Field Program Director.

c. Supporting Aircraft:

During the pre-operational period, a chase and communications relay platform aircraft will be required. A Cessna 210 aircraft, currently in position at Area-51, will satisfy this requirement.

5. CONCEPT - PRE-OPERATIONAL PERIOD

a. Developmental Flight Testing:

(1) The first of the AV's developmental flight tests will begin in June 1970. Following that date, approximately 6-8 months will be devoted to completing the flight tests required to establish the total system airborne parameters of the AV's. Prior to the

first AV flight, the first air ground control station (AGCS-1) will have been constructed. Concurrent with the AV flight test activities there will be an on-going developmental and product improvement program underway for the AGCS-1.

(2) During the early RD&E period (June 70 - Jan 71) it is envisaged that an aircraft (U-3-T-33-C130) will be used as the interim communications link between the AV's and the AGCS. Subsequent to this testing period, but prior to achieving a limited operational capability with the AV's, it is planned to supplement the aircraft commo link with a satellite communications link. It is possible that at some point during the RD&E phase the transition from aircraft communications link to an in being satellite communications link [   ] can be made.

(3) During the fourth quarter FY-71 (April 71 - June 71) it may be possible to conduct as many as three limited range operational missions. The capability to conduct operational missions in FY-71 will be dependent upon the completion status of the AGCS-2, the status of training, the satellite command and control link, and other factors having direct bearing on mission capability.

b. Personnel Manning Concept:

(1) Billets for the AQUILINE field unit should be primarily civilian. Complexity of training requirements inherent in management and operation of the airborne vehicle and ground control station, coupled with the expertise required to maintain and support the vehicle and sensor systems, will make recurring recruitment of personnel very impractical. Use of semi-permanent contract and staff personnel that can be retained with the AQUILINE program will enhance the continuing operational capability of the project and will improve necessary project security.

(2) During the early stages of the program (FY-70), initial recruitment of the AQUILINE's field detachment will have been completed. Supervisory personnel by title are: Field Program Director, Manager Flight Systems, and a Manager Systems Support Officer. These individuals will become the nuclei of the AQUILINE operational unit and will be responsible for effecting the orderly and efficient transition of the program from the RD&E phase to an operational ready status.

(3) The initial months of FY-71 will be devoted to further personnel recruitment, training, and further flight testing of the AV-1's/AGCS. It is envisaged that by January 1971, the personnel complement of the AQUILINE's field unit will be approximately 39 personnel. This strength level includes Agency contract and staff positions. It will be augmented by commercial contractors as required.

(4) It is envisaged that Headquarters, OSA, as presently manned, can assimilate the AQUILINE's program into its pre-operational structure with only minimal increases in manning. These Headquarters tasks have been identified as follows: Program Director, Manager Flight Systems, Manager System Support, and an Automation Data Processing Specialist. Support for the above OSA management personnel assigned to Project AQUILINE will be provided from existing OSA and Agency staff resources.

c. Unit Operational Readiness Training:

(1) During FY-70 the Program Director (PD), the Manager Flight Systems (MFS), and the Manager Systems Support (MSS) will begin training with the AQUILINE program. This training will be on the job type training with the prime and sub-systems contractors. Additionally, these individuals will be in attendance as observers on all developmental tests that will occur during the early stages of the program.

(2) During FY-71 the Field Units Training Program will begin after recruitment of the field personnel has been completed. This training will center around the unit's Flight Teams. It is planned for this training to be divided into two parts; vehicle and system assembly, and flight operations. The purpose of the initial training is to best describe the field unit's training requirements, and to outline the functions of the Flight Team during a typical actual operation.

(3) Pre-Mission Countdown:

(a) Project Headquarters receives targeting requirements for AQUILINE.

(b) Project Headquarters alerts field unit for deployment and operational mission. Targets, suggested flight plan, special systems, etc., are sent to field.

AQUI-0001/69
Copy ___ of ___
Page 7 of ___

*(c) One Flight Team, under the direction of the Manager Flight Systems, assembles the mission data and programs the AGCS computers. As soon as sufficient target information has been programmed into the AGCS, the team will begin simulated mission training.

*(d) While the first team is involved in the flight phase preparations, the second team will be responsible for assembling, performing required ground checks (and flight checks if required) on the AV and its special systems. This team will be under the auspices of the Support System Manager during these pre-mission checkouts of the AQUILINE vehicle.

*(e) At Headquarters direction, the Flight Teams, Launch and Recovery Teams, the AGCS, the AV's, and necessary support personnel equipment will be deployed to a forward location.

*(f) Once deployed, the Flight Teams will have the capability to launch, control, and recover the AQUILINE vehicle on operational missions.

*Denotes training requirements.

6. OBJECTIVES - OPERATIONAL PERIOD

During this period the following major tasks will be accomplished:

a. The continued testing of equipment systems and procedures in order to improve the operational capability and reliability of the overall program.

b. The development of the micro-miniaturized special systems and other weight reduction programs for the purpose of achieving the maximum designed ranges with the AQUILINE vehicle.

c. The continued training of the Flight Teams and support personnel.

d. Execute covert aerial technical intelligence collection missions at selected high priority targets.

TOP SECRET
AQUILINE

7. CONCEPT - OPERATIONAL PERIOD (1 January 71 -   )

   a. A total of eighteen (18) AQUILINE vehicles will be required to support planned operations. All vehicles will be located at Area-51, which will be used as the permanent training and support base for forward stagings as required. Following is the anticipated disposition of the assigned vehicles:

     (1) Six engineering development vehicles are to be used as test vehicles under ORD management and control until Research and Development Engineering is complete. Remaining vehicles, after flight tests by ORD, will be retrofitted and made available to the AQUILINE Field Program Director as replacement vehicles.

     (2) One vehicle in modification and retrofit.

     (3) One vehicle for training (minus payload).

     (4) Four vehicles in the operational fleet to be maintained in an operational readiness status.

     (5) Twelve vehicles as operational inventory.

   b. Operational missions will be directed and controlled by Project Headquarters against approved AQUILINE target requirements.

   c. Operational missions will be planned by the field unit based on directions provided by Project Headquarters. Mission routes will be prepared and assigned to teams that will prepare for deployment. The deployment teams will simulate their operational missions at the training site. At the conclusion of training by each team, they will be given an operational readiness evaluation by Project Headquarters, who will certify that the team is ready to deploy to an advanced location in preparation for a subsequent mission execution by Project Headquarters. When the mobile teams are deployed to an advanced operation location, the following supporting actions will be required:

     (1) Necessary ground control and support personnel will be prepositioned at a forward location.

     (2) The mission vehicle(s) and spares will be ferried to the forward base from Area-51.

AQUI-0001/69
Copy ___ of ___
Page _9_ of ___

AQUILINE
TOP SECRET

TOP SECRET
AQUILINE

(3) Mission flight planning (flight plan, controller's charts, route maps, route photos, computer program tapes, etc.) will be prepared at Area-51 and ferried to the forward base.

(4) The mission(s) crew(s) will be airlifted to the forward operating location in sufficient time to provide necessary crew and systems check-out prior to execution of planned missions by Project Headquarters.

8. OPERATIONAL MISSION PLANNING

a. Upon receipt of mission requirements from Project Headquarters, the Field Program Director at Area-51 will direct accomplishment of mission planning and preparation of the mobile AQUILINE teams to satisfy the levied mission requirements. Mission route planning information required to prepare for AQUILINE missions will be supplied by all community services. AQUILINE performance factors, determined during the Pre-Operational Period, will be used in planning for initial operational missions.

b. Missions will be planned and flown along preplanned and rehearsed routes. Mission preplanning and preparation will be accomplished by the teams that will deploy to satisfy dictated mission requirements. During mission preparation, maximum cross-training and coordination will be conducted between the deployment operations teams to insure maximum flexibility during field operations.

9. OPERATIONAL COMMAND/CONTROL

a. Once mission generation has begun Project Headquarters will direct and control AQUILINE operational missions through the use of Policy Directives, Mission Directives, Tactical Doctrine and Reports Control Manual. The responsibility for mission implementation and detailed supervision will be vested in the designated deployed Flight Director.

b. A Command and Execution Chart is included as Attachment

c. An Operational Communications Chart is included as Attachment

AQUI-0001/69
Copy _____ of _____
Page 10 of _____

AQUILINE
TOP SECRET

.0. OPERATIONAL MISSION GENERATION

The following major actions will be accomplished in the generation of each operational mission. Timing of these actions may vary dependent upon the operational employment concept used as more experience is gained in defining mission "countdown" requirements.

    a. Upon receipt of approval to execute an operational mission, Project Headquarters will direct that an AQUILINE mobility team be dispatched to the pre-planned advanced staging location. The mobility team and associated equipment will be in position, ready to react to mission execution within 96 hours.

    b. Project Headquarters will alert the appropriate overseas locations as required of an impending operation. The notification will provide arrival times of the mobility team to the advanced location.

    c. Based on weather watch information, Project Headquarters will provide weather updating information to the deployed mobility team.

    d. The mobility team will be prepared to launch the AQUILINE vehicle within two hours after receipt of mission launch execution from Project Headquarters.

    e. The senior deployed mobility team's Flight Director will report mission readiness status to Project Headquarters twenty-four hours after arrival at the advanced operating location. Subsequent to the initial status report, mission readiness status will be forwarded to Project Headquarters every eight hours until the go-no-go message is received. The senior Flight Director at the deployed operating location will retain the final prerogative of cancelling a mission for reasons of local weather or other system operating conditions.

    f. At H-hour, the AQUILINE will be launched on the operational mission. During the mission, the duty Flight Director will keep Project Headquarters informed via message traffic (operational immediate precedence) every four hours on vehicle status and mission progress.

AQUI-0001/69
Copy ____ of ____
Page _11_ of ____

AQUILINE
TOP SECRET
Approved for Release: 2019/11/05 C02387106

g.   The Project Headquarters Weather Staff will begin transmitting AQUILINE mission weather reports as soon as the
mobility team is in place and communication is established
with Project Headquarters. Weather information necessary
to support the alerted operational mission will be transmitted
to the mobility teams every twelve hours, and will be updated,
as required, by operational immediate precedence during the
operational missions.

11.   SURVIVABILITY

a.   The probability of detection and intercept of the AQUILINE
vehicle during operational missions is being thoroughly studied
and evaluated in a "Survivability Program" conducted by the McDonnel
Douglas Missile and Space Systems Division. Capability of enemy
defensive systems to destroy the vehicle, once acquired, are also
being studied.

b.   Preliminary evaluations indicate that avoidance of detection
by defensive systems will be the prime consideration in providing
an acceptable survivability rate for the AQUILINE vehicle. A
computer program to determine lowest risk routes for the AQUILINE
vehicle is being developed.

12.   WEATHER SUPPORT

a.   Training:

(1)   Weather support for all Area-51 training missions will be
provided by the weather facilities at Area-51.

(2)   Upon request, Global Weather Central will provide route
and area forecasts which are beyond the capability of Area-51
Weather Station. All requests will be sent through Project
Headquarters Weather Staff, except matters which require
immediate action.

b.   Operational Missions:

(1)   Weather forecasts will be provided by WECEN as required
by Project Headquarters. Upon receipt of these forecasts,

AQUI-0001/69
Copy ____ of ____
Page 12 of ____

briefings will be prepared and presented to Project Headquarters
staff personnel for mission planning, decision making, and
direction of missions. Cloud cover above 400 feet is considered
acceptable for photographic missions due to the low altitude
capability of the vehicle. For ELINT or other type missions,
lower cloud cover is not expected to interfere with the mission,
since positions can be determined by means other than visual
reference to the ground.

(2) AQUILINE missions are of long duration; consequently, the
forecast reliability will be a factor in the later stages of a
mission. Updated forecasts for command and control will be a
necessity. Short range forecasts will be passed to the field
station by Project Headquarters Weather Staff. Long range forecasts will be developed at Project Headquarters to determine
directed decisions on route and target changes. Missions flown
in no data regions will rely on television and Mission Flight
Director readout to avoid unacceptable weather.

13. LOGISTICAL SUPPORT

a. Supply:

(1) Supply policies and procedures are based primarily on the
support that is provided through contractor-source supplies
and equipment. Project Headquarters develops and issues supply
policies and procedures for compliance by the field activity
in meeting special requirements. Except in special situations
attributable to the nature or exigencies of the program, minimum
reliance is made on availability of DOD procured assets.

(2) Initial spares provisioning for the air vehicle and its
associated systems and ground support equipment are determined
by the contractors, and reviewed and approved by Project
Headquarters. Follow-on provisioning, as dictated by operational
experience and spares consumption factors, includes a joint
review by the contractors, the field activity, and Project
Headquarters; as approving authority.

(3) Programming and budgeting for spares procurement and for the
repair and overhaul of equipment and components are performed at
Project Headquarters. Operational concepts, including anticipated
flying time, missions planned, and operating locations, as well as
engineering and technical performance factors, form the basis for
programming these budget requirements.

AQUI-0001/69
Copy ____ of ____
Page 13 of ____

(4) Stock levels of hardware, spares and systems components are initially established upon the recommendations made by the contractors and will be approved by Project Headquarters. Consideration is given to providing the contractor's repair facility with sufficient bonded stock to enable the expeditious turn-around of project repairables. Adjustments to stock levels are made as indicated by operational experience and usage data.

(5) The field activity possesses self-contained, self-sustaining supply operation. It is, to all intents and purposes, capable of operating as an activity independent of other support elements in the same locale. At its home station (Area-51) it is provided such additional support as may be required in performance of logistical functions beyond its organic capability.

(6) Functions basic to the supply operation in the field activity are provided in property accounting, issues and receipts, packing and crating, warehousing, and related logistics areas, as fit the needs of the activity.

b. Transportation:

(1) Motor vehicles are not assigned as permanent organizational equipment to the field activity. Personnel transportation support is provided by the home station and at operating locations in keeping with local policies. Commercial transportation is available where time and operational factors are of essence.

(2) Project Headquarters manages and directs the movements of all heavy and bulky items of material from the contractor's facilities to the operating location. Routine requirements are normally shipped parcel post, railway express agency, and/or commercial air freight.

c. Maintenance:

(1) Contractor personnel are responsible for performance of maintenance on the air vehicle and its associated systems and support equipment, under the supervision of the Manager Systems Support in conjunction with the Flight Team.

(2) Maintenance planning factors as pertain to periodic inspections, time between overhauls, quality control and time change requirements are developed by the contractors and defined as operational experience is gained.

TOP SECRET
AQUILINE

b. Special Communications Support:

(1) Weather information (WECEN to Project Headquarters) is transmitted by digital data with photographic printout, backed up by teletype.

(2) Voice circuits, as well as teletype, will be used between the Ground Control System and launch/recovery sites to coordinate activities.

(3) Command and control of the vehicle is the major function of the Ground Control System. An airborne radio relay system will be used in the test phases. Operational deployment of the vehicle will require a satellite radio relay system. Supporting voice and teletype communications will be provided in the radio relays to coordinate vehicle launch and recovery operations.

CONCEPTUAL SECURITY SUPPORT

Appropriate security support, to include physical, personnel and operational security, is being provided during the Pre-Operational Period and will be provided during the Operational Period. Additionally, security of the entire industrial effort now rests with another Agency component, but will be continued by OSA Security Staff at an appropriate future date.

AQUILINE
TOP SECRET

a. Physical Security:

(1) Secure perimeter of operating, training, and testing locations from unauthorized entry.

(2) Provide appropriate surveillance of vehicles, fuel, subsystems, and other sensitive, associated systems and assets.

(3) Conduct periodic counter-audio inspections of Detachment areas, installations and associated communications equipment.

(4) Assure implementation of appropriate security controls for safeguarding the movement and storage of classified equipment and documents.

(5) Establish physical security program to ensure integrity of sight sensitive characteristics of AV and related systems.

b. Personnel Security:

(1) Assure that personnel assigned to or visiting industrial work areas and operating locations have been granted the appropriate security clearance and are approved for access to the location by Project Headquarters.

(2) Requests for program clearances will be processed in accordance with existing OSA Security Staff criteria.

(3) Establish briefing controls whereby the project knowledge of cleared personnel will be restricted on an individual "must know" basis.

(4) Monitor the security consciousness of all project-cleared personnel, and advise Project Headquarters of any individual's conduct, personal or official, which might tend to compromise the unit or mission.

(5) Establish an organized system of periodic security reindoc-trinations for all cleared personnel.

(6) Investigate security violations and incidents, and recommend appropriate disciplinary action to Project Headquarters.

TOP SECRET
AQUILINE

c. Operational Security:

  (1) Employ deceptive techniques when and where appropriate to protect the mission, assets and personnel.

  (2) Maintain liaison with local law enforcement and security forces and solicit their assistance in establishing effective security support.

  (3) Establish security procedures for emergency situations.

  (4) Promulgate mission and unit cover stories to personnel at operating locations.

  (5) Assure sterilization of mission configured vehicle.

  (6) Provide couriers for expeditious movement of mission product to the processing facility and to Headquarters.

  (7) Security Officer member of the Mobility Team will provide security advice and guidance to Mobility Team Commander and will ensure implementation of above security responsibilities.

AQUI-0001/69
Copy ____ of ____
Page 18 of ____

AQUILINE

AQUILINE

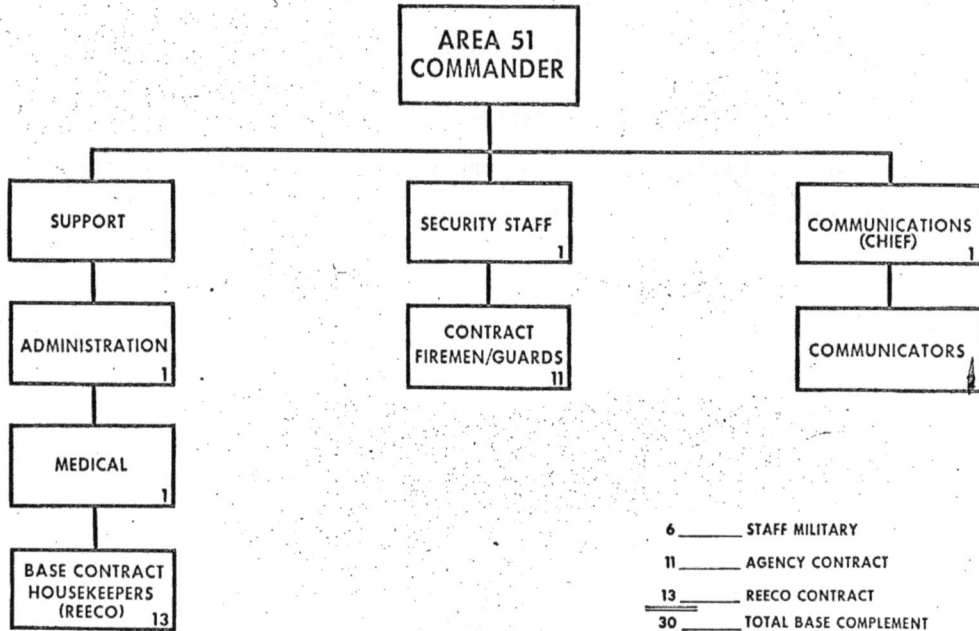

```
                        AREA 51
                       COMMANDER

        ┌──────────────────┼──────────────────┐

     SUPPORT          SECURITY STAFF      COMMUNICATIONS
                               1            (CHIEF)    1

  ADMINISTRATION        CONTRACT          COMMUNICATORS
             1       FIREMEN/GUARDS                    2
                               11

     MEDICAL
           1

  BASE CONTRACT
  HOUSEKEEPERS
    (REECO)   13
```

6	STAFF MILITARY
11	AGENCY CONTRACT
13	REECO CONTRACT
30	TOTAL BASE COMPLEMENT

DEPLOYMENT LOCATIONS

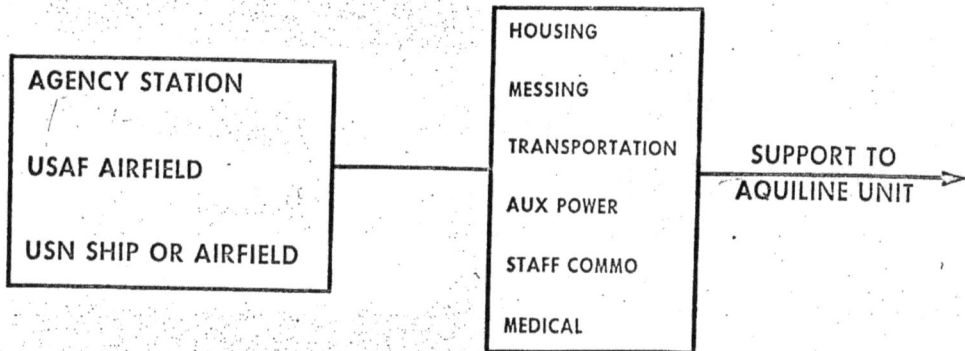

AGENCY STATION

USAF AIRFIELD

USN SHIP OR AIRFIELD

HOUSING

MESSING

TRANSPORTATION

AUX POWER

STAFF COMMO

MEDICAL

SUPPORT TO
AQUILINE UNIT →

AQUILINE

CONCEPTUAL AQUILINE ORGANIZATION AT AREA 51

(FY 71 - FY 72)

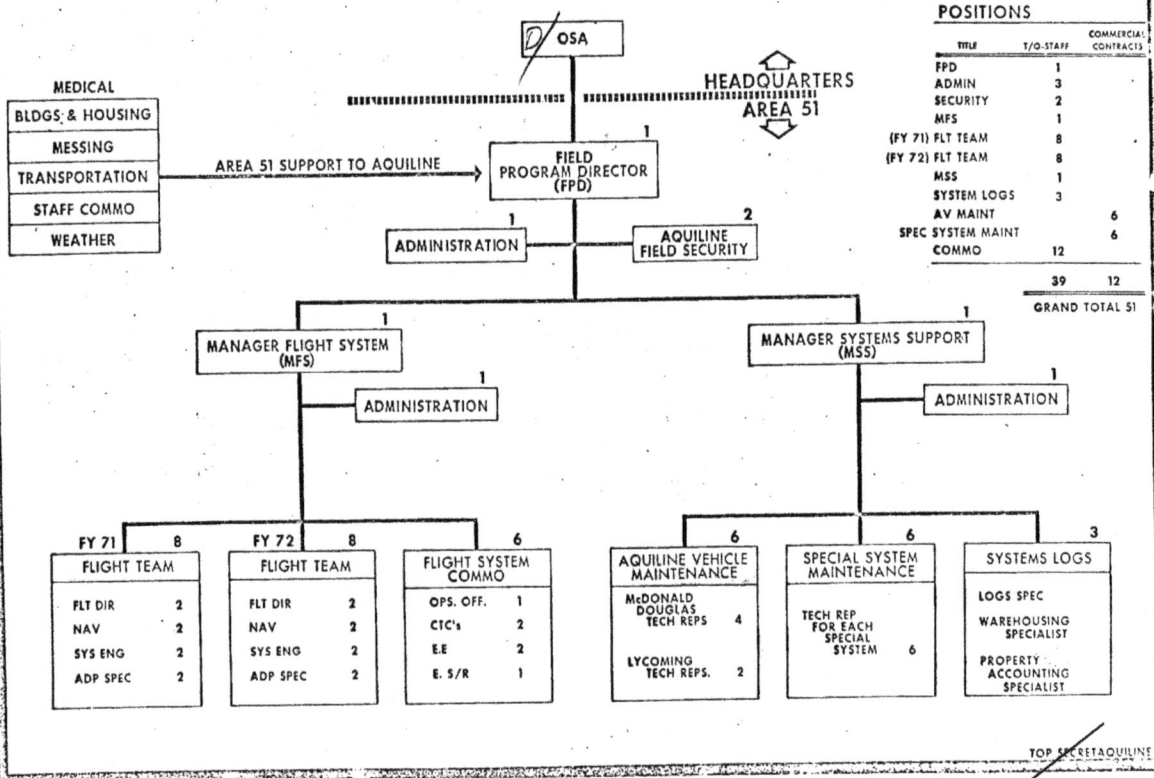

POSITIONS

TITLE	T/O-STAFF	COMMERCIAL CONTRACTS
FPD	1	
ADMIN	3	
SECURITY	2	
MFS	1	
(FY 71) FLT TEAM	8	
(FY 72) FLT TEAM	8	
MSS	1	
SYSTEM LOGS	3	
AV MAINT		6
SPEC SYSTEM MAINT		6
COMMO	12	
	39	12

GRAND TOTAL 51

MEDICAL

| BLDGS & HOUSING |
| MESSING |
| TRANSPORTATION |
| STAFF COMMO |
| WEATHER |

AREA 51 SUPPORT TO AQUILINE →

HEADQUARTERS AREA 51

D/OSA

FIELD PROGRAM DIRECTOR (FPD)   1

ADMINISTRATION   1

AQUILINE FIELD SECURITY   2

MANAGER FLIGHT SYSTEM (MFS)   1

ADMINISTRATION   1

MANAGER SYSTEMS SUPPORT (MSS)   1

ADMINISTRATION   1

FY 71   8
FLIGHT TEAM

FLT DIR	2
NAV	2
SYS ENG	2
ADP SPEC	2

FY 72   8
FLIGHT TEAM

FLT DIR	2
NAV	2
SYS ENG	2
ADP SPEC	2

FLIGHT SYSTEM COMMO   6

OPS. OFF.	1
CTC's	2
E.E	2
E. S/R	1

AQUILINE VEHICLE MAINTENANCE   6

| McDONALD DOUGLAS TECH REPS | 4 |
| LYCOMING TECH REPS. | 2 |

SPECIAL SYSTEM MAINTENANCE   6

| TECH REP FOR EACH SPECIAL SYSTEM | 6 |

SYSTEMS LOGS   3

LOGS SPEC

WAREHOUSING SPECIALIST

PROPERTY ACCOUNTING SPECIALIST

AQUILINE
CONCEPTUAL OVERSEAS DEPLOYMENT
(FY 71)
SINGLE LOCATION FOR LAUNCH-CONTROL-RECOVERY

DEPLOYED AQUILINE TEAM COMPOSITION

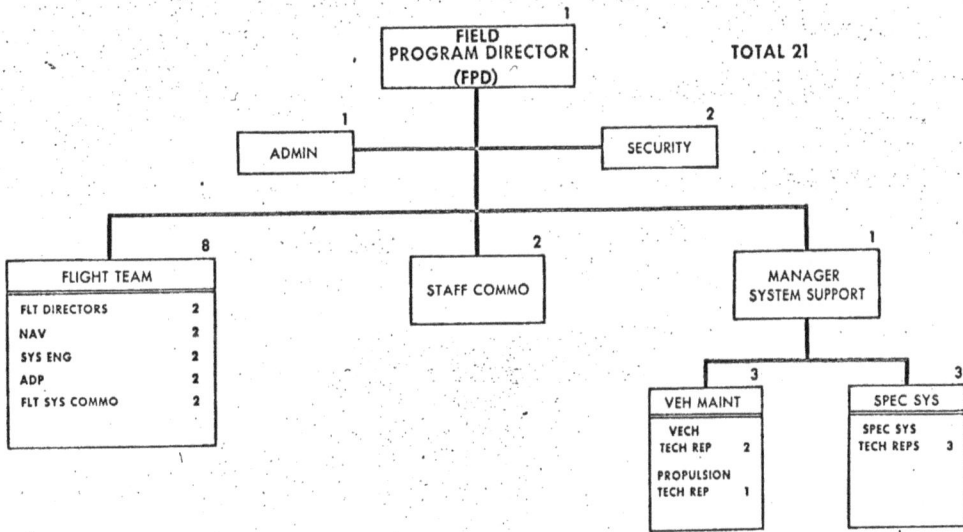

TOTAL 21

FIELD PROGRAM DIRECTOR (FPD) — 1

ADMIN — 1

SECURITY — 2

FLIGHT TEAM — 8
FLT DIRECTORS	2
NAV	2
SYS ENG	2
ADP	2
FLT SYS COMMO	2

STAFF COMMO — 2

MANAGER SYSTEM SUPPORT — 1

VEH MAINT — 3
VECH TECH REP	2
PROPULSION TECH REP	1

SPEC SYS — 3
SPEC SYS TECH REPS	3

AQUILINE

CONCEPTUAL OVERSEAS DEPLOYMENT

SEPARATE LOCATIONS FOR LAUNCH-CONTROL-RECOVERY (FY 72)

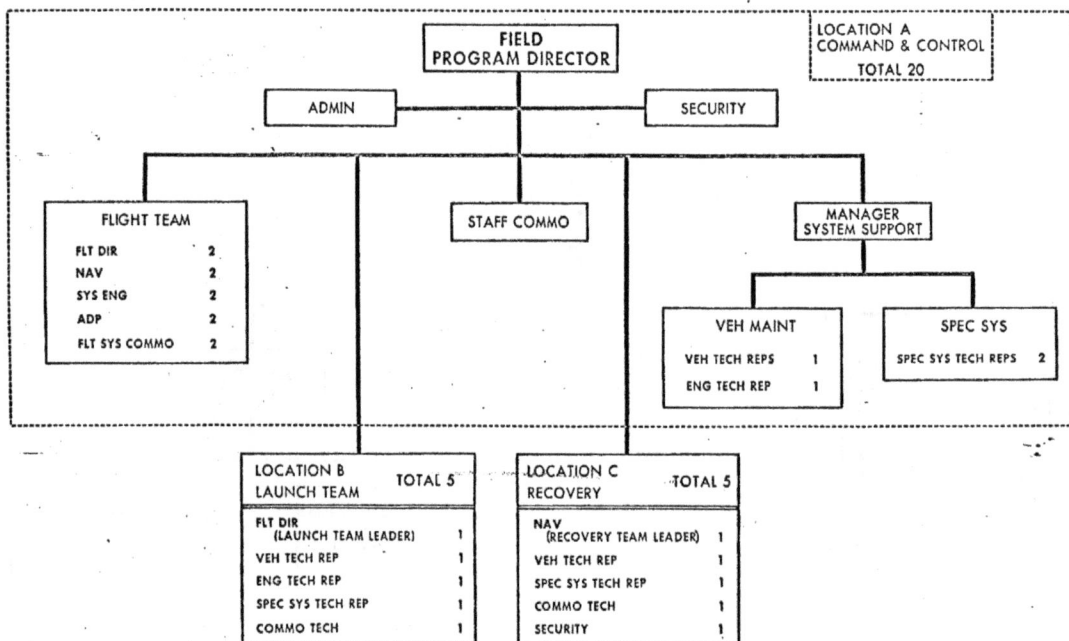

LOCATION A
COMMAND & CONTROL
TOTAL 20

FIELD
PROGRAM DIRECTOR

ADMIN

SECURITY

FLIGHT TEAM

FLT DIR	2
NAV	2
SYS ENG	2
ADP	2
FLT SYS COMMO	2

STAFF COMMO

MANAGER
SYSTEM SUPPORT

VEH MAINT

VEH TECH REPS	1
ENG TECH REP	1

SPEC SYS

SPEC SYS TECH REPS	2

LOCATION B LAUNCH TEAM — TOTAL 5

FLT DIR (LAUNCH TEAM LEADER)	1
VEH TECH REP	1
ENG TECH REP	1
SPEC SYS TECH REP	1
COMMO TECH	1

LOCATION C RECOVERY — TOTAL 5

NAV (RECOVERY TEAM LEADER)	1
VEH TECH REP	1
SPEC SYS TECH REP	1
COMMO TECH	1
SECURITY	1

AQUILINE

CONCEPTUAL AREA 51 COMPLEMENT DURING DEPLOYMENT
(TRAINING TESTING)
(FY 72)

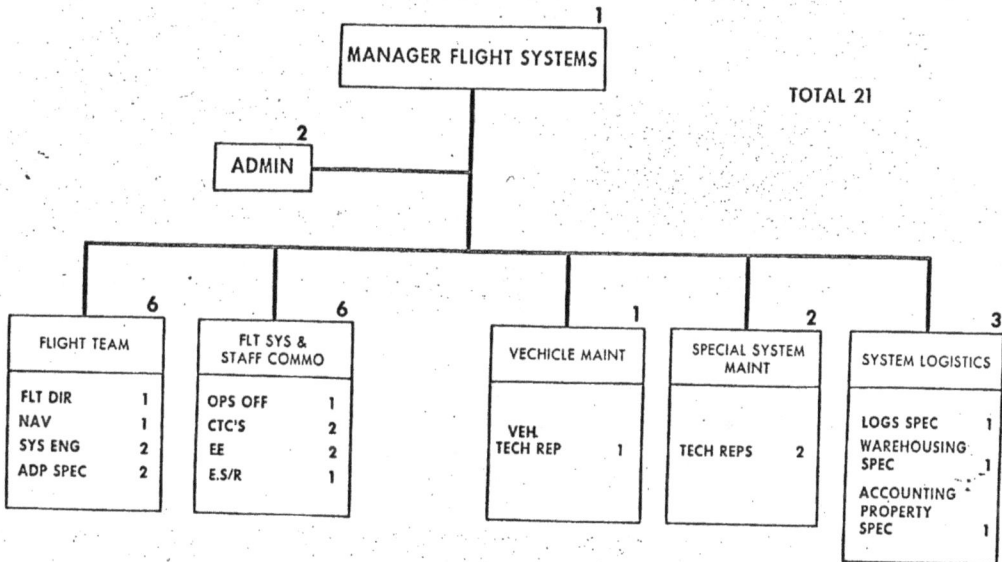

```
                    1
        MANAGER FLIGHT SYSTEMS                    TOTAL 21

        2
      ADMIN
```

FLIGHT TEAM (6)	FLT SYS & STAFF COMMO (6)	VECHICLE MAINT (1)	SPECIAL SYSTEM MAINT (2)	SYSTEM LOGISTICS (3)
FLT DIR 1	OPS OFF 1	VEH. TECH REP 1	TECH REPS 2	LOGS SPEC 1
NAV 1	CTC'S 2			WAREHOUSING SPEC 1
SYS ENG 2	EE 2			ACCOUNTING PROPERTY SPEC 1
ADP SPEC 2	E.S/R 1			

AQUILINE
OPERATIONAL COMMUNICATIONS

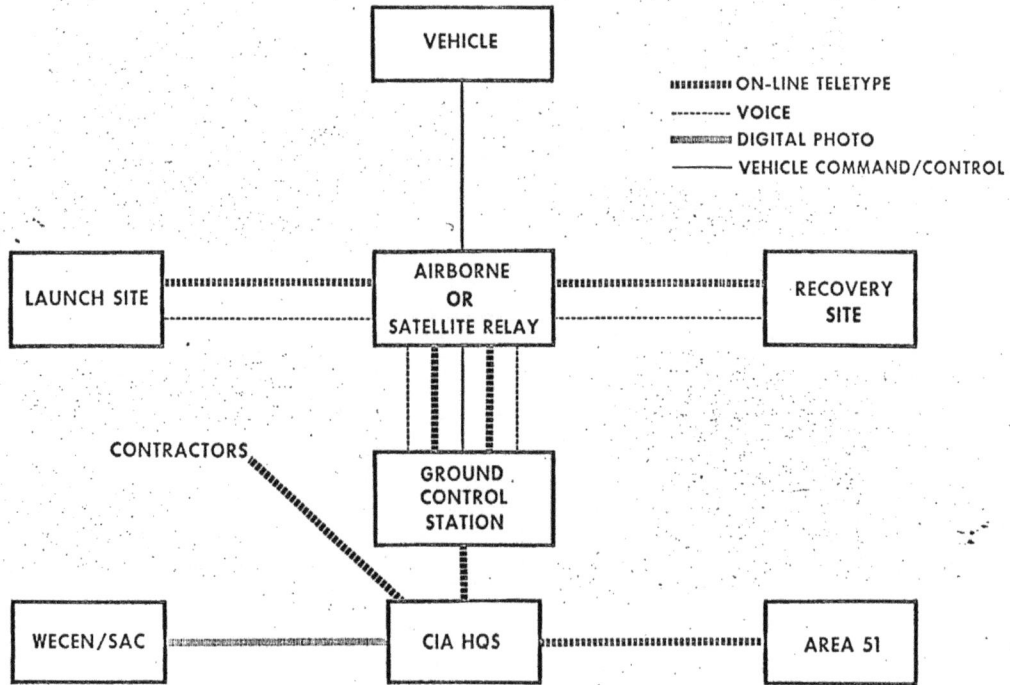

VEHICLE

Legend	
▪▪▪▪▪▪▪	ON-LINE TELETYPE
--------	VOICE
▬▬▬	DIGITAL PHOTO
———	VEHICLE COMMAND/CONTROL

LAUNCH SITE — **AIRBORNE OR SATELLITE RELAY** — **RECOVERY SITE**

CONTRACTORS

GROUND CONTROL STATION

WECEN/SAC — **CIA HQS** — **AREA 51**

TOP SECRET AQUILINE

TOP SECRET AQUIL

PROJECT AQUILINE PAYLOADS

SYSTEM	CAPABILITY	WEIGHT	POWER REQ
COMINT PACKAGE	20 MIN CAPACITY	5 LBS	60 WATTS AT 28 VDC
ELINT PACKAGE	6 HRS CAPACITY	5 LBS	50 WATTS AT 28 VDC
IR SCANNER	6 HRS CAPACITY	3½ LBS	2.5 WATTS AT 28 VDC
PHOTO CAMERA	10 MIN CAPACITY	5 LBS	20 WATTS AT 28 VDC

OFFICIAL ROUTING-SLIP

TO	NAME AND ADDRESS	DATE	INITIALS
1	SS		
2	SA/COVER		
3	SA/AS		..
4			
5	C/SS		
6	Aquiline		

ACTION	DIRECT REPLY	PREPARE REPLY
APPROVAL	DISPATCH	RECOMMENDATION
COMMENT	FILE	RETURN
CONCURRENCE	INFORMATION	SIGNATURE

Remarks:

Attached is a draft of the proposed charter for
AQUILINE. Request your comments by COB
8 August. This paper will also be coordinated
with ORD. Hope to have final paper for D/SA
and D/R&D signature by 15 August.

FOLD HERE TO RETURN TO SENDER

FROM: NAME, ADDRESS AND PHONE NO.	DATE
AQUI/O/OSA	

UNCLASSIFIED	CONFIDENTIAL	SECRET

DRAFT

MEMORANDUM FOR: Director of Special Activities

Director of Research and Development

SUBJECT : Project AQUILINE Policy, Functions and Responsibilities

REFERENCE : Project AQUILINE Concept of Operations, AQUI 0001-69

GENERAL

The AQUILINE Concept of Operations expressed in reference is approved. This memorandum prescribes policy and delineates functions and responsibilities for that Program.

STATEMENT OF POLICY

A. Sponsorship, support and management of AQUILINE will be wholly through CIA resources and auspices.

B. The objective is to provide CIA with an Intelligence vehicle uniquely fitted to mobile, covert employments. AQUILINE Project Managers will program and insure the execution of the development and operational activities necessary for the collective attainment of this objective.

FUNCTIONS AND RESPONSIBILITIES

A. Director of Research and Development will:

(1) Serve as Program Manager and have overall development responsibility for satisfactory completion of the Research and Development phase of Project AQUILINE.

(2) Collaborate with Office of Special Activities and other interested Agency Organizations to establish and insure that the operational employment requirements of the users are made an integral part of the development considerations.

SECRET

(3) Provide technical monitors and technical assistance, as required, to Office of Special Activities for the life of the program.

B. Director of Special Activities will:

(1) Serve as Program Manager and have overall responsibility for the operational phase of Project AQUILINE.

(2) Establish specific requirements for the logistic and maintenance support of the flight test and operational phases of the program.

(3) Collaborate with Office of Research and Development to insure that the system and operational support programs include logistic and maintenance considerations which can be supported and operated during the operational phase.

(4) Conduct the contracting and procurement for all aspects of the operational phases of the program.

(5) Establish specific requirements for the overall security of the test, training and operational phases of the program.

(6) Establish and backstop the overall cover plans and policy for the test, training and operational phases of the program.

(7) Organize, man, train and command the field unit responsible for the operational employment of the program.

(8) Conduct operational tests and evaluations of the project equipments and assigned field unit personnel for the purposes of determining the operational status of the project.

(9) Plan, develop and procure adequate and timely training for the field unit personnel.

(10) Develop, prepare and implement the concept of operations, operational policy, operational plans and overall program doctrine for the operational phases of the project.

CARL E. DUCKETT

SECRET

PROJECT AQUILINE

RESEARCH AND DEVELOPMENT STUDY

BEST COPY

3.3(h)(2)

AQUILINE

PROJECT AQUILINE

RESEARCH AND DEVELOPMENT STUDY

29 August 1967

~~SECRET~~

TABLE OF CONTENTS

~~SECRET~~

Small powered glider intelligence collection system . . .

Figure 2
Inboard Profile

MARK I

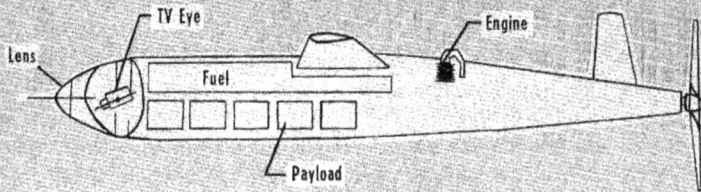

- Lens
- TV Eye
- Fuel
- Payload
- Engine

Figure 1
Radar Cross Section Model

Length - 4.75 feet

Wingspan - 6 feet

PROJECT AQUILINE
RESEARCH AND DEVELOPMENT STUDY

I   Nature and Purpose of the Study

In response to a Bureau of the Budget request, a research and development study has been prepared on Project AQUILINE. The AQUILINE system is a new concept in the collection of intelligence which encompasses development of the vehicle as well as the associated subsystems.

Research and development on the AQUILINE system was initiated to increase our capability for collection of intelligence against prime targets. Our present airborne collection systems are large and must fly very high and very fast to survive. The AQUILINE concept is to have a small vehicle which will fly low and slow and still have sufficient range. The successful development of the AQUILINE collection system depends heavily upon our ability to develop advanced microtechnology, microminiature sensors and power sources, sophisticated communications and control systems as well as an efficient, small aircraft.

This study is organized into four major sections. Section II presents a history of the program through fiscal year 1967

SECRET

including a description of its intelligence collection potential. Section III outlines the planned development program
for fiscal years 1968 and 1969. Section IV presents a detailed
description of the basic technology involved in the development
and a summary of the development concept. The final section
presents operational concepts and estimates program costs and
timing.

SECRET

~~SECRET~~

II   History

A.   Program Initiation.

During the past four years, the Office of Research and
Development has been investigating advanced concepts by which
"black box" sensors could be emplaced at strategic targets in
China, Russia, North Vietnam, and other denied areas. These
emplaced "black boxes" would collect intelligence from missile
test ranges, nuclear test facilities, BW/CW test areas, and
other prime targets. The collected information could be sent
in real time or be stored for later readout via radio to overflight aircraft or relay satellites.

A major difficulty in the present emplacement systems is
that the emplacement vehicle must execute the penetration and
drop the black box at a high altitude in order to avoid detection and/or interception. Consequently, black box payloads
designed for emplacement in this manner are large and heavy--a
few hundred pounds not being unusual. In addition, as the
opposition develops more sophisticated defense systems, our
opportunities to deliver black boxes using our present assets
will be grossly limited.

A solution to our present difficulty would be to employ a
system that would allow low altitude drops of small, light-

~~SECRET~~

3

SECRET

weight, low power solid state sensors. This would enhance the probability of the black box surviving the emplacement as well as decreasing the probability of it being detected. At present, solid state and microminiaturization technologies have progressed to the point where these small, light-weight, low power black boxes can be developed. To emplace these black boxes, however, requires a small, low flying emplacement vehicle system capable of long range surreptitious penetration. The AQUILINE project was initiated out of this requirement.

B. Program Concept.

The AQUILINE concept encompasses a very small bird-like emplacement and collection system. To determine AQUILINE system feasibility, internal and external studies were conducted. The early conceptual studies were conducted by the Naval Ordnance Test Station (NOTS), Douglas Aircraft Company, and others (see Figures 1 and 2). Mission analyses and cost effect- iveness studies indicated that the AQUILINE concept was feasible and held great promise as an advanced emplacement and collection system. Further, the studies established that the vehicle could exist for long periods of time in target areas and would be practically undetectable. Even if detected, it would be expensive and difficult to countermand. Its low altitude and low speed characteristics added to a long loiter time capability

SECRET

4

would permit detailed examination of the target areas and permit a wide variety of intelligence missions. Further, its small size and innocuous nature would make it more politically palatable in tense situations than conventional aircraft. It would be unmanned, smaller, and cheaper and, therefore, expendable on special missions. Because of these characteristics, it would be deployable against targets not accessible by any means at the present time. In early stages of development, it could complement existing high altitude systems by providing more detailed examination of selected short-range targets by flying below the cloud cover.

Concentrated studies have been performed on a wide range of aerodynamic lift devices including balloons, ballistic glider, powered glider and helicopter types for this application. The powered glider was selected because of the following considerations:

1. _Vehicle_. A small aerodynamically clean vehicle can be produced which will contain the miniature payloads and subsystems required for the mission contemplated.

2. _Propulsion_. A variety of propulsion systems such as two-cycle engines, four-cycle engines, fuel cell and radioisotope powered systems can be used to propel the vehicle. The four-cycle and radioisotope powered systems have a potential range of thousands of miles.

~~SECRET~~

3. Observability. Tests of mockup models demonstrate that such a vehicle and its subsystems could have low enough observability (visual, acoustic, radar and IR) to immerse itself in the indigenous signal environment of the target area, loitering unobtrusively while performing its mission.

4. Guidance and Navigation. Several guidance and navigation systems such as CHECKROTE, radio direction finding, transit satellites and Loran or Omega could direct this vehicle to within a few miles of the distant target.

5. TV Eye. The development of a subminiature TV Eye is feasible both in the visible and IR. The TV Eye can be employed for guidance and navigation as well as surveillance duties.

6. Communication Link. Secure communications for data transmission and vehicle control can be achieved at line-of-sight ranges and are feasible over the longer ranges by using relays such as a small vehicle of the same type, satellites or CHECKROTE.

7. Payloads. Photographic, IR, ELINT, audio, [ ] and droppable black box payloads being developed by various divisions in ORD can be employed in this system.

8. Mobility and Flexibility. Because of its size,

~~SECRET~~

6

~~SECRET~~

weight, and speed, the vehicle can be launched from a small boat or aircraft or a simple portable launcher.

9. <u>Range</u>. A range of ⬚ for the Initial Operational Capability (IOC)* version can be achieved. However, with a four-cycle internal combustion engine or fuel cells ranges of thousands of miles can be provided. Radioisotope engine versions could have unlimited range (30-day flight duration, 36,000 miles).

10. <u>Operations Research</u>. Computer programs for vehicle configuration systems integration, systems vulnerability and mission analysis have been initiated and can be further developed to insure the effectiveness of operational systems. Eventually the computer programs can be carried out in the Intelligence Processing Research and Development (IPRD) facility of ORD.

C. <u>FY 1967 Development Program</u>.

During fiscal year 1967, development of an emplacement/collection system configured as a small powered glider (AQUILINE) began with a budget of ⬚ dollars. The development concept of the AQUILINE system was refined and improved with:

1. The initiation of an IOC prototype development program.

*Used to designate the first generation vehicle and associated subsystem.

~~SECRET~~

7

Approved for Release: 2020/02/11 C03055187

SECRET

2. The continuation of advanced system studies by
Douglas Aircraft (System Contractor).

3. Institution of development programs in the subsystem areas of aerodynamics, propulsion, navigation,
communications, antennas, survivability studies, intelligence collecting payloads, and ground control equipment.

A flight test range was established and instrumented to
allow flight test of the airframe, its subsystems, and payloads
under development. The flight of the fully instrumented IOC
system is scheduled for October 1967. The IOC system will
include remotely controlled autopilot, navigation and communications equipment (including a slow-scan TV camera and associated
radio transmitter) and will be equipped to carry test payloads
up to five pounds to a range of

SECRET

8

Approved for Release: 2020/02/11 C03055187

~~SECRET~~

III Program Objectives

    A. <u>Overall Objective.</u>

The AQUILINE development program is designed to be evolutionary, i.e., its collection capability will be increased as advances in technology become available. Specifically, the program will require advances in the state-of-the-art in the critical areas of aerodynamics, propulsion, navigation, communication and payload instrumentation. <u>A major goal of the program is the ability to define an optimum collection system to be employed against a particular intelligence target using the technology currently available</u> (see Figure 3). A more detailed description of this aspect of the program is contained in Section IV below.

By late fiscal year 1968, the initial operational vehicle will be capable of flying   . missions at altitudes up to 10,000 feet carrying a payload of five pounds. Prototype hardware will enable the vehicle to be positioned and controlled within a CEP of 70 feet at distances to   . These capabilities are sufficient to perform intelligence collection missions against typical peripheral targets in USSR, China, and Cuba.

Computer programs have been developed to supply the detailed

~~SECRET~~
9

~~SECRET~~

design information needed to construct an AQUILINE vehicle and its subsystems. The computer program will optimize the vehicle and payloads for a specific mission against a specific target. and gives the probability of success for the mission.

B. FY 1968 Goals.

During fiscal year 1968, research and development on an Advanced Operational Capability (AOC) will be initiated. This program will consider four-cycle internal combustion engine designs, advanced subsystem elements, and payload instrumentation resulting from current microelectronics research and development efforts. The initial AOC goal will be for [   ] round-trip missions. Possible target areas would be the coastal regions of the Barents Sea, China, Vietnam, and Cuba. Low altitude imagery, ELINT and SIGINT collection devices are typical payloads which could be carried.

C. FY 1969 Goals.

The AQUILINE system capabilities for fiscal year 1969 will be increased by an advanced four-cycle engine which will extend the range to [   ] Emerging navigational technologies such as [   ] OMEGA* will provide the capability of using the AQUILINE vehicles in one-way missions against Lop Nor, Shuang-ch'eng-tzu and Sary Shagan. One specific objective for fiscal

*A navigation concept which utilizes the long range Navy OMEGA radio transmissions, retransmitted through a synchronous satellite to the ground station for decommutation and position location.

~~SECRET~~

10

year 1969 will be to emplace a black box within a CEP of
1/2 n.m. at 2400 n.m.

D.   Ultimate Goals.

During fiscal year 1970 and beyond, research and development will be oriented toward increasing the range, navigational
accuracy, data communication and storage capacities, loiter
time at target and the overall reliability of the system. Improved payloads which are lighter in weight will be under
development to collect a wider range of intelligence data under
varying conditions. In addition, initial operational experience
obtained from earlier deployed AQUILINE systems will be used to
guide future AQUILINE development.

~~SECRET~~

IV Program Plan

A. Approach.

The program plan used for development of an AQUILINE
system during fiscal year 1967 will be replaced by an overall
system's program in fiscal year 1968. This is necessary for
a variety of reasons. During fiscal year 1967, there were three
program areas:

    1.   IOC prototype development.

    2.   Interface (conceptual development)

    3.   Subsystem development

Three vehicles, each with increasing capability, were designed
and constructed under the IOC prototype development program
[   ] If in fiscal year 1968 we
were to follow this same schedule of building increasingly
refined test vehicles, we would quickly exceed fiscal year 1968
funding of [   ]. In addition, our increased understanding of the various subsystem requirements and a better estimate
of the costs involved in achieving these requirements has
placed ever increasing strain on our limited funds.

Further, mission analysis studies revealed that in order
to achieve acceptable probabilities of success against any particular target, a specially designed vehicle system should be
constructed and deployed. In an environment of continually
changing intelligence requirements, it becomes extremely difficult

SECRET

and prohibitively expensive to predict the mission requirement and the operation schedule. To plan for an AQUILINE development which provides as milestones an increasing inventory of vehicle systems designed for general purpose missions seems to us to be an inappropriate and expensive approach to the Agency's particular problem. None of these vehicle systems, in all probability, would be the optimum vehicle required to perform an intelligence mission when the need arises. To adjust the AQUILINE development plan to the available funds and to the specific capability needs of the Agency, a new plan has been formulated and put into effect.

B.   Development Plan.

As shown in Figure 3, the program emphasis is now being put on developing a capability in terms of the developing state-of-knowledge which can be assessed on command by management. This is done by establishing the two computer programs shown. The scheme works as follows. For fiscal year 1968 the control of the program is vested in the Advanced Conceptual Development team (Douglas Aircraft working under the direction of the Contracting Officer's Technical Representative*). The information library for the developmental program is a computer program endowed in its subroutines with all of the known or estimated (temporarily) characteristics of the IOC AQUILINE vehicle system. At the periphery of this information base are the various sub-

*COTR

SECRET

13.

system project engineers (Douglas) who are charged with generating requirements, subsystem development and updating and refining the information stored in that particular subsystem computer sub-routine. The computer can at any time be instructed to read out the current capability of the IOC family of vehicles under de-velopment. This information, for instance, would include the range, payload capability and "signature" (i.e., IR, radar, visual and acoustic signal) emanating from the vehicle system.

A second computer program has been established in order to make maximum use of this information. The information for this computer is derived from reiterated survivability studies. The mission survivability computer program predicts the ability (probability) of the selected AQUILINE vehicle to penetrate undetected through the radar, visible, and acoustic defenses of a hostile country. In order to describe the radar defenses, the location and characteristics of each radar, including radar horizon and ground clutter, are read into the computer program. The visible and acoustic defenses are described by the population density distribution. A candidate mission profile and vehicle are then chosen for gathering intelligence from a selected target behind the defense system. The mission profile is described by the position-time-function of the flight path (altitude, velocity, position vs. time), the cloud cover, the background-sky contrast and the sun-aircraft relationship along the route. The candidate aircraft is described by its radar cross section (as a function of viewing angle), its physical size and the acoustic and infrared characteristics of the power plant. With these data, the computer program determines the probability of undetected penetration through the radar, visible and acoustic defenses. Should any of these probabilities prove unacceptable, a new mission profile and/or vehicle can be chosen which concentrates specifically on that aspect of penetration.

C. Flight Tests.

In order to assure that the information stored in the computer yields an accurate representation of the physical characteristics of the vehicle, two additional components of the development plan must be provided. These are the Prototype Systems Development (IOC) and Test Range Programs. Within the Prototype Systems Development Program, a number of test vehicles are designed and fabricated. (Five vehicles are planned for fiscal year 1968.) These vehicles are designed primarily to be test flown in a particular manner such as to augment or update the flight performance information stored in the computer. The vehicles are also used to carry developmental subsystems in experimental flight tests. The vehicles, then, are designed to be representative of the IOC family of vehicles, modified slightly to accommodate other requirements of the program.

SECRET

A test range for flight testing the developing
AQUILINE system has been established at Randsburg Wash, a
secure range on the Naval Ordnance Test Station at China
Lake, California. The facilities and facilities support
are being supplied by the Navy under a task order from the
Agency. The prime contractor (Douglas) has established and
maintains the instrumentation on the test range.

D. Summary of Development Concept.

In summary then, what the program attempts to provide
is a developing capability in intelligence collection
systems which can be assessed on command by management at
any time and from which they can define the optimum AQUILINE
collection system for a specific current intelligence
requirement.

In essence, the program plan is to develop a series of
AQUILINE subsystems (Figure 4) which will be fabricated,
tested in flight, and evaluated. The characteristics of
these subsystems will be permanently stored in the computer
memory. Each subsystem R&D program has its own goal milestones which are calculated to be integrated with the total
system capability development.

Each of the major subsystems may be expanded to indicate
the long-range plans in that area. In Navigation (Figure 4,

SECRET

16

~~SECRET~~

Item III-C), for example, R&D programs are being carried
out or planned for all of the fundamental techniques listed.
This broad approach is necessary because no one technique
currently offers the potential to satisfy all of the probable
requirements.

In conjunction with the subsystem capability development,
mission environmental information for some of the most likely
targets is being collected from other offices and stored for
evaluation and collation with specific system configurations.
Sociological studies in conjunction with wildlife information
would aid in a determination of the probability of detection
and recognition. The population distribution would be a measure
of likelihood of detection while the birdlife studies would
reveal the likelihood of the vehicle registering as a bird or
a normally appearing object to the observer. It also is obvious
that survivability is dependent on current meteorological data,
geographic features and intrusion defense posture. The political
situation would affect the determination for detection and
reaction of recognition by local governments, thus affecting the
calculated risk that may be taken.

Collation of all the subsystem data and environmentals
would be an impossible task without the aid of modern computer
techniques. However, the computer technique used in this program

~~SECRET~~

SECRET

can compare all the R&D results achieved to date and provide
answers to optimize the future AQUILINE development plan for
any of three alternatives:

    1. Most efficient use of available R&D funds.

    2. Most effective pacing of subsystem develop-
ments for orderly buildup of·system capability.

    3. Most effective combination of platform and
subsystem elements in a possible crash program to
develop a particular mission-oriented system.

  E. Management and Funding.

During fiscal years 1966 and 1967, the program was broken
down into its major components in accordance with Figure 5.
During fiscal year 1967, although the funding was increased to
[   ] dollars including AQUILINE-related efforts, the
program from an Agency management point of view had not progressed
to the point where it was considered a system endeavor. (A
system plan will be initiated in fiscal year 1968 and is discussed
later.) The funding for the program was provided in a piece-
meal fashion, project by project as the program areas became
defined. In order to manage the many separate contract packages
as an integrated program development, an AQUILINE budget sheet
was used for funding control. Figure 6 is a representative copy
of this budget showing the total budget funds, the office's
plan to commit these funds, and the status of commitment of funds

SECRET

18

under the general program. By this means, management was kept apprised of the progress of the overall program and the effort that the new dollars committed were to fund.

The funding for AQUILINE in fiscal year 1968 is based on a master AP/ORD program with a system contractor (See Figure 3). Several individual AP/ORD support contracts with other contractors and a moderate number of AQUILINE related projects (mainly payload R&D) monitored by other divisions are funded separately in support of the program. The basic funding program supports many tasks in subsystem development, environmental studies, mission analysis, and flight testing. Individual funding of these tasks in fiscal year 1967 created unnecessary complications in contract negotiations and management as well as increasing the problems of coordinating and synchronizing the technical developments of each subsystem. A new technique will be used for fiscal year 1968 program funding and control. This plan will provide the required program development flexibility and still assure adequate control by the COTR of the rate of expenditure of funds.

A master contract will be let with the McDonnell-Douglas Company. The request for fiscal year 1968 funds to Agency management will indicate the total contract price and costs of the four major subcontract elements. This breakdown of costs will

be similar to that shown in Figure 4. There are a number of
major subcontracts which will be let by McDonnell-Douglas in
fiscal year 1968. In fiscal year 1967 the composite fee
negotiated with McDonnell-Douglas was ☐ based on a ratio of
Prime to Subcontract effort of approximately ☐ A new composite fee will be negotiated with the prime contractor based
on the new Prime/Subcontract ratio.

In addition, the master contract will establish a funding limitation on a quarterly basis. Within this funding
limitation, McDonnell-Douglas will request funds on a task
basis against which costs, technical milestones and delivery
schedules will be submitted to the COTR. On approval by the
COTR, the contract officer will authorize funds for the task.
With this mechanism both the technical and financial progress
of the program will be more closely monitored. At the same
time, the COTR will have the required flexibility, found
necessary during early stages of the program, to adjust the
direction of the total effort in accordance with the developing
technology.

The preceding plan was considered more appropriate to
the AQUILINE development program than a PERT COST analysis.
However, PERT TIME analysis is maintained on both the advanced
system development and prototype system development elements of
the program.

~~SECRET~~

The prime contractor has formulated a detailed fiscal
year 1968 system program plan (Figure 8) for a [   ]
dollar budget. AP/ORD proposes to use this system plan by
funding the highest priority tasks to a current budget ceiling
of [   ] dollars. Therefore, additional funding, if
it becomes available throughout the year, can be wisely used
and coordinated with the overall AQUILINE program. A summary
of the projected AQUILINE costs through fiscal year 1973 is
shown in Figure 9.

~~SECRET~~

SECRET

V   Operational Development

The development of an operational AQUILINE system requires development of the aircraft system and payloads as well as ground control equipment, operations support facilities and personnel.

Although plans for fiscal year 1968 include study and parametric definition of the ground control equipment and operations support requirements, the plan is once again to develop only those components which have commonality to all possible missions.

All aspects of the problem would be researched, however, and a prototype of the basic ground control equipment would be developed. Keeping in mind that the costs of acquiring an operational capability are not funded, and that what is indicated is ORD's ability to respond technologically to a requirement for an operational system, the projected operational capability for AQUILINE is shown in Figure 7.

The development of the AQUILINE concept has required a hard look at the future of technical intelligence collection. As a result, it has been catalytic in the generation of a variety of new development projects. Although many of these new areas, i.e., small IR scanners, microminiaturization of ELINT receivers, recorders, communication and navigation equipment, etc., have application in the AQUILINE program, they also meet more general

SECRET

22

needs of the Agency. In any funding analysis it would be improper, therefore, to assess the AQUILINE program on a direct basis for the development costs in these areas. Figure 9 apportions the total costs of the program in accordance with this point of view.

The AQUILINE system is being designed to provide an unusual degree of flexibility in both the types of mission and the operational modes that it can accommodate. Therefore, without defining the type of intelligence to be collected, the target, and the operation scenario, it is difficult to project the costs of an operation.

ORD has, however, projected the cost of a 100 mission/1 year operation. The breakdown, shown in Figure 10, considers two alternate vehicles: a) an internal combustion engine propulsion system with a max. range of 2400 n.m.; and b) a radioisotope fueled engine propulsion system with 36,000 n.m. or 30-day flight duration capability.

The mix and quantity of payloads were selected to support 100 missions against typical targets of present and future interest. Spares are included in the quantities shown, with repair and maintenance included in O&M costs as shown.

Mission analysis studies have shown that 50 IC systems is a good estimate of the number of vehicles needed to conduct

100 single target missions. Twenty-five radioisotope fueled
vehicles would be required for the same number of targets since
it is assumed that a system with a thirty-day flight endurance
capability could cover more than one target/mission.

Although the total estimated cost of one year of sustained
operations for the IC and RI systems is $ [   ] and $ [   ]
respectively, one can, using Figure 10, determine the approximate
cost of other mixes of payloads/missions, and/or vehicles should
one desire. (Costs, however, are based on the quantity shown.)

DEVELOPMENT PLAN

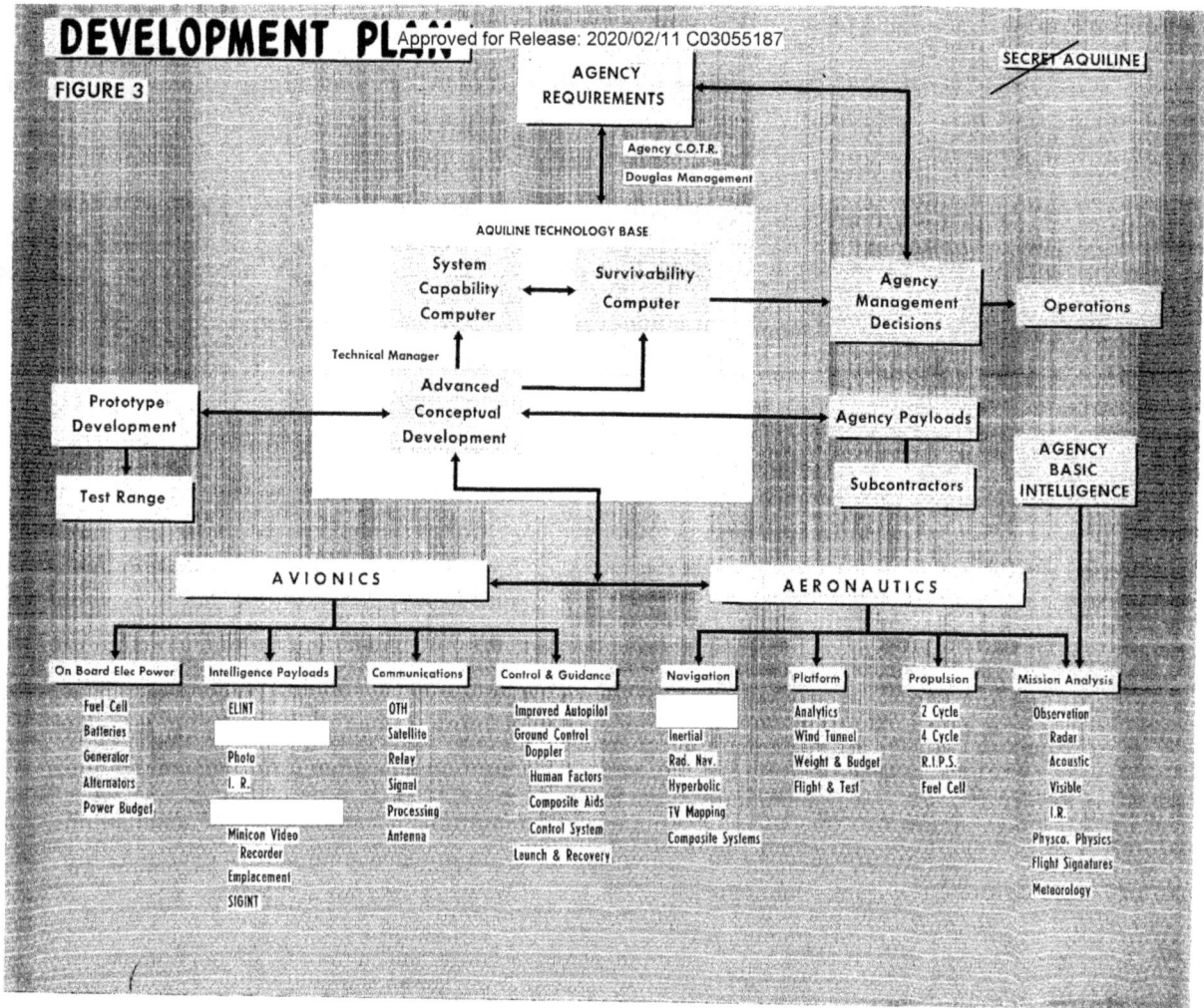

SECRET AQUILINE

FIGURE 3

AGENCY REQUIREMENTS

Agency C.O.T.R.
Douglas Management

AQUILINE TECHNOLOGY BASE

System Capability Computer ←→ Survivability Computer → Agency Management Decisions → Operations

Technical Manager

Advanced Conceptual Development

Prototype Development

Test Range

Agency Payloads

Subcontractors

AGENCY BASIC INTELLIGENCE

AVIONICS

AERONAUTICS

On Board Elec Power	Intelligence Payloads	Communications	Control & Guidance	Navigation	Platform	Propulsion	Mission Analysis
Fuel Cell	ELINT	OTH	Improved Autopilot		Analytics	2 Cycle	Observation
Batteries		Satellite	Ground Control Doppler	Inertial	Wind Tunnel	4 Cycle	Radar
Generator	Photo	Relay	Human Factors	Rad. Nav.	Weight & Budget	R.I.P.S.	Acoustic
Alternators	I. R.	Signal	Composite Aids	Hyperbolic	Flight & Test	Fuel Cell	Visible
Power Budget		Processing	Control System	TV Mapping			I.R.
	Minicon Video Recorder	Antenna	Launch & Recovery	Composite Systems			Physco. Physics
	Emplacement						Flight Signatures
	SIGINT						Meteorology

SECRET

AQUILINE BUDGET WORK SHEET

	TITLE	PROJECT NO.	CONTRACTOR	FY 1966	FY 1967	BUDGETED FY 1968	UNBUDGETED FY 1968
I	Prototype System Development	A-4001-A-01	Douglas	--			
II	Advanced Systems Definition Studies						
	A. Douglas	A-4001-A-02	Douglas	☐			
	B. AP/ORD Conceptual Support/Other Contractors		TBD	--			
III	Subsystem Development						
	A. Advanced Aerodynamics						
	1. Coanda Studies	A-4030-A-01	IITRI	--			
	2. Advanced Vehicles	O-7020	TBD				
	3. Wind Tunnel Tests	O-7020					
	B. Advanced Propulsion						
	1. Souped-up 2-Cycle Eng.		Marquardt				
	2. 4-Cycle D&E	A-4001-A-01	DAC/Lyc				
	* 3. 4 Cycle						
	* a. Reciprocating	PC	Eng. Tech.				
	* b. Wankel (Rotary)	PC	OMC				
	4. Free Piston		SRI				
	5. R.I.P.S.	A-4110-A-01	DAC/GM				
	6. Coanda Thrust Generators						
	C. Navigation Systems Dev.	A-4060-A-01	Litton	☐			
	1. Improved Autopilot		DAC				
	2. Inertial Systems						
	a. Component Develop.		Teledyne				
	b. Radio Navigation Update		TBD				
	3. Radio Hyperbolic Systems						
	a. ☐-OMEGA☐		DAC/RSI				
	b. OMEGA, ☐ Loran						
	1) LOP		DAC/TBD				
	2) Stored Phase Profile		DAC/TBD				
	4. Radio Trilateration	A-4100-A-01	DAC/Cubic				

SECRET

GROUP 1
Excluded from automatic
downgrading and
declassification

SECRET

AQUILINE BUDGET WORK SHEET---2

TITLE	PROJECT NO.	CONTRACTOR	FY 1966	FY 1967	BUDGETED FY 1968	UNBUDGETED FY 1968
5. Satellite Systems		DAC/TBD				
* 6. TV Mapping/Correlation Optics						
7. Altimeter						
a. Improved Barometric						
b. Radio						
c. Imagery Derived V/H		DAC				
D. Communications						
1. Signal Processing						
(Spread Spectrum, etc.)	TBD	TBD				
2. Data Storage/Handling	A-4120-A-01	Philco				
3. On-Board Electronics						
Development	A-4001-A-01	Douglas, ITT				
4. Detectability and						
Security Studies		DAC/TBD				
* 5. O.T.H. Communications		RP/EPL				
6. Satellite Commo		ESL				
7. Relays		TBD				
E. Antennas						
1. Integrated Antenna Study		DAC/TBD				
2. Antenna Development						
F. Survivability						
1. Vehicle Signature						
Studies and Configura-						
tion Iteration	A-4180-A-01	Douglas				
*a. Visual		TBD				
*b. E/M		TBD				
*c. Thermal		TBD				
*d. Acoustic	PC	Battelle				
2. Mission Analysis		DAC				
3. Meteorology		TBD				
G. Ground Control Station Dev.						
1. Equipment Requirements						
Study/RD&E						
a. Control & Guidance	O-7025-A-01					
b. Data Receiving and						
Processing						
*c. Man-Machine Interface	BMSD					

SECRET

GROUP 1
Excluded from automatic

SECRET

AQUILINE BUDGET WORK SHEET---3

TITLE	PROJECT NO.	CONTRACTOR	FY 1966	FY 1967	BUDGETED FY 1968	UNBUDGETED FY 1968
2. Launch & Recovery (Air, Land & Water) Requirements Study						
a. Prototype Dev.						
1) Air						
2) Land	A-4200-A-01					
3) Water						
H. TV Eye						
* 1. Slow Scan	Optics					
* 2. Solid State (Mosaic)	AP					
* 3. Digiton	Optics					
* 4. IR Scanner	O-1210-A-03					
* 5. Real Time Vidicon	Optics					
* 6. Image Motion Compensator, Image Motion Stabilization, and Image Intensifier	Optics					
I. Payloads						
* 1.	Optics					
* 2. ELINT	A-4210-A-01	Scope, T.I.				
* 3. TV Eye	Optics					
* 4.	RP	Mitras				
* 5. SIGINT	AP	Telcom				
* 6. Photo Payload	Optics	TBD				
* 7.						
* 8. Payload Emplacement System	AP	TBD				
* 9. Min. Video Recorder	AP	Ampex				
J. Operations Research		Winston				
IV Range Test Support	A-4160	Navy				
A. O&M on Facilities		Douglas				
B. O&M on Instrumentation		Douglas				
C. AQUILINE Test Bed Vehicles & Spares		Douglas				

SECRET

SECRET

AQUILINE BUDGET WORK SHEET---4

TITLE	PROJECT NO.	CONTRACTOR	FY 1966	FY 1967	Budgeted FY 1968	UNBUDGETED FY 1968
D. Douglas Support of AQUILINE Related Projects		Douglas				
1. OMEGA WANDERING BOY						
2.						
3. ELINT						
4. TV Eye						
5.						
6. SIGINT						
7. Photo Payload						
8. Air Sampling						
9. Propulsion						
10. Payload Emplacement						

TOTALS: AQUILINE

        * AQUILINE RELATED

SECRET

AQUILINE

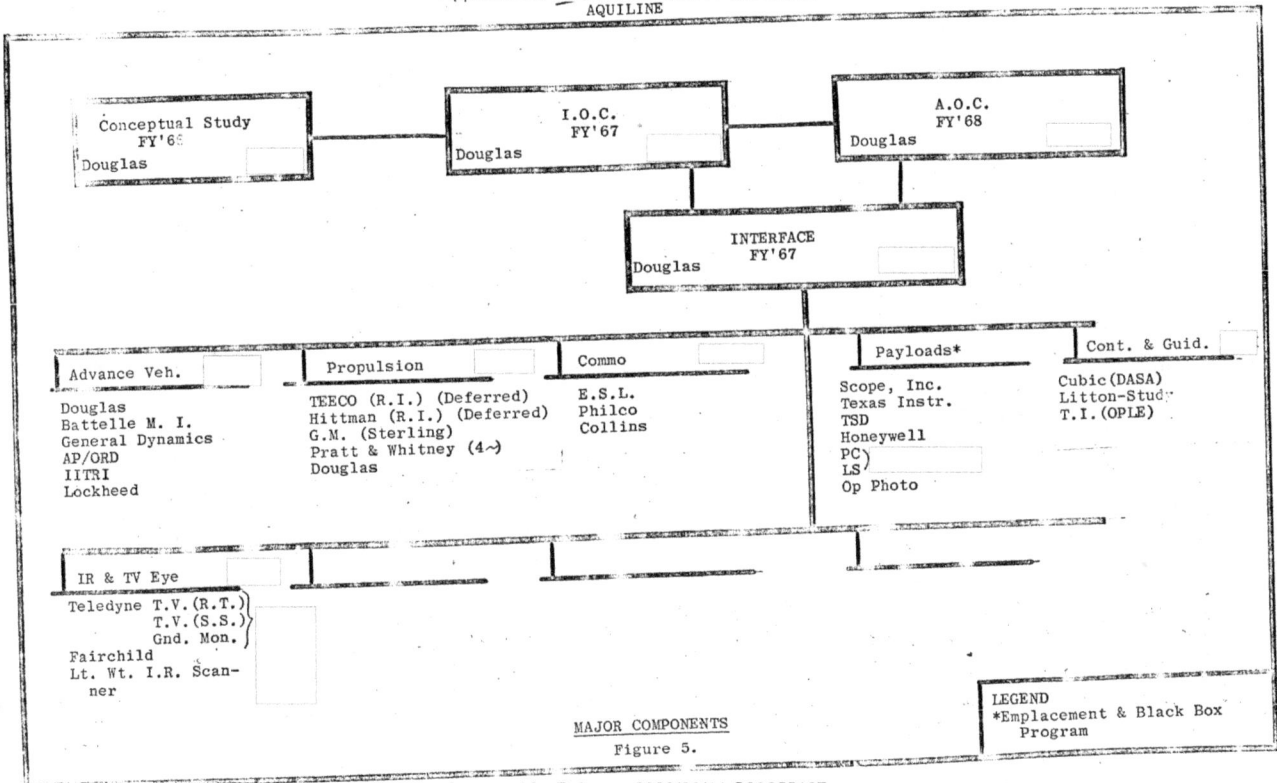

MAJOR COMPONENTS

Figure 5.

LEGEND
*Emplacement & Black Box
Program

AQUILINE BUDGET

Project	R/D No.	FY'67 Budget	Committed Amount	Committed Date	Proposed Spending Amount	Proposed Spending Date	Contractor
VEHICLE SYSTEMS							
I.O.C.	A4011-A01			Nov.			Douglas Aircraft
Interface	A4000-A02			Nov.			Douglas Aircraft
CONTROL & GUIDANCE							
Navigation Study	A4060-A01			Oct. 10			Litton
Test Range Navigation Equipment	A4100-A01			Jan. 12			Douglas/Cubic
Inertial Navigation Systems Dev.	A4060-A02						
Radio Nav. (OMEGA)	A4130-A01					Feb.	Texas Instruments
COMMUNICATIONS							
Sensor (Data Storage & Processing)	A4120-A01			Jan. 16			Philco Corporation
Line of Sight Study	A4070-A01						
GROUND SUPPORT							
Test Range Support (NOTS)						As req'd.	To be determined
Launcher						Jan.	Douglas Aircraft
PROPULSION	A4110-A01						
4 Cycle I.C.						Jan.	Douglas/Pratt-Whitney
Radio-Isotope						Jan.	Douglas/General Motors
ADVANCED PLATFORMS	A4030-A01					Feb.	ITTRI/Douglas Aircraft
ANTENNA SYSTEM	A4180-A01						Radiation Systems, Inc.
IR AND TV EYE							
Real Time TV				Sept.		Jan.	Teledyne
Slow Scan TV						Jan.	Teledyne
Scan Conv. & Gnd. Mon.	O7025-A01					Jan.	Teledyne
Light Weight IR Scanner	O1210-A03						
TOTAL BUDGET							
TOTAL TO BE COMMITTED							

Figure 6.

Group 1
Excluded from automatic
downgrading and
declassification

AQUILINE OBJECTIVES

	1967	1968	1969	1970	1971
RANGE	600 N. M.	1200 N. M.	2400 N. M.	25000 N. M.	UNLIMITED
PROPULSION	2- Cycle Internal Combustion	4-Cycle Internal Combustion	Advanced 4-N Internal Combustion	Radioisotope	
TARGETS		Barents Sea Chinese and Vietnam Coastal Area Cuba	Lop Nor Shuang-Ch'Eng-tzu Sary Shagan 80% of Targets of Interest	USSR China Land, Sea and Air Launch	ANY TARGET
MISSION CAPABILITY		Reconnaissance Ferret Cep 4 N. M. Interim Commo	Black Box Emplace-ment Cep 1/2 N. M. Secure Commo	Black Box Emplacement Reconnaissance Cep 1/2 N. M. T.V. Terminal 100 Secure Commo Unlimited loiter	ADAPTIVE
INTELLIGENCE REQUIREMENT		Low Altitude Imagery Elint Sigint	Event Indicator Missile Telemetry Nuclear Staging and Yield	Monitor Missile and Nuclear Ranges Intelligence Processing	

SECRET/AQUILINE

FIGURE 7

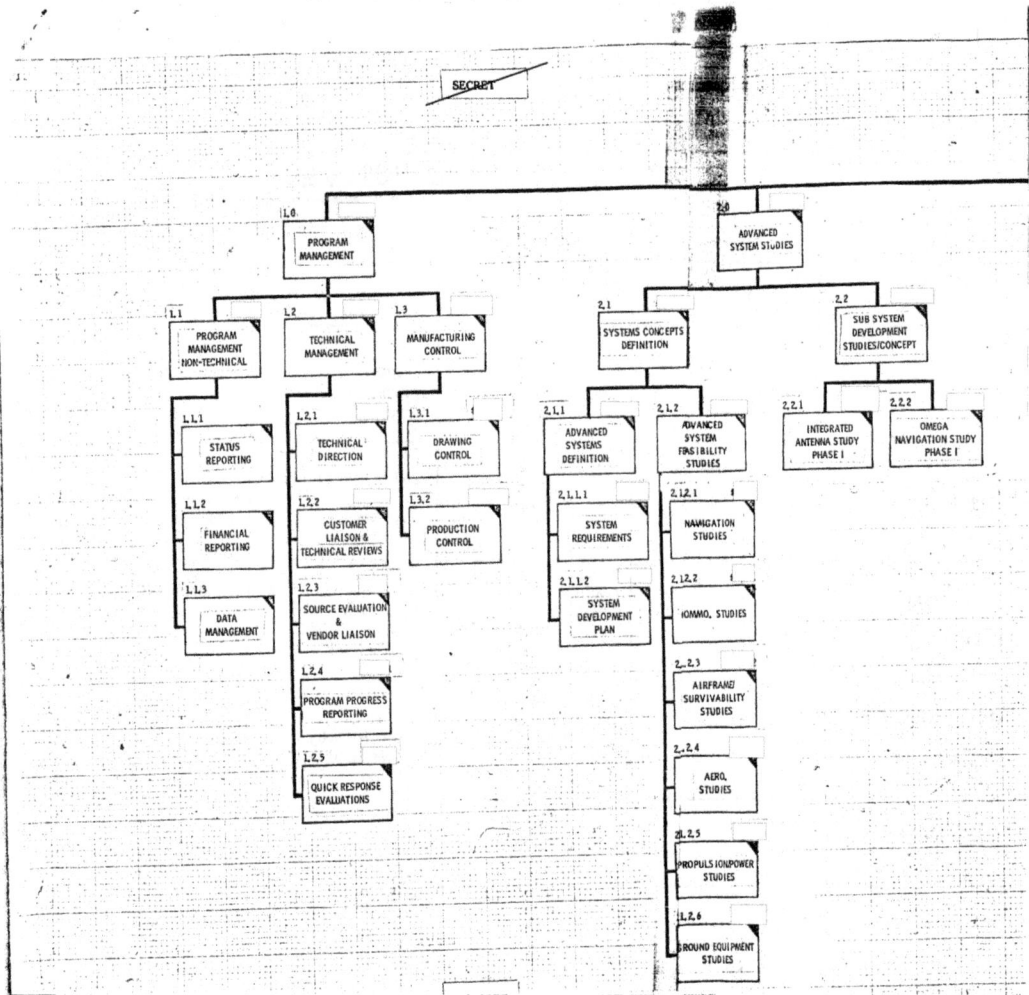

SECRET

AUG 8 1967

4.0 AQUILINE PROGRAM FY-68 — (A)

3.0 SUB SYSTEM DEVELOPMENT & EVALUATION — (B)

3.1 IOC IMPROVEMENTS PROJECTS

3.2 SUB SYSTEM PROTOTYPE DEVELOPMENT/ IMPROVEMENTS

3.1.1 AIRFRAME IMPROVEMENTS

3.1.2 GSE IMPROVEMENTS

3.1.3 IOC POWER SOURCE IMPROVEMENTS

3.1.4 IOC ELECTRONICS IMPROVEMENTS

3.2.1 CAMEL I PROTOTYPE DEVELOPMENT (4 CYCLE)

3.2.2 OMEGA NAVIGATION SYSTEM DEVELOPMENT

INTERIM AUTOPILOT DEVELOPMENT

AIRFRAME SURVIVABILITY DEVELOPMENT

3.2.5 WIND TUNNEL TEST PROGRAM

3.2.6 COMMO. SYSTEM BREADBOARD DEVELOPMENT

3.1.3.1 IOC PROPULSION IMPROVEMENT

3.1.3.2 IOC ELECTRICAL POWER IMPROVEMENT

3.1.4.1 CONTROL SYSTEM IMPROVEMENTS

3.1.4.2 NAVIGATION/COMMO. SYSTEM IMPROVEMENTS

3.2.5.1 DIMENSIONAL TESTS

3.2.5.2 BOUNDARY LAYER CONTROL TESTS

3.2.5.3 AOC GLIDER TESTS

KEY

MATRIX NO. → X.X (Same as Statement of Work)

$ XXX — COST OF TASK (Sum of sub tasks)

COST IS FIRM IF DARK CORNER
COST IS ROM IF NOT DARKENED

TITLE

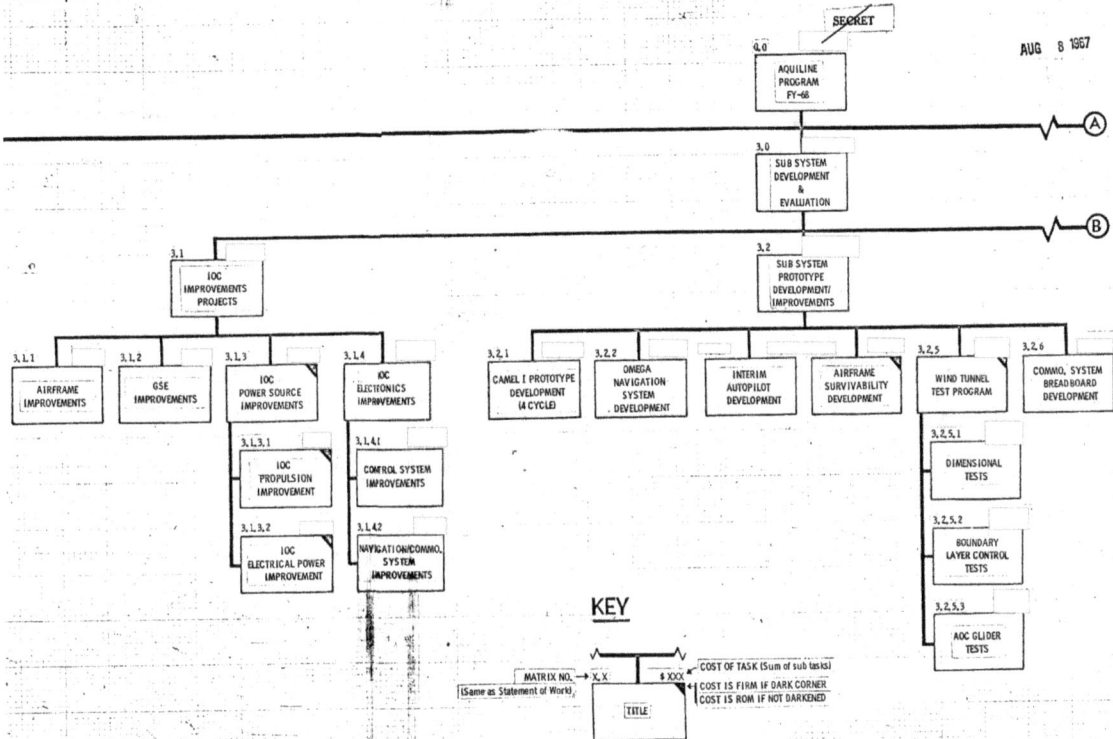

WORK BREAKDOWN STRUCTURE
AQUILINE PROGRAM FY-68

EXCLUDED FROM AUTOMATIC REGRADING; DOD DIR 5200.10 DOES NOT APPLY

DOCUMENT CONTROL
No. 790 Copy No. 1
DOUGLAS AIRCRAFT COMPANY, INC.

Fig 8.

SECRET

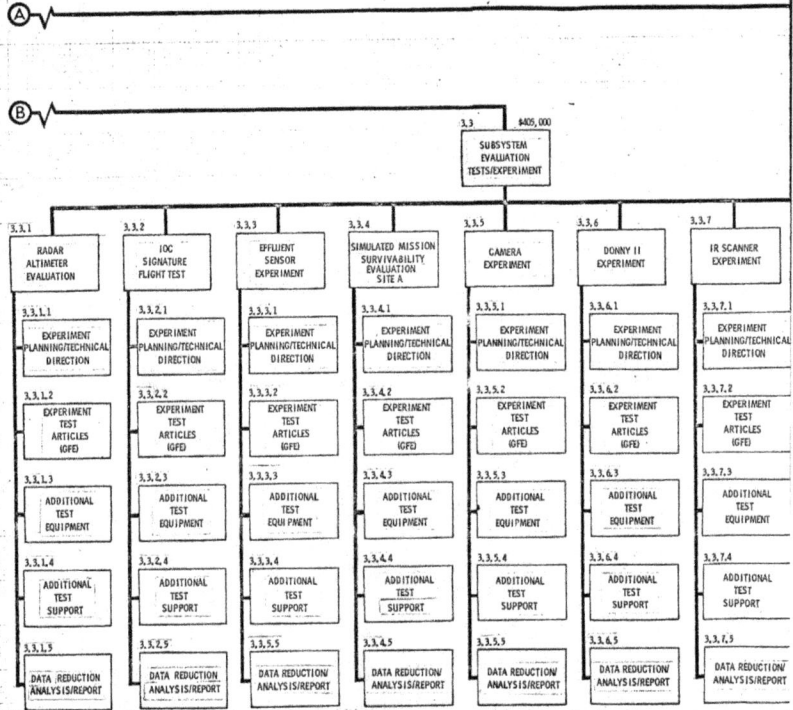

SECRET

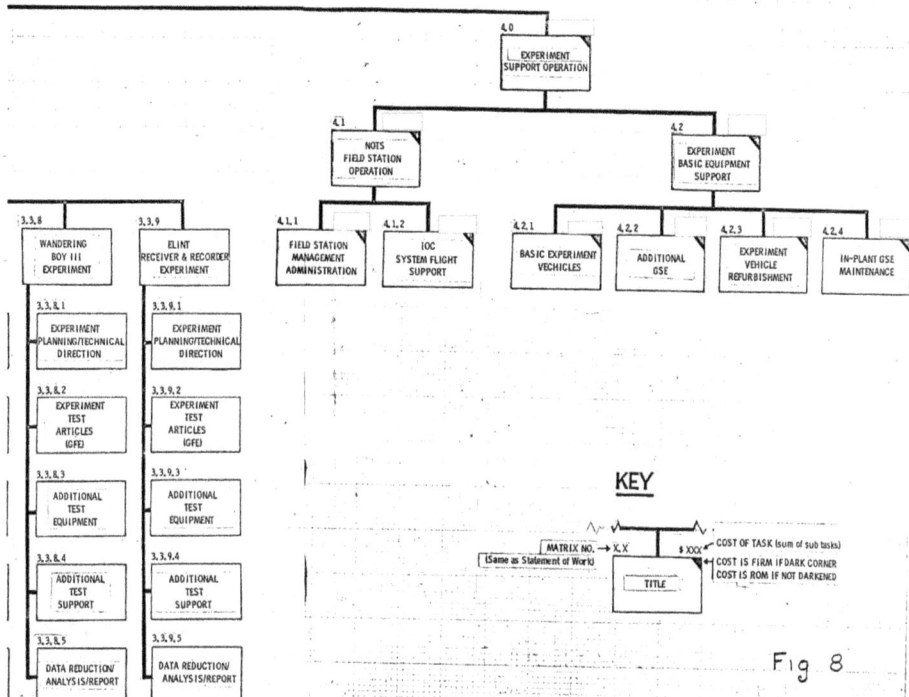

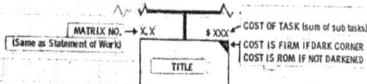

KEY

MATRIX NO. → X.X
[Same as Statement of Work]

COST OF TASK (sum of sub tasks)

$ XXX — COST IS FIRM IF DARK CORNER
COST IS ROM IF NOT DARKENED

TITLE

Fig 8

Note
THE ROM COST FOR 3.3 IS BASED ON AN AVERAGE COST OF $8,000 PER EXPERIMENT. NOT ALL 9 EXPERIMENTS WILL BE STARTED DURING FY'68.

EXCLUDED FROM AUTOMATIC REGRADING; DOD DIR 5200.10 DOES NOT APPLY
GROUP I

SECRET

10

SECRET

AQUILINE

Summary of Projected Costs (X 1000)

TITLE	FY'66	*FY'67	*FY'68	FY'69	FY'70	FY'71	FY'72	FY'73
BASIC SYSTEM DEVELOPMENT								
I Prototype Sys. Dev.								
II Advanced Sys. Def.								
III Subsystem Dev.								
IV Test Range								
Subtotal								
AQUILINE SUPPORT DEVELOPMENT								
III Subsystem Dev. Payload Dev.								
Subtotal								
TOTAL PROGRAM BY F.Y.								

*Budgeted

SECRET.

Figure 9.

GROUP 1
Excluded from automatic
downgrading and
declassification

SECRET

PROJECTED AQUILINE OPERATIONAL COSTS

System Element	Costs (50 Vehicles / 100 Missions)				Costs (25 Vehicles / 100 Missions)			
	No. Req'd.	@ x $1000	Internal Combustion 600-2400 n.m.	Totals	No. Req'd.	@ x $1000	Radioisotopes 36,000 n.m. or 30-day Flt.	Totals
I Payloads								
Camera								
Elint (Repeater)								
Elint (On-board record)								
Nuclear BB/Empl.								
Missile BB/Empl.								
BB Interrogate								
1 yr. O&M and Training								
II Vehicle								
TV Eye								
Radio Navigation								
Electronics (Rec./Trans)								
Autopilot and Contr.								
Airframe								
Altimeter								
Batteries								
Engine & Generator								
Fuel Inventory/Flt.								
1 yr. O&M and Training								

Figure 10.

SECRET

SECRET

PROJECTED AQUILINE OPERATIONAL COSTS (cont'd)

System Element	Costs (50 Vehicles / 100 Missions)				Costs (25 Vehicles / 100 Missions)			
	No. Req'd.	@ x $1000	Internal Combustion 600-2400 n.m.	Totals	No. Req'd.	@ x $1000	Radioisotopes 36,000 n.m. or 30-day Flt.	Totals
III Ground Station (Comm. Cont., Data Storage & Readout)								
Mobile (Sea & Air)								
Land Based								
Satellite Piggyback								
Electronics								
Relays & Support								
Aircraft								
1 yr. O&M and Training								
IV Data Proc. & Mission Plan.								
Film								
Video								
Analysis								
Waveform								
GRAND TOTALS								

SECRET

3.3(h)(2)

TRANSMITTAL SLIP	DATE
TO:	
ROOM N	

REMARKS:

FROM:	
ROOM NO.	EXTENSION

FORM NO. 241
1 FEB 55   REPLACES FORM 36-8
WHICH MAY BE USED.   (47)

~~SECRET~~

PROJECT AQUILINE

RESEARCH AND DEVELOPMENT STUDY

23 August 1967

~~SECRET~~

SECRET

TABLE OF CONTENTS

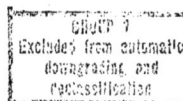

GROUP 1
Excluded from automatic
downgrading and
reclassification

SECRET

SECRET

PROJECT AQUILINE

RESEARCH AND DEVELOPMENT STUDY

I   Nature and Purpose of the Study.

This study has been prepared in response to a request by the Bureau of the Budget for the background, the history of the development and operational concepts of this important project area. The vehicle development and associated component subsystems have been organized into the total project concept under the AQUILINE cryptonym.

Project AQUILINE was initiated in response to intelligence requirements which would only be satisfied by unmanned reconnaissance systems. The need for a new level of capability encompassed not only photographic missions but also required the emplacement of collection payloads hundreds of miles into denied areas. The system concept incorporates the use of the most advanced microtechnology, e.g., microelectronics, microminiature sensors and power sources, sophisticated communications and control systems.

This study is organized into four major sections. The first presents a history of the program up through fiscal year 1967 including a description of the intelligence collection potential. The second section outlines the planned development

SECRET

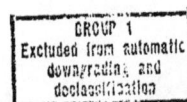

SECRET

program for fiscal year 1968 and fiscal year 1969. Section

III presents a detailed description of the basic technology

involved in the development cycle and a summary of the develop-

ment concept. The final section presents several operational

concepts and estimates program timing and costs.

SECRET

2

II   History.

A. Program Initiation.

For the past four years, DD/S&T/ORD has been considering advanced concepts by which "black box" sensors could be emplaced at strategic targets in China, Russia, North Vietnam, and other denied areas. These emplaced "black boxes" would collect a variety of ELINT, COMINT, SIGINT air sampling and other technical intelligence. The information would be stored for later read out via radio to overflight aircraft or relay satellites. A major difficulty in the emplacement concept has been the need for the "mother ship" to execute the penetration and drop at a high altitude in order to avoid detection and/or interception. Black box payloads designed for emplacement in this manner tended to be large and heavy -- a few hundred pounds not being unusual.

Discussions by ORD with other offices within the Agency (OSA, OSP, FMSAC, OSI, OEL, and other potential users within the clandestine services) gave substance to the developing AQUILINE concept. It was agreed that low altitude drops of small, light-weight, low power solid state sensors would have a high probability of surviving the emplacement. Indeed, the same qualities could decrease the probability of detection of the black box once emplaced.

Solid state and microminiaturization technologies had
progressed by 1965 to the point where these black boxes could
be developed. A low flying emplacement vehicle capable of
long range surreptitious penetration was in its genesis in the
Office of Research and Development.

B. Program Concept.

During this period ORD, internally and through conceptual
studies conducted by the Naval Ordnance Test Station (NOTS),
Douglas Aircraft Company, and others, was defining and developing the concept of a very small bird-like emplacement system
(see Figures 1 and 2). Mission analyses and cost-effectiveness
studies indicated that this approach had great promise in
meeting the requirements of the advanced penetration system
sought by the Agency. The studies produced a completely new
concept in collection platforms. Conceptually, the platform
could exist for long periods of time in target areas and would
be practically undetectable. Even if detected, it would be expensive and difficult to defend against. Its low altitude and
low speed characteristics added to a long loiter time capability
would permit detailed examination of the target areas and permit
a wide variety of intelligence missions. Further, its small
size and innocuous nature would make it more politically palatable
in tense situations than conventional aircraft. It would be
unmanned, smaller, and cheaper, and, therefore, expendable on

SECRET

special missions. Because of these characteristics, it would
be deployable against targets not accessible by any means at
the present time. It would be long-range insurance against the
loss of current vehicle assets, which will devaluate with time
due to improved enemy defenses and the loss of foreign real estate.
In an early stage of development, it could complement existing
high altitude systems by providing more detailed examination of
selected targets -- especially under cloud cover.

Concentrated study was performed on a wide range of aerodynamic lift devices including balloons, ballistic glider,
powered glider and helicopter types for this application. The
powered glider was selected because of the following considerations:

1. Vehicle. A small aerodynamically clean
vehicle can be produced which will contain the miniature
payloads and subsystems required for the missions
contemplated.

2. Propulsion. A variety of propulsion systems
such as two-cycle engines, four-cycle engines, fuel
cell and radioisotope powered systems, are practicable
for propelling the vehicle thousands of miles.

3. Observability. Tests of mock-up models
demonstrate that such a vehicle and its subsystems

could have low enough observability (visual, acoustic, radar and IR) to immerse itself in the indigenous signal environment of the target area, loitering unobtrusively while performing its mission.

4. Guidance and Navigation. Several guidance and navigation systems such as CHECKROTE, radio direction finding, transit satellites and Loran or Omega could direct this vehicle to within a few miles of the distant target.

5. TV Eye. A subminiature TV Eye is practical, both in the visible and IR, to assist in guidance and navigation as well as perform surveillance duties.

6. Communications Link. Secure communications for data transmission and vehicle control are achievable at line-of-sight ranges and feasible over the longer ranges by using relays such as a small vehicle of the same type, satellites or CHECKROTE.

7. Payloads. Photographic, IR, ELINT, audio, air sampling, and droppable black box payloads being developed by various ORD divisions point up the diversified potential of the system.

8. Mobility and Flexibility. Because of its size, weight, and speed, the vehicle can be launched from a small boat or aircraft, or a simple portable launcher.

SECRET

9. Range. The range of the IOC version will be
[   ]; however, four-cycle internal combustion
engines or fuel cells will provide ranges to thousands
of miles. Radioisotope engine versions would have unlimited range (30-day flight duration -- 36,000 mi.).

10. Operations Research. Computer programs for
vehicle configuration, systems integration, systems
vulnerability and mission analysis have all been studied
and can be developed further to insure the effectiveness
of operational systems. Eventually this could be done
in the IPRD facility of ORD.

C. FY 1967 Development Program.

During the fiscal year 1967, development of an emplacement/
collection system configured as a small powered glider (AQUILINE)
began with a budget of [   ] dollars. During the year, the
development concept of the AQUILINE system was refined and improved with:

1. The initiation of an IOC* prototype development program.

2. The continuation of advanced system studies
by Douglas Aircraft (System Contractor).

3. Institution of development programs in the
subsystem areas of aerodynamics, propulsion, navigation,

*IOC - Initial Operational Capability. This term is used
to designate the first generation vehicle and associated
subsystem.

SECRET
7

communications, antennas, survivability studies, intelligence collecting payloads, and ground control
equipment.

A flight test range was established and instrumented to
allow flight tests of the airframe, its subsystems, as well as
developing payloads. The flight of the fully instrumented IOC
system is scheduled for October 1967. This system will include
remotely controlled autopilot, navigation and communications
equipment (including a slow-scan TV camera and associated radio
transmitter) and will be equipped to carry test payloads up to
five pounds to a range of

III   Program Objectives.

A.   Overall Objective.

The AQUILINE development program has been designed to provide an evolutionary series of aerial collection systems capabilities. The program will require advancements in the state-of-the-art in the areas of aerodynamics, propulsion, navigation, communication and payload instrumentation. A major goal is for the program to provide the capability of defining the optimum collection system available from the development program at any time which may be used against specific intelligence targets to satisfy specific requirements. (Figure 3 -- Development Plan.) A more detailed description of this aspect of the program is contained in Section IV below.

By late fiscal year 1968, the Initial Operational Vehicle will be capable of flying [   ] missions at altitudes up to 10,000 feet, carrying a payload of five pounds. The system will have achieved prototype hardware capable of positioning and controlling the vehicle to within a CEP of 70 feet at distances to [   ]. These capabilities are sufficient to perform intelligence collection missions against typical peripheral targets in China, Cuba, and the USSR. When interrogated, the AQUILINE computers will be capable of supplying the detail design information on a specific embodiment of the IOC prototype which

SECRET

~~SECRET~~

would be optimized to these objectives. In addition, the computer will calculate the probability of success for the mission.

B. FY 1968 Goals.

During fiscal year 1968, an Advanced Operational Capability (AOC) will be researched. This program will consider four-cycle internal combustion engine designs, advanced subsystem elements, and payload instrumentation resulting from current microelectronics R&D efforts. The initial AOC* goal will be [   ] round-trip missions against coastal areas in Cuba, the Barents Sea, China, and Vietnam. Reconnaissance and ferret-type missions could provide low altitude imagery, ELINT and SIGINT. Feasibility of these objectives were studied in a simulated operational test against Tallinn.

C. FY 1969 Goals.

The range of objectives for fiscal year 1969 will be expanded by the results of advance four-cycle engine development which will extend the range of these systems to [   ] Emerging navigational technolgies, such as the [   ] OMEGA** will provide the capability of using these vehicles in one-way missions against Lop Nor, Shuang-ch'eng-tzu and Sary Shagan. Typical objectives for fiscal year 1969 will be the development of a black box emplacement capability within a CEP of 1/2 n.m. These missions have intelligence capabilities against missile telemetry, nuclear staging and yield.

*AOC - Advanced Operational Capability.
**A navigation concept which utilizes the long range Navy OMEGA
   radio transmissions, retransmitted through a synchronous
   satellite to the ground station for ___ mmutation and position
   location.

~~SECRET~~

~~SECRET~~

D. Ultimate Goals.

During fiscal year 1970 and beyond, program objectives are to develop capabilities for collecting intelligence from any remote area through the development of radioisotope-powered vehicles having [   ] ranges and unlimited loiter times. Land and sea launch capabilities against any target in the USSR and China are current goals. Improved sensors and intelligence processing payloads will be adaptive to mission variations as determined by specific requirements.

~~SECRET~~

11

~~SECRET~~

IV Program Plan.

A. Approach.

The program plan used for development of an AQUILINE
system during fiscal year 1967 will be replaced by an overall
system's program in fiscal year 1968. This is necessary for
a variety of reasons. During fiscal year 1967, there were three
program areas:

1. IOC prototype development

2. Interface (conceptual development)

3. Subsystem development

Three vehicles, each with increasing capability, were designed
and constructed under the IOC prototype development program

If in fiscal year 1968 we were
to follow this same schedule of building increasingly refined
test vehicles, we would quickly exceed fiscal year 1968 funding
of   In addition, our increased understanding of
the various subsystem requirements, and a better estimate of the
costs involved in achieving these requirements has placed ever
increasing strain on our limited funds.

Further, mission analysis studies revealed that in order
to achieve acceptable probabilities of success against any
particular target, a specially designed vehicle system should be
constructed and deployed. In an environment of continually
changing intelligence requirements, it becomes extremely difficult

~~SECRET~~

12

~~SECRET~~

and prohibitively expensive to predict the mission requirement
and the operation schedule. To plan for an AQUILINE development
which provides as milestones an increasing inventory of vehicle
systems designed for general purpose missions seems to us to be
an inappropriate and expensive approach to the Agency's particular problem. None of these vehicle systems, in all probability,
would be the optimum vehicle required to perform an intelligence
mission when the need arose. To adjust the AQUILINE development
plan to the available funds and to the specific capability needs
of the Agency, a new plan has been formulated and put into
effect.

B. Development Plan.

As shown in Figure 3, the program emphasis is now being
put on developing a capability in terms of the developing state-
of-knowledge which can be assessed on command by management.
This is done by establishing the two computer programs shown. The
scheme works as follows: For fiscal year 1968 the control of the
program is vested in the Advanced Conceptual Development team
(Douglas Aircraft working under the direction of the COTR). The
information library for the program is a computer endowed in its
subroutines with all of the known or estimated (temporarily)
characteristics of the IOC AQUILINE vehicle system. At the periphery of this information base are the various subsystem project
engineers (Douglas) who are charged with generating requirements,

~~SECRET~~

subsystem development and updating and refining the information
stored in that particular subsystem computer subroutine. The
computer can at any time be instructed to read out the current
capability of the IOC family of vehicles under development.
This information, for instance, would include the range, payload
capability and "signature," (i.e., IR, radar, visual and acoustic
signal) emanating from the vehicle system.

A second computer program has been established in order
to make maximum use of this information. The information for
this computer is derived from reiterated survivability studies.
The mission survivability computer program predicts the ability
(probability) of the selected AQUILINE vehicle to penetrate
undetected through the radar, visible, and acoustic defenses of
a hostile country. In order to describe the radar defenses, the
location and characteristics of each radar, including radar
horizon and ground clutter, are read into the computer program.
The visible and acoustic defenses are described by the population
density distribution. A candidate mission profile and vehicle are
then chosen for gathering intelligence from a selected target
behind the defense system. The mission profile is described by
the position-time-function of the flight path (altitude, velocity,
position vs. time), the cloud cover, the background-sky contrast
and the sun-aircraft relationship along the route. The candidate

aircraft is described by its radar cross section (as a function
of viewing angle), its physical size and the acoustic and
infrared characteristics of the power plant. With these data,
the computer program determines the probability of undetected
penetration through the radar, visible and acoustic defenses.
Should any of these probabilities prove unacceptable, a new
mission profile and/or vehicle can be chosen which concentrates
specifically on that aspect of penetration.

C. Flight Tests.

In order to assure that the information stored in the
computer yields an accurate representation of the physical
characteristics of the vehicle, two additional components of the
development plan must be provided. These are the Prototype
Systems Development (IOC) and Test Range Programs. Within the
Prototype Systems Development Program, a number of test vehicles
are designed and fabricated. (Five vehicles are planned for
fiscal year 1968.) These vehicles are designed primarily to be
test flown in a particular manner such as to augment or update
the flight performance information stored in the computer. The
vehicles are also used to carry developmental subsystems in experimental flight tests. The vehicles, then are designed to be
representative of the IOC family of vehicles, modified slightly
to accommodate other requirements of the program.

A test range for flight testing the developing
AQUILINE system has been established at Randsburg Wash, a
secure range on the Naval Ordnance Test Station at China
Lake, California. The facilities and facilities support
are being supplied by the Navy under a task order from the
Agency. The prime contractor (Douglas) has established and
maintains the instrumentation on the test range.

D. Summary of Development Concept.

In summary then, what the program attempts to provide
is a developing capability in intelligence collection
systems which can be assessed on command by management at
any time and from which they can define the optimum AQUILINE
collection system for a specific current intelligence
requirement.

In essence, the program plan is to develop a series of
AQUILINE subsystems (Figure 4) which will be fabricated,
tested in flight, and evaluated. The characteristics of
these subsystems will be permanently stored in the computer
memory. Each subsystem R&D program has its own goal milestones which are calculated to be integrated with the total
system capability development.

Each of the major subsystems may be expanded to indicate
the long-range plans in that area. In Navigation (Figure 4,

SECRET

16

Approved for Release: 2020/02/11 C03055186

~~SECRET~~

Item III-C), for example, R&D programs are being carried
out or planned for all of the fundamental techniques listed.
This broad approach is necessary because no one technique
currently offers the potential to satisfy all of the probable
requirements.

In conjunction with the subsystem capability development,
mission environmental information for some of the most likely
targets is being collected from other offices and stored for
evaluation and collation with specific system configurations.
Sociological studies in conjunction with wildlife information
would aid in a determination of the probability of detection
and recognition. The population distribution would be a measure
of likelihood of detection while the birdlife studies would
reveal the likelihood of the vehicle registering as a bird or
a normally appearing object to the observer. It also is obvious
that survivability is dependent on current meteorological data,
geographic features and intrusion defense posture. The political
situation would affect the determination for detection and
reaction of recognition by local governments, thus affecting the
calculated risk that may be taken.

Collation of all the subsystem data and environmentals
would be an impossible task without the aid of modern computer
techniques. However, the computer technique used in this program

~~SECRET~~

17

Approved for Release: 2020/02/11 C03055186

SECRET

can compare all the R&D results achieved to date and provide
answers to optimize the future AQUILINE development plan for
any of three alternatives:

    1. Most efficient use of available R&D funds.

    2. Most effective pacing of subsystem develop-
ments for orderly buildup of system capability.

    3. Most effective combination of platform and
subsystem elements in a possible crash program to
develop a particular mission-oriented system.

E. <u>Management and Funding.</u>

During fiscal years 1966 and 1967, the program was broken
down into its major components in accordance with Figure 5.
During fiscal year 1967, although the funding was increased to
[   ] dollars including AQUILINE-related efforts, the
program from an Agency management point of view had not progressed
to the point where it was considered a system endeavor. (A
system plan will be initiated in fiscal year 1968 and is discussed
later.) The funding for the program was provided in a piece-
meal fashion, project by project as the program areas became
defined. In order to manage the many separate contract packages
as an integrated program development, an AQUILINE budget sheet
was used for funding control. Figure 6 is a representative copy
of this budget showing the total budget funds, the office's
plan to commit these funds, and the status of commitment of funds

SECRET

SECRET

under the general program. By this means, management was kept apprised of the progress of the overall program and the effort that the new dollars committed were to fund.

The funding for AQUILINE in fiscal year 1968 is based on a master AP/ORD program with a system contractor (See Figure 3). Several individual AP/ORD support contracts with other contractors and a moderate number of AQUILINE related projects (mainly payload R&D) monitored by other divisions are funded separately in support of the program. The basic funding program supports many tasks in subsystem development, environmental studies, mission analysis, and flight testing. Individual funding of these tasks in fiscal year 1967 created unnecessary complications in contract negotiations and management as well as increasing the problems of coordinating and synchronizing the technical developments of each subsystem. A new technique will be used for fiscal year 1968 program funding and control. This plan will provide the required program development flexibility and still assure adequate control by the COTR of the rate of expenditure of funds.

A master contract will be let with the McDonnell-Douglas Company. The request for fiscal year 1968 funds to Agency management will indicate the total contract price and costs of the four major subcontract elements. This breakdown of costs will

SECRET

SECRET

be similar to that shown in Figure 4. There are a number of
major subcontracts which will be let by McDonnell-Douglas in
fiscal year 1968. In fiscal year 1967 the composite fee
negotiated with McDonnell-Douglas was ☐ based on a ratio of
Prime to Subcontract effort of approximately ☐ . A new composite fee will be negotiated with the prime contractor based
on the new Prime/Subcontract ratio.

In addition, the master contract will establish a funding limitation on a quarterly basis. Within this funding
limitation, McDonnell-Douglas will request funds on a task
basis against which costs, technical milestones and delivery
schedules will be submitted to the COTR. On approval by the
COTR, the contract officer will authorize funds for the task.
With this mechanism both the technical and financial progress
of the program will be more closely monitored. At the same
time, the COTR will have the required flexibility, found
necessary during early stages of the program, to adjust the
direction of the total effort in accordance with the developing
technology.

The preceding plan was considered more appropriate to
the AQUILINE development program than a PERT COST analysis.
However, PERT TIME analysis is maintained on both the advanced
system development and prototype system development elements of
the program.

SECRET

20

The prime contractor has formulated a detailed fiscal year 1968 system program plan (Figure 8) for a [   ] dollar budget. AP/ORD proposes to use this system plan by funding the highest priority tasks to a current budget ceiling of [   ] dollars. Therefore, additional funding, if it becomes available throughout the year, can be wisely used and coordinated with the overall AQUILINE program. A summary of the projected AQUILINE costs through fiscal year 1973 is shown in Figure 9.

'SECRET'

V   Operational Development

The development of an operational AQUILINE system
requires development of the aircraft system and payloads as
well as ground control equipment, operations support facilities
and personnel.

Although plans for fiscal year 1968 include study and
parametric definition of the ground control equipment and
operations support requirements, the plan is once again to
develop only those components which have commonality to all
possible missions.

All aspects of the problem would be researched, however,
and a prototype of the basic ground control equipment would be
developed. Keeping in mind that the costs of acquiring an
operational capability are not funded, and that what is indicated is ORD's ability to respond technologically to a requirement for an operational system, the projected operational
capability for AQUILINE is shown in Figure 7.

The development of the AQUILINE concept has required a hard
look at the future of technical intelligence collection. As
a result, it has been catalytic in the generation of a variety
of new development projects. Although many of these new areas,
i.e., small IR scanners, microminiaturization of ELINT receivers,
recorders, communication and navigation equipment, etc., have
application in the AQUILINE program, they also meet more general

'SECRET'

needs of the Agency.   In any funding analysis it would be

improper, therefore, to assess the AQUILINE program on a

direct basis for the development costs in these areas.

Figure 9 apportions the total costs of the program in accord-

ance with this point of view.

S.S. (/)

Gen Ross Brief
1400 22 aug
C

PROJECT

AQUILINE

AQUILINE

STATUS OF PROGRAM

ORD Activities:

Contract Signed with MDAC   July 1969

Personnel to Area 51   February 1970

Flight Test Begins   April 1970

Flight Test Ends   November/December 1970

Contract Expires   February 1971

Developing Satellite Relay Program

Preparing Paper on Project Impact on Agency Budget (FY-70 - FY-74)

OSA Activities:

Preparing and Coordinating with ORD

DDS&T Policy Paper for Program

Security and Cover Plan

Maintenance and Logistics Plan

Personnel Manning Plan

Communications Support Plan

Support Airlift Requirements (Test Phase) Plan.

Assisting on Agency Budget Impact Paper

AQUILINE Major Activities Chart

SECRET

SECRET

DDS&T POLICY PAPER FOR PROJECT AQUILINE

Purpose:　　　　To establish in a single paper the basic program

policy plus define OSA and ORD functions and

responsibilities during life of program.

Method of Approach:

　　　　Prepared by OSA.

　　　　Coordinated in Draft with SPG/ORD.

　　　　Paper to DSA and DRD for coordination and

　　　　approvals.

　　　　Paper to DDS&T for approval.

Suggested Effective Date:　　1 October 1969

Description:

　　　　Policy

　　　　Functions

　　　　Responsibilities

SECURITY AND COVER PLAN

Purpose: To establish overall program Security and Cover Plan.

Method of Approach:

        Prepared by OSA (agreed to by SPG/ORD).

        Coordinated in Draft with SPG/ORD.

        Final paper to DSA and DRD for coordination

        and approval.

        Final paper to DDS&T for approval.

        Brief Pery Panel - September 1969.

Suggested Effective Date: 1 January 1970

Description:

        Security Plan

        Cover Plan

MAINTENANCE AND LOGISTICS PLAN

Purpose: To establish Maintenance and Logistics Plan

for OSA AQUILINE Field Unit.

Method of Approach:

Prepared by OSA.

Approved by DSA.

Implemented by D/M/OSA in coordination

with SPG/ORD and OL/DDS.

Suggested Effective Date: 1 July 1970

Description:

Maintenance Plan

Logistic Plan

SECRET

PERSONNEL MANNING PLAN

Purpose: To provide for orderly acquisition of Personnel

for Project AQUILINE.

Method of Approach:

Prepared by OSA.

Approved by DSA.

Implemented by COMPT, D/OPS and D/M/OSA..

Suggested Effective Date: 30 September 1969

Description:

Headquarters Manning Plan

Field Manning Plan

SECRET

~~SECRET~~

COMMUNICATIONS SUPPORT PLAN

Purpose: To define and plan for OSA Communications responsibilities for Project AQUILINE.

Method of Approach:

Prepared by OSA.

Coordinated with SPG/ORD.

Briefed to Mr. Scott.

Paper to DSA and ORD for approval.

Suggested Effective Date: 31 September 1969

Description:

Staff Communications.

Command Control Communications.

~~SECRET~~

(8)

AGENCY BUDGET IMPACT PAPER

Purpose: ORD is preparing paper on 1970-1974 AQUILINE

budget for OPPB and BOB review.

Method of Approach:

SPG Policy Meeting with Mr. Duckett.

SPG in coordination with .

OSA prepares paper for OPPB.

Suggested Effective Date: Approximately 5 September 1969

Description:

This paper will be basis for the FY-1971 OSA AQUILINE

Budget.

SECRET

SUPPORT AIRLIFT REQUIREMENTS PLAN

Purpose: To establish and provide support airlift for project

AQUILINE.

Method of Approach:

Feasibility Study made at Intermountain.

Prepared by OSA.

Coordinated with SPG/ORD.

Coordinated with Air Branch SOD.

Approved by DSA-ORD-SOD.

Overall approval by DDS&T and DDP.

Suggested Effective Date: 1 January 1970.

Description:

Civilian airlift support.

Personnel Transport.

Relay platform.

Chase aircraft.

SECRET

S E C R E T

3.5(c)
3.3(h)(2)

19 February 1969

MEMORANDUM FOR: Mr. Samuel A. Mitchell

SUBJECT: Project AQUILINE

        I was under the impression that the scheduled meeting on
20 February was to discuss the total project concept the outcome
of which would then govern the position that OSA would take with
respect to the manner in which the project would be approached.
Since it is impracticable to forecast fallout of a discussion such
as that contemplated, the Contracts Management Division's primary
concern with Project AQUILINE is whether or not the contract management concept of contracting heretofore practiced in OSA will be
applied to the project or whether the logistic procurement concept
will be applied. In the event the decision is made that the logistic
procurement concept will apply then certain consequences of necessity
will follow which will affect the manner in which OSA will be forced
to manage this project. Within the framework of the logistic procurement concept is the ⌐   ⌐ contracting officer limitation, the
utilization of the logistic supply system, the utilization of the
Industrial Contract Audit Division, Office of Finance, the submission
of actions in excess of ⌐   ⌐ and overruns in excess of ⌐   ⌐ of the
contract to the Contract Review Board, the utilization of the Blue
Book approval technique, etc. It is evident that our existing contracting
methods would not be practicable if we were required to proceed along
the lines cited, therefore, it would seem to be in the best interest of
the program and OSA to request the DDS&T for authority to operate not
only the contracting phases, but the support, security, etc., along
the OSA program/project concept.

C/CMD/OSA

S E C R E T

SECRET

1 5 FEB 1968

AQUILINE

PROJECT AQUILINE

(Prepared for Briefing to be given by Col. White, Feb. 1968)

1. <u>AQUILINE</u>. A program for the development of a miniature surreptitious aircraft vehicle system which with its growth capabilities would penetrate with relative impunity thousands of miles into denied areas such as the Soviet Union, Red China, Cuba, etc., to collect critical technical intelligence, support in-place agents, or perform other such CIA missions.

The vehicle system, Viewgraph #1, can drop payloads [   ] [   ] collect data (photographic IR scanner images, ELINT, COMINT, [   ] [   ] and relay or carry the data back to Central Control.

2. <u>SYSTEM ADVANTAGES</u>.

a. It is small, flies low and slow, having small visual, acoustic, and radar observables; can outfox defenses rather than overpower them.

b. Inexpensive and unmanned; low risk and investment.

c. Inoffensive and unassuming characteristics compared to overflight aircraft and large drones, make it more politically palatable for use.

d. Close proximity of payloads to target provide unique signal collection advantages to augment those obtainable by much more sophisticated and expensive programs such as satellites and high flying aircraft.

SECRET

~~SECRET~~

e. The R&D program costs include the cost of the pay-loads which can be emplaced or borne by other water, land and air platforms, including agents and animals.

3. <u>PROGRAM OBJECTIVES</u>. Viewgraph #3 provides a summary of the projected costs both from a research and development and an operational applications standpoint.

a. One vehicle system has already undergone R&D flight tests, and should by the end of fiscal year 1968 have demonstrated its operational potential. During fiscal year 1970, the operations group will test operational models of this vehicle having a flight endurance capability of [ ] [ ] Operational tests will continue through fiscal year 1971, during which time a four-cycle engine system of higher reliability and greater range will become available. Lightweight, long-range navigations systems and associated Ground Control Stations now under development will give this system an operational range of [ ] [ ] in 1972 and [ ] in 1973. An improved version of this four-cycle engine will provide a system by 1974 having an operating range of [ ].

b. It is anticipated that the first R&D flight tests of a vehicle system combining a radioisotope propulsion system will begin in fiscal year 1973. On paper this vehicle system would have an altitude capability of [ ] and a flight endurance of 50 days or approximately [ ] Preliminary operational flight tests on this vehicle will occur in

~~SECRET~~

~~SECRET~~

fiscal year 1974 and will be available for operational use
the following year. It will have vast utility for over-water
applications; its radiation hazards will be so low as to
permit consideration of its use for over-land missions.

~~SECRET~~

AQUILINE MILESTONES

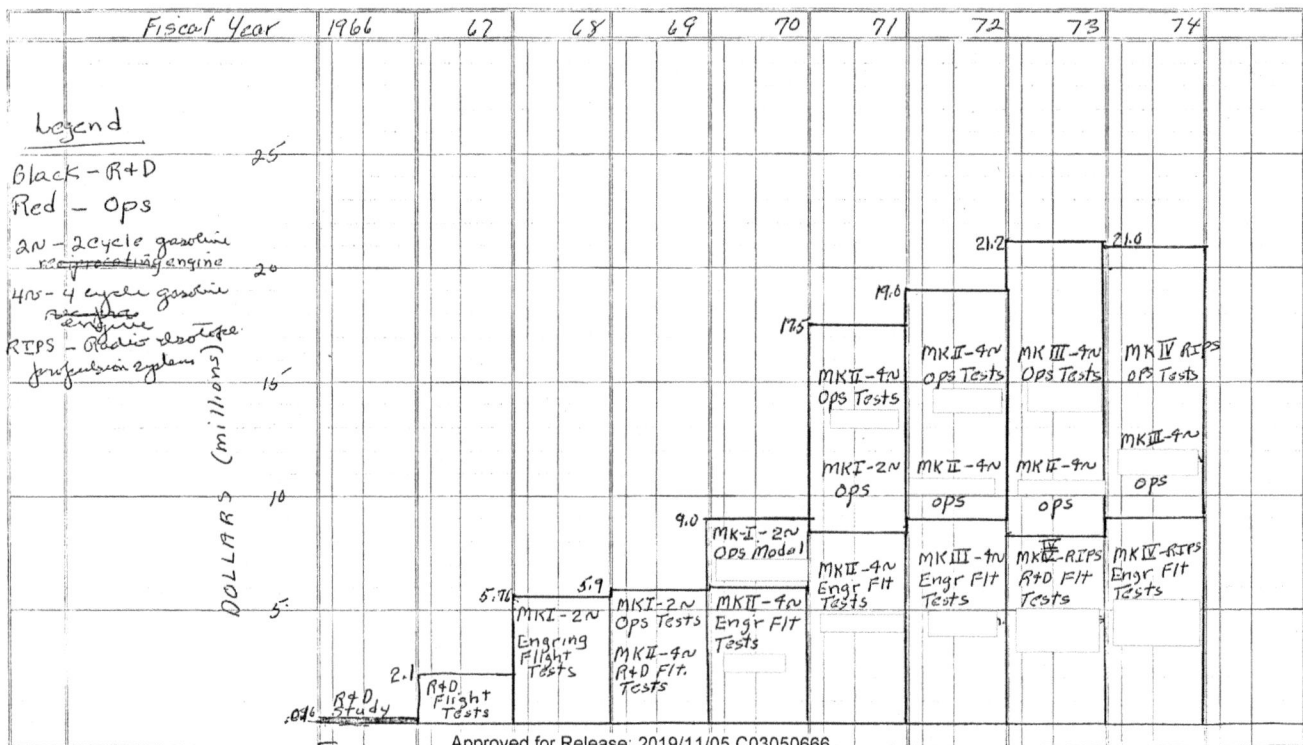

AQUILINE MILESTONES

Fiscal Year	1966	67	68	69	70	71	72	73	74

Legend

Black — R+D
Red — Ops

2N — 2 cycle gasoline reciprocating engine

4N — 4 cycle gasoline engine

RIPS — Radio Isotope propulsion system

DOLLARS (millions)

25 —
20 —
15 —
10 —
5 —

.046 — R+D Study
2.1 — R+D Flight Tests
5.76 — MKI-2N Engring Flight Tests
5.9 — MKI-2N Ops Tests / MKII-4N R+D Flt. Tests
9.0 — MK-I-2N Ops Model / MKII-4N Engr Flt Tests
12.5 — MKII-4N Ops Tests / MKII-4N Engr Flt Tests
19.0 — MKII-4N Ops Tests / MKI-2N Ops / MKIII-4N Engr Flt Tests
21.2 — MKII-4N Ops Tests / MKII-4N Ops / MKIII-4N R+D Flt Tests
21.0 — MKIII-4N Ops Tests / MKII-4N Ops / MKIV-RIPS R+D Flt Tests
MKIV RIPS Ops Tests / MKIII-4N Ops / MKIV-RIPS Engr Flt Tests

Rf

22 JUN 1971

DD/S&T-1970-71

3.5(c)

MEMORANDUM FOR: Director, Research and Development
Director, Special Activities

SUBJECT: Project AQUILINE

1. Attached hereto is a copy of Executive Director-Comptroller's memorandum regarding the meeting with the DCI on project AQUILINE.

2. I invite your attention particularly to paragraph three in which the Executive Director-Comptroller has agreed to make $[   ] of FY 1971 Funds available for the next 90 days and also to his limitation on the use of any FY 1972 funds for project AQUILINE.

(Signed) F. W. M. Janney

For:

Carl E. Duckett
Deputy Director
for
Science and Technology

Attachment:
As stated

SECRET

DD/~~~ (848-71)

18 June 1971

MEMORANDUM FOR: Director of Planning, Programming, and Budgeting

SUBJECT : Project AQUILINE

1. On 16 June 1971 Carl Duckett and I met with the Director and General Cushman to report on the status of Project AQUILINE and to seek guidance on the course of action we should now pursue. Carl reported on the last test flight, during which the plane crashed, and also pointed out the following:

a. $ ___ would be approximately enough money to continue the project on a bare-bones approach for approximately ninety days.

b. If we decide to go ahead with the project, the $ ___ in the Fiscal Year 1972 budget will probably not be enough. At this point in time we do not know how much more would be needed.

c. If we go ahead with the project, Fiscal Year 1973 will be the peak budget year, and we shall need at least $ ___ and probably $ ___ for the project during that fiscal year.

d. In the light of SALT negotiations, Ping-Pong diplomacy, and the like, we need to satisfy ourselves to the extent possible that, assuming we produce a viable operational asset, we shall be permitted to use it over denied areas.

2. In the discussion which followed, the Director agreed that during the next ninety days we should, working with the contractor, wring out the project thoroughly, using the bare-bones approach recommended by Carl. During this time frame we should also make a presentation to the 40 Committee to find out whether we shall be

GROUP 1
~~~

Approved for Release: 2020/02/11 C05646579

~~SECRET~~

able to use the vehicle operationally. We should do everything necessary to make a decision and bite the bullet one way or the other no
later than 30 September. The Director also said that, if the project
goes ahead, if it is successful, and if we have reason to believe that
we shall be permitted to use it, he will have no hesitancy in requesting
the necessary funds in the Fiscal Year 1973 budget.

3. In a subsequent conversation with Carl Duckett on 18 June,
I agreed to make the $[   ] of Fiscal Year 1971 money available
now with the understanding that (a) this will take care of the bare-bones
approach approved by the Director for the next ninety days and (b) that
no Fiscal Year 1972 funds will be used for Project AQUILINE until the
decision to proceed or terminate is made sometime between now and
the end of September.

/s/ L. K. White

L. K. White
Executive Director-Comptroller

cc: DDCI
DD/S&T

~~SECRET~~

Approved for Release: 2020/02/11 C05646579

TOP ~~SECRET~~

BYE-6396-69

e. Sub-category: Other
1) Element: Multi-sensor

PROJECT: AQUILINE

Objectives: To provide a multi-sensor collection and advanced emplacement capability for collection of intelligence.

Program Plan:

Method of Approach: FY 1970 - During fiscal year 1970, OSA will continue to participate with ORD in the development program. During FY 1970, ORD will be developing and operating the prototype air-ground control station. This will be in conjunction with the development and flight test of the AQUILINE vehicle. The schedule now envisioned indicates that system and sensor tests will start in the first quarter of FY 1970 and the actual flight test of the vehicle carrying its associated systems and payloads will occur during the later part of that fiscal year. OSA will continue to participate through this phase of the development program. Three key personnel for AQUILINE will be required by OSA during fiscal year 1970 to enable adequate participation in the ORD Test Program. These people will be: a Field Program Director; a Manager, Flight Systems; and a Manager, System Support. It is imperative that these positions be filled at the earliest possible date, as these individuals will be the nucleus of the AQUILINE Operational Detachment and will be responsible for effecting an orderly transition of AQUILINE from R&D to operationally ready status. The three positions indicated are in excess of the presently authorized fiscal year 1970 ceiling. OSA will also require $[   ] not included in the fiscal year 1970 Budget for support of these operations.

Present plans call for AQUILINE to be conducted as a unilateral U.S. project entirely funded by CIA. There is no need for foreign participation inasmuch as the vehicle is unmanned and it is not expected that foreign-controlled bases will be required. The characteristics of the vehicle are such that it can be launched either by catapult or rocket-assisted take off from U.S. vessels or from any small U.S. base abroad. It is probable that foreign-based launchings can be made without detection or at least without identification. An important element in the security of the vehicle's operation is that its existence, configurations and unique operating characteristics not be known. Thus, every effort is being made to avoid any publicity or knowledge of the vehicle. To this end, flight tests are to be made only at Area 51, and all activities will be conducted as "NOFORN".

FY 1971 - The Flight Test Program conducted by ORD will continue into early FY 1971. The procurement of the second air-ground control system during this period will be the pacing item in attainment of an early operational capability. ORD is proposing to have 7 vehicles for its flight test program. At the conclusion of the flight test program ORD has proposed that the remaining flight test vehicles be rehabilitated and turned over to OSA for use in training, testing and refinement of operational concepts. Anticipating a high attrition rate among flight test vehicles, it is assumed that only 3 vehicles will be available from ORD at

TOP ~~SECRET~~   Handle Via
                                        BYEMAN-TALENT-KEYHOLE-COMINT
                                          Control Systems Jointly

BYE-6396-69

the conclusion of their test period.

It is planned to rehabilitate the 3 aircraft left over from the ORD test program, to procure 4 additional aircraft and to use the air-ground control system available from the ORD test program for training, testing and development of operational deployment concepts. During this phase of the OSA operation, it is proposed that an airborne relay system be utilized for confirmation of systems effectiveness, guidance reliability, etc. It must be realized that the maximum range attainable from use of an airborne relay system will be only about _____ of which, in an operational environment, only _____ could be over denied territory. Necessarily, the relay aircraft must remain outside of denied territory, and the size of components in the operational vehicle is such that only UHF communications are available for its control and navigation. Thus to enable employment of the AQUILINE aircraft to its maximum design capability, it will be necessary to employ satellite relays for communications, control, and data feed-back. If relay systems can be incorporated into satellites being used for other programs, it may be possible to set up a satellite relay system without procurement of a dedicated satellite. If however, a dedicated satellite must be procured, it is estimated this will cost in the neighborhood of _____ In order to acquire an operational capability by late fiscal year 1971, it will therefore be necessary to procure, in addition to the AQUILINE aircraft, a second transportable air-ground control system, a satellite data link, 2 navigation terminals, and terminal control equipment. If a dedicated satellite is necessary, this also should be procured during fiscal year 1971 in order to establish an operational deployment capability in that fiscal year. Twelve additional people will be required to support the training, testing and development of operational concepts and to support possible deployment. Funding requested is sufficient to support this program wherever based, on an austere basis plus minimal coverage for deployment contingencies.

FY 1972 - It is planned to fly a minimum of 12 operational missions. This will necessitate procurement of 6 AQUILINE vehicles, associated systems and payloads, 1 additional ground navigation terminal, and 1 additional satellite data link during this fiscal year. The missions will be controlled from one of two air-ground systems; either the ORD procured prototype or the later, OSA procured, highly mobile system. This will enable one deployment to be conducted, plus training and testing of new or improved aircraft systems and sensors, etc. It will further give marginal dual deployment capability if operations are not conducted at the home base. To maintain a deployment capability plus a home base operating capability will require 8 additional positions.

FY 1973, FY 1974, FY 1975 - No further personnel increases are planned for this period. It is proposed to procure 3 vehicles in each fiscal year to enable accomplishment of up to 12 operational missions per fiscal year, and to continue testing of improved systems and sensors, and refinement of operational concepts and procedures.

Coordination, Joint Planning, Requirements: Coordination is now being effected within DDS&T for joint planning during the

TOP ~~SECRET~~

Handle Via
BYEMAN-TALENT-KEYHOLE-COMINT
Control Systems Jointly

133

Approved for Release: 2020/02/11 C05646611

TOP ~~SECRET~~

BYE-6396-69

remaining development phase. Joint planning will be established
as necessary with other components of CIA to insure support for
this program. Joint planning will also be established, if deemed
necessary, with other members of the intelligence community.
There is no requirement for coordination outside the intelligence
community or with foreign services.

The AQUILINE vehicle will satisfy specific future
requirements of the intelligence community for collection of
information in normally denied areas. As opposition defenses
increase in capability, the present vehicles may lose some of
their utility in obtaining information over these areas. The
AQUILINE vehicle will, if developed as projected, enable an almost
completely surreptitious penetration. It is planned to attain a
capability, combined with satellite relay systems, to satisfy
requirements for real time intelligence, precise emplacement
capability, etc.

Risks: The obvious risk is loss of an unmanned aircraft
over denied territory and the resulting political implications
therefrom. The risk in this case is minimized by the fact that
the aircraft is much less provocative than any other, being very
small and having no armament. This constitutes a low risk capability
with an extremely high information gathering potential.

Alternatives: Four alternative levels of effort were
considered for FY 1970, and beyond through FY 1975. The first
consideration was attainment of an operational capability at the
earliest possible date. The development program as outlined by
ORD indicated that a relatively sophisticated operational capability
could be attained during FY 1970, provided a major expenditure of
FY 1969 funds took place. The assets could be acquired to meet
such a capability in the most highly desirable form, i.e., a fixed
base plus two mobile units capable of simultaneous deployment.
This would envision an aircraft with a range of over [   ],
computerized flight, [   ]. Operation
at these ranges with the requirements for precise navigation and
precise position control of the aircraft can only be achieved by
taking advantage of potentially available satellite relay systems,
highly sophisticated ground control equipment and data quality
transmission equipment. The cost of establishing such a system
would be approximately $[   ]. This was considered to be
impractical for numerous reasons among which are:

1. At this point in the development it cannot be said
for certain that the equipment in the configuration required for
this type of operation would be available within the specified
time period.

2. Obtaining the personnel required to man such a
capability would have had to start early in FY 1969.

3. The impracticability of obtaining FY 1969 money in
the amount indicated.

The second alternative considered was the establishment
during FY 1970 of a less ambitious capability consisting of two
mobile units with less sophisticated navigation and control

TOP ~~SECRET~~

Handle Via
BYEMAN-TALENT-KEYHOLE-COMINT
Control Systems Jointly

BYE-6396-69

equipment but still requiring satellite relay systems for control of the aircraft at the extreme ranges. Equipment for this alternative would cost in the neighborhood of $13 million for the first year's operation. To establish this capability in FY 1970 would require expenditure of approximately $ [   ] of FY 1969 money. This was deemed impractical. Additionally, as indicated above, it was uncertain as to whether the equipment would be developed to the extent necessary to insure reliable production systems.

The third alternative considered establishing one mobile unit during FY 1970. This unit would be considered capable of operating at ranges up to [   ], which still require satellite relay systems and sophisticated control and navigation equipment, which may or may not be available in the time required.

The fourth alternative is to rehabilitate 3 aircraft left over from the ORD test program, procure 4 additional aircraft, use the ground control available from ORD test program for training, testing and developing operational deployment concepts. This would provide a testing capability for systems and sensors for range extension and for improved aircraft performance. By late fiscal year 1971, the transportable air-ground control system being procured during this year will become available. Since the AQUILINE System must have available a satellite relay to enable employment to design capability, it may be necessary during this fiscal year to procure a dedicated satellite. If this is necessary, such a system, procured in FY 1971, also will be available by late in that fiscal year. This will provide, by late FY 1971, an initial operational deployment capability.

Resources Required:

Unfunded Requirements and Over-ceiling Positions, FY 1970:
Funding: ($thousand)

	FY 70
Pers Svc.	
Contracts	
Other	
Travel	
Trans	
Supplies	
Equip	
Total	

Positions:

	FY 70
Ceiling	3
Non-Ceiling	—
Field Prog. Dir.	1
Mgr. Flt. Sys.	1
Mgr. Sys. Sup.	1

Handle Via
BYEMAN-TALENT-KEYHOLE-COMINT
Control Systems Jointly

TOP SECRET

BYE-6396-69

Requirements FY 1971 - 1975:
Funding: ($thousand)

	FY68	FY69	FY70	FY71	FY72	FY73	FY74	FY75
Pers Svc.	-	-	-					
Contracts	-	-	-					
Other	-	-	-					
Travel	-	-	-					
Trans	-	-	-					
Contract	...	.	-					
Aircraft	-	-	-					
Computers		-	-					
O&M&Tng	-	-	-					
Supplies	-	-	-					
Equip.	-	-	-					
Total	-	-	-					

* Includes [   ] in FY 1971 for dedicated [   ]

Positions:

	FY68	FY69	FY70	FY71	FY72	FY73	FY74	FY75
Ceiling	-	-	-	19	27	27	27	27
Non-ceiling	-	-	-	-	-	-	-	-
Total	-	-	-	19	27	27	27	27
Field Prog. Dir.	-	-	-	1	1	1	1	1
Manager Flt. Sys.	-	-	-	1	1	1	1	1
Manager Sys. Sup.	-	-	-	1	1	1	1	1
Security	-	-	-	2	2	2	2	2
Clerical	-	-	-	3	3	3	3	3
Operations		-	-	2	4	4	4	4
				2	4	4	4	4
		-	-	2	4	4	4	4
		-	-	2	4	4	4	4
System Logistics								
Log. Spec.	-	-	-	1	1	1	1	1
Whse. Spec.	-	-	-	1	1	1	1	1
Prop. Acc.	-	-	-	1	1	1	1	1
Total	-	-	-	19	27	27	27	27

TOP SECRET

Handle Via
BYEMAN-TALENT-KEYHOLE-COMINT
Control Systems Jointly

136

C02074113 .

~~TOP SECRET~~

3.3(b)(1)
3.5(c)

~~TOP SECRET~~
IDEALIST/AQUILINE

BYE 9283-71
Copy 1 of 6
9 April 1971

MEMORANDUM FOR: Chief, Budget and Finance Division, OSA

SUBJECT: Quarterly Review of Status of Funds and
Forecasts of Fourth Quarter FY-1971

1. In accordance with your request, attached is the Operations portion of the Quarterly Review briefing. _____ will brief this portion.

2. Request charts be prepared for each page of the attachment.

3. Please forward copies of final briefing charts to the Deputy for Operations prior to 13 April 1971, for his review.

Deputy for Operations, OSA

Attachment:
As stated

IDEALIST/AQUILINE
~~TOP SECRET~~
~~TOP SECRET~~

Handle via BYEMAN
Control System

C02074113.

Approved for Release: 2019/11/05 C06774183

TOP SECRET
TOP SECRET
IDEALIST/AQUILINE

BYE 9283-71
Page 2

SAS/O/OSA: [   ] (9 April 1971)
Distribution:
  1 - C/BFD w/atts.
  2 - D/O/OSA w/atts.
  3 - SAS/O/OSA w/atts.
  4 - IDEA w/IDEALIST att. only
  5 - AQUI w/AQUILINE att. only
  6 - RB/OSA w/atts.

IDEALIST/AQUILINE
TOP SECRET
TOP SECRET

Handle via BYEMAN

Approved for Release: 2019/11/05 C06774183

~~TOP SECRET~~
~~TOP SECRET~~
AQUILINE

AQUILINE
ATTACHMENT TO
BYE 9283-71
Page 1

AQUILINE

(AS OF 31 MARCH 1971)

Flight Planning   Management of mission algorithm develop-
                    ment assumed by OSA.

Documentation   Reports Control Manual completed in draft
                    and being coordinated.

Project Management An initial meeting between MDAC manage-
                    ment and OSA was conducted on 31 March and
                    1 April for purpose of constructing FY-72
                    Program philosophies, concepts, etc.

AQUILINE
~~TOP SECRET~~
~~TOP SECRET~~

Handle via BYEMAN
Control System

~~TOP SECRET~~
~~TOP SECRET~~
AQUILINE

Target Area Planning
Program (TAPP)
[   ] study contract on capability and
survivability in target areas five-week
progress report presented.

Simulated Missions
Preliminary plans for typical short-range
missions prepared.

AQUILINE
~~TOP SECRET~~
~~TOP SECRET~~

Handle via BYEMAN
Control System

C02074113

AQUILINE
ATTACHMENT TO
BYE 9283-71
Page 3

AQUILINE

FOURTH QUARTER FORECAST FY-71

Contract Negotiations   1. May: Definitize FY-72 Program Plans.

2. June: FY-72 contract with prime contractor negotiated and signed.

3. June: Contract for FY-72 air support signed.

Training   Preliminary team (MDAC and OSA) training initiated. FY-72 training program completed and readied for implementation in FY-72.

System Validation   System validation plan ready for implementation.

Flight Planning   1. Initial Flight Plan Module of computer program checked out and running.

2. UNIVAC 9200 Remote Job Entry installed in Tyler providing direct link with Headquarters computers.

AQUILINE
~~TOP SECRET~~
~~TOP SECRET~~

Secy files

Adm - 2.1

~~SECRET~~
AQUILINE

3.3(h)(2)
3.5(c)

BYE-9443-72
Copy _6_ of _14_

MEMORANDUM FOR: Director of Central Intelligence

SUBJECT: Request for Funds for Closeout of AQUILINE Contract
with McDonnell Douglas Astronautics Company

REFERENCE: Memo for DCI from DDS&T, dated 1 November 1971;
Subject: Termination of Project AQUILINE
(BYE-6507-71, Attachment I)

1.   This memorandum contains a request for the approval of the Director
of Central Intelligence. The specific request is contained in paragraph 6.

2.   In accordance with the directive received from the Executive
Director-Comptroller (reference memorandum), the AQUILINE Program was
extended through 15 November 1971 with the funds previously authorized -
$[   ] through 7 November and $[   ] through 15 November. Effective
12 November, MDAC was notified that all planned contract activity was to
cease and they were to prepare their program closeout bid for presentation
and negotiation. On 22 and 23 November, negotiations were conducted at
MDAC which covered: program closeout costs and time; the determination of
contract incentive bonuses allowable under the incentive clauses of the
contract; MDAC fee and associated other open items remaining on Contract[   ]

3.   Attachment II is the negotiated MDAC proposal for program closeout in
the amount of $[   ] In addition to this closeout bid, it was determined
that MDAC was due and should be awarded $[   ] as incentive payment for
satisfactory completion of the tasks as stipulated in Contract[   ] incentive
clauses. Therefore, of the $[   ] authorized by the Executive
Director-Comptroller for terminating the MDAC efforts, only $[   ] will
be required ($[   ] for the contract extension 7 through 15 November
and $[   ] for closeout costs). The following table presents the total
picture on the results of the 22 and 23 November negotiations:

Event or Activity

Contract Value at 30 September 1971 (Less Fee) $[   ]
Contract Extension Thru 31 October 1971
Contract Extension Thru 7 November 1971
Contract Extension Thru 15 November 1971

GROUP 1
Excluded from automatic
downgrading and
declassification

**DD/S&T
FILE COPY**

AQUILINE
~~SECRET~~

HANDLE VIA BYEMAN
CONTROL SYSTEM

SECRET
AQUILINE

BYE-9443-72
Page 2

Event or Activity

Contract Value 15 November (Less Fee) $ [   ]
MDAC Expenditures and Commitments Thru 15 November ___

Contract Funds Available at 15 November $ [   ]

Fee Thru July 31, 1971 as Negotiated
22 November $ [   ]
Fee July 31 Thru 15 November as
Negotiated 22 November   ___

Total Negotiated Fee $
Minus 22 November Disallowed
Costs (Material handling, ops
hourly increase at Field Site,etc.)   ___

                Subtotal $

Balance of Contract Funds Available at 15 November   [   ]
(Funds of $[   ] Minus Fee of $[   ])

Contract Closeout Cost (At No Fee) $ [   ]
Incentive Bonus   ___

                Subtotal $

Additional Funding Required for Closeout and
Incentives ($[   ] Minus $[   ] of
Available Funds) $ [   ]

    4. It is anticipated that all closeout actions of MDAC Contract [   ]
will be completed not later than 15 February 1972.

    5. Contract monitor for this closeout program will be [   ]
[   ]. Security classification of this contract will remain
SC-1.

AQUILINE   HANDLE VIA BYEMAN
SECRET   CONTROL SYSTEM

SECRET
AQUILINE

6. It is specifically requested that you authorize the expenditure of funds in the amount of $188,700.00 for the purpose of closing out Contract ☐ and payment of incentive bonuses of that contract.

CARL E. DUCKETT
Deputy Director
for
Science and Technology

Attachments:
  I and II As Stated

SIGNATURE RECOMMENDED:

Director of Special Activities

1 FEB 1972
—————————————
Date

The request contained in paragraph 6 is approved:

/S/
—————————————————————
Director of Central Intelligence

28 Feb 72
—————————
Date

AQUILINE
SECRET

HANDLE VIA BYEMAN
CONTROL SYSTEM

SECRET
AQUILINE

DPM/AQUI/OSA[   ] (2 December 1971)
Distribution:
 Orig - DPM/AQUI/OSA (w/atts)
    2 - DDCI (w/atts)
    3 - Ex.Dir.-Comptroller (w/atts)
    4 - ER (w/atts)
    5 - DDS&T Chrono (w/atts)
  6&7 - DDS&T Registry (w/o atts)
    8 - SA/DDS&T (w/atts)
    9 - PMS/ORD (w/atts)
   10 - O/PPB/DDS&T (w/atts)
   11 - D/SA (w/atts)
   12 - C/B&FD/OSA (w/atts)
   13 - CMD/OSA (w/atts)
   14 - RB/OSA (w/o atts)

AQUILINE
SECRET

HANDLE VIA BYEMAN
CONTROL SYSTEM

REQUEST TO PROCUREMENT DIVISION FOR SERVICES
(other than property or building maintenance and repairs)   DD/S&T#

OFFICE/DIV/BR	REQUEST NO.	DATE OF REQUEST	I CERTIFY THAT FUNDS IN THE ESTIMATED AMOUNT OF $
DDS&T/OSA/AQUI			AVAILABLE CHARGE TO FAN.
PROJECT TITLE		EXTENSION B- 5682 R- 229	SIGNATURE OF BUDGET OFFICER DATE
AQUILINE			

CONTRACTOR (if known)	PROPOSAL NO. AND DATE	CONTRACT & TASK ORDER NO. (if known)
McDonnell Douglas Astronautics Company	24 Nov 1971	

TYPE OF SERVICE REQUESTED		APPLICABLE ONLY TO REPAIRS AND MODIFICATIONS
X RESEARCH/DEV	TRANSFER OF FUNDS TO OTHER GOVT. AGENCY (specify if applicable)	TECHNICAL INSPECTION IS REQUIRED BY
GRANT		☐ RECEIVING DEPOT T & I ☐ TECHNICAL MONITOR
REPAIR		☐ ITEMS TO BE PICKED UP OR ☐ SERVICES PERFORMED AT:
MAINTENANCE		ITEMS TO BE REDELIVERED TO:
MODIFICATION		

STERILITY	CONTRACT CLASSIFICATION	WORK CLASSIFICATION	HARDWARE CLASSIFICATION	REPORTS CLASSIFICATION
SC 0				
X SC 1	SECRET	SECRET	SECRET	SECRET
SC 2				

SHORT SUBSTANTIVE TITLE AND/OR DESCRIPTION OF SERVICE TO BE PERFORMED

Closeout of MDAC Contract [   ]

Total Closeout Cost After Negotiation $188,700.00

(See reverse for specific information required on R&D requests)

APPROVAL

DESIGNATION	SIGNATURE	DATE
D/SA		25 JAN 1972
A DDS&T		3 FEB 1972
Ex.Dir.-Compt.		28/__/72

PROCUREMENT DIVISION USE

DATE RECEIVED IN PD	RECORDED BY	SECTION ASSIGNED TO	NEGOTIATOR

FORM 2420 REPLACES FORMS 2420 AND 2416 WHICH MAY BE USED.
3-67

UNCLASSIFIED ☐ CONFIDENTIAL ☐ ATTACHMENTS OR STATEMENTS XX SECRET ☐ (specify)

1. JUSTIFICATION FOR SOURCE SELECTION

N/A

2. PROPOSAL

3. DELIVERABLE ITEMS

REPORTS REQUIRED ____ NO. OF COPIES ☐ MONTHLY ☐ INTERIM ☐ QUARTERLY ☒ FINAL

HARDWARE (*state type and number*) All GFE and Contract Purchased Equipment

OTHER All Program Documentation

4. GFE REQUIRED

None

5. SPECIAL INSTRUCTIONS

All Program assets, hardware, documentation, GFE, etc. at contractor's Huntington Beach facility will be packaged and shipped to Area 51 for semi-permanent storage.

☐ UNCLASSIFIED ☐ CONFIDENTIAL XX SECRET ☐ ____ (specify)

REFERRED TO OFFICE	RECEIVED				RELEASED		SEEN BY	
	SIGNATURE	DATE	TIME	DATE	TIME	NAME & OFFICE SYMBOL	DATE
DCI					11/ /		

Handle Via Indicated Controls

BYEMAN

Access to this document will be restricted to those persons
cleared for the specific projects;

....

....

WARNING

This document contains information affecting the national security of the United States within the meaning
of the espionage laws U. S. Code Title 18, Sections 793 and 794. The law prohibits its transmission or
the revelation of its contents in any manner to an unauthorized person, as well as its use in any manner
prejudicial to the safety or interest of the United States or for the benefit of any foreign government to the
detriment of the United States. It is to be seen only by personnel especially indoctrinated and authorized
to receive information in the designated control channels. Its security must be maintained in accordance
with regulations pertaining to BYEMAN Control System.

TOP SECRET

PPB _71-1641_

BYE-6507-71
Copy ,

MEMORANDUM FOR: Director of Central Intelligence

SUBJECT: Termination of Project AQUILINE

1. You will recall that following my preliminary
report to you on the status of AQUILINE, you gave me
guidance to terminate the program because of the high
costs needed in FY 72 and 73 to reach operational
readiness. We have completed our study of how termination
might best be accomplished, and this memorandum defines
two options for your consideration. My recommendation is
contained in paragraph 4.

2. Option I provides for the immediate termination
of the project and storage of all assets. Under this
option, there would be no further expenditures of funds
for aircraft construction, testing, final reports or program
documentation. It will take about two months and $
to implement this option. An additional $ would
allow full program and technical documentation to be
accomplished during the termination period, which would
provide the basis for reactivation and use at some later
date by this or some other organization. Under the original
contract, MDAC is also due approximately $ for payment
of incentives on that contract. Therefore, the total cost
of this option would be $ or, if program documentation
is desired, $.

3. Option II would provide for a four months'
termination period and would cost $ about
$ more than Option I. During this period several
flight tests would be conducted using the in-plant test
facilities and field test assets now in being. It would
also provide full technical documentation. The flight tests
would be conducted at Area 51 over a test range instrumented
with simulated Soviet air defense radars to define radar
detectability and with observers and sensors, to determine

HANDLE VIA BYEMAN
CONTROL SYSTEM ONLY

visual and aural detectability. Additionally these tests
would give us a better understanding of some of the more
important technology such as navigation and command control.
I feel sure we will want to use some of these developed
items in other Agency programs.

4. I would like to put the AQUILINE technology on the
"shelf" in a way that would satisfy us all that we have tied
all the loose ends together and have made it available for
confident assessment for future uses. I therefore recommend
Option II. We had budgeted $ [   ] for the program this
year, of which $ [   ] remains unobligated.

5. This recommendation for termination would not be
complete without reference to the fact that we still have
an important need for a technique for deep penetration for
covert emplacement and technical intelligence collection.
We therefore would like to continue to explore ways to
exploit some of the AQUILINE technology and other system
concepts for using this technology. With your permission,
we will from time to time be proposing the expenditure of
relatively small amounts of money in these areas.

                          Carl E. Duckett
                          Deputy Director
                               for
                        Science and Technology

DCI has approved Option I.
I understand $80,000 was authorized
to carry the project thru 12 Nov 71.
Hence, the total amount authorized
for final termination is $ [   ]

                                   Ex. Dir - Comp
                                   12 Nov 71

NAUTICS COMPANY

SECRET AQUILINE

5301 Bolsa Avenue, Huntington Beach, CA 92647 (714) 896-3311

ROUTING

JWC_____

JOS_____

KB_____

RH_____

JS_____

_____

_____

NOV 24 1971

Subject: CONTRACT [   ] FIRM CPFF PROPOSAL FOR PROGRAM CLOSEOUT

Reference:

Dear Sir:

　　　　Pursuant to prior discussions with the Contracting Officer and in reply to reference TWX, the Contractor is transmitting herewith his firm CPFF proposal covering closeout activities of subject Contract. This proposal consists of an estimated cost of $ [   ]. Details of this proposal are contained in the enclosure.

　　　　The Contractor has prepared this proposal assuming it is additive to the baseline Aquiline Program effort which was concluded on 12 November 1971. Closeout activities were initiated, per Customer direction, on 15 November 1971.

Contracts-Program Control
Special Programs

CMC:pr

Enclosure as noted

cc: [   ] /Program Manager, w/Enclosure

SECRET

DOCUMENT CONTROL
NO. 6664 Copy No. 1

GROUP 1
EXCLUDED FROM AUTOMATIC
DOWNGRADING AND

MCDONNELL DOUGLAS

FIRM CPFF PROPOSAL

FOR

PROGRAM CLOSEOUT

Prepared Under Contract Number [REDACTED]

By

McDonnell Douglas Astronautics Company

Western Division

McDonnell Douglas Corporation
Huntington Beach, California

SECRET AQUILINE

CONTENTS

SECRET

SECRET AQUILINE

SECTION 1

SECRET

SECRET AROLINE

SECRET

SECRET AQUILINE

2-1

SECRET

ACQUILINE

SECTION 4

COST PROPOSAL

SECRET

ADMINISTRATIVE

SECRET

4-3

SECRET

4-4

SECRET

3.5(c)
3.3(h)(2

SECRET

DD/S&T# 1606-68

AQUILINE

16 APR

Executive Registry
68-1876

ADM-12.6

MEMORANDUM FOR: Executive Director-Comptroller

SUBJECT   :   Revised AQUILINE Program

I.   This memorandum contains recommendations for
concurrence. The recommendations are contained in
paragraph IV.

II. Program Review

        A. A comprehensive review and evaluation
of the AQUILINE program objectives, accomplishments
to date, current status, and future prospects has
been conducted by the Directorate of Science and
Technology. This review has included extensive
consultations with the Science and Technology Panel.
As a direct result of this activity, a redirection
of the program appears highly desirable in order to
achieve significantly earlier availability of a truly
operational system. An outline of the recommended
program revision, together with the supporting
rationale, will be developed in this memorandum.

        B. Program History Summary. The program was
initiated in FY 1966 with a 96K study effort to
analyze system requirements, vehicle performance
requirements, and provide preliminary designs.

        1. During 1967 this development program
was hardened and broken into three phases:

                a. Phase 1 (target date August 1968).
Design, fabricate and test a small vehicle
with two cycle engine to verify concept
feasibility.

AQUILINE
SECRET

GROUP 1
Excluded from automatic
downgrading and
declassification

AQUILINE

b. Phase II (target date
December 1969). Design, fabricate
and test a small airplane with
improved subsystems and a four-cycle
engine. Phase II was to demonstrate
a limited operational capability to
[   ].

c. Phase III (target date
mid-FY 1972). Design, fabricate
and test a small bird configured
aircraft with full operational
capability to [   ].

III. The Revised Program

A. In Phase I four test flights with vehicle #1
verified launch, recovery and general handling
feasibility. Vehicle #2 crashed on initial flight in
January 1968. A wiring error was established as the
cause. A thorough program review was then conducted
both in the Directorate and with the S&T Panel to
review concept feasibility and intelligence value
against current and projected requirements. The Panel
was enthusiastic but saw no advantage in proceeding
with Phase II. The Directorate review established a
series of intelligence requirements which could not
be provided by other programs.

1. The Panel concluded that base
technology gave assurance there was no
technical reason not to start immediately
on Phase III.

2. Phase II would not have produced a
bird-like vehicle and would therefore have had
a significantly lower order of penetration
survivability.

3. Proceeding directly to Phase III
would, by establishing a single well-defined
goal, be more efficient from a cost standpoint.

B. The recommended revised development program will
produce the ultimate vehicle. Initial range of [   ]

AQUILINE   Page 2

AQUILINE

will be extended to [   ] simply by microminiaturizing proven subsystems. The airframe would not need redesign

     1. The target flight of the first bird-like vehicle with the ultimate degree of penetration survivability and [   ] range extending as payload weight is reduced would be scheduled for April 1970 -- more than two years ahead of the previous target date.

    C. Program Milestones. In addition to technical milestones, two others have been incorporated to facilitate over-all management decision:

     1. Six months from program start there will be a Preliminary Design Requirements Document permitting a stop-go decision on the basis of capabilities firmly predicted and specified in this document.

     2. There is a design release nine months from start after which the remaining program could go for competitive bids if desirable.

    D. Revised Costs.

     1. 1.3M of the FY 1968 2.6M will be redirected to the air-bird system.

     2. 1.2M of the FY 1969 old Phase II flight testing and support would be similarly redirected.

     3. Proforma cost schedule for [   ] bird-like vehicle capability:

(In Millions)

	FY 66	FY 67	FY 68	FY 69	FY 70	Total
Minima						
Maxima						

These figures include:

    a. Basic vehicle and subsystem development costs.

AQUILINE   Page 3

AQUILINE

b. Ground Control Station prototype (limited operational) development costs.

c. Payload development costs for those items in paragraph above.

4. It is anticipated that expenditures will peak in FY 1969 beyond that year's previously established budget level of [   ] It will then be required to increase funds in that year with a corresponding reduction in funds required in FY 1970 in order to meet cash flow requirements. Total costs through FY 1970 would remain as shown. A Management option that is available would be to slip the first flight milestone from 1 April 1970 to approximately 1 July 1970 in order to allow total application of FY 1970 funds to the first flight milestone.

IV. Recommendations

A. The following actions are recommended as soon as possible in order to start the recommended AQUILINE Operational System development:

1. Authorize FY 1968 prime contract reprogramming.

2. Authorize four-cycle engine development.

3. Authorize Loran navigation receiver development.

4. Authorize 5 mc video recorder development continuation.

5. Approve FY 1967 McDonnell/Douglas overrun.

B. It is noted that the Executive Director-Comptroller has approved 4 and 5 above.

CARL E. DUCKETT
Deputy Director
for
Science and Technology

CONCUR:

Executive Director-Comptroller

22 Apr. 68

AQUILINE

Page 4

TRANSMITTAL SLIP	DATE 22 April 1968

TO: DD/S&T

ROOM NO.	BUILDING HQ	A&'

REMARKS:

Carl:

    Please see DDCI's comment. The stop-go decision to which he refers should be made by DDCI or DCI. Please keep this in mind and arrange a briefing at the appropriate time.

LKW

FROM: Executive Director - Comptroller

ROOM NO.	BUILDING HQ	EXTENSION 6767

FORM NO. 241
1 FEB 55

REPLACES FORM 36-8
WHICH MAY BE USED.

(47)

MEMORANDUM FOR: Exec. Dir.

DDCI comment:

    Paragraph III C. 1. also provides for one more backward glance. By that time the CCPC and Wood studies should provide additional basis for consideration.

    I say let's go ahead with the revised program and look once more at six months from program start as suggested.

/s/ T

22 Apr 68
(DATE)

FORM NO. 101
1 AUG 54

REPLACES FORM 10-101
WHICH MAY BE USED.

(47)

MEMORANDUM FOR: Admiral Taylor

    The attached memorandum was prepared at my request following our briefing of last week on Project AQUILINE. I am inclined to authorize Carl to proceed along the lines he recommends if you agree that this is the right course of action. I think we should not be too concerned at this point in time about the cash flow requirements mentioned in paragraph III. D. 4. We can cross this bridge when we come to it.

L. K. White

19 April 1968

(DATE)

FORM NO. 101   REPLACES FORM 10-101
1 AUG 54   WHICH MAY BE USED.

(47) 3

3.5(c)
3.3(h)(2)

BYE 8767-69
Copy #3 of 4

28 January 1968

MEMORANDUM FOR: Comptroller, OSA

SUBJECT : Transmittal of AQUILINE Program Call FY 71 - FY 75

Forwarded herewith is Project AQUILINE, Program Call for FY 71 - FY 75.

Chief, Communications Division
OSA/DDS&T

Attachment:
As stated

Distribution:
Copy #1 - Compt/OSA w/att
2 - Commo/OSA
3 - RB/OSA
4 - Chrono

Handle Via
BYEMAN
Control System Only

TOP SECRET

GROUP 1
Excluded from automatic downgrading and declassification

CATEGORY   : Communications

SUB-CATEGORY: Operations

ELEMENT   : Domestic Activity

SUB-ELEMENT : AQUILINE

1. PROGRESS TOWARD OBJECTIVES:

During the period Nov 1967 through Dec 1968, OSA Communications
Division maintained a close liaison with ORD in the development of
system parameters needed to design the ground control, staff communications, and data relay systems. A smooth transition from development
phase to operational phase will be accomplished by the ORD/OSA working
group.

2. OBJECTIVES:

To install, operate, and maintain two types of communications
services. ' Provide staff communication circuits from the ground control
station to Headquarters and supplementary communications from the ground
control station to both the launch and recovery sites. Secure teletype
and voice will be provided in the supplementary circuits to facilitate
pre-launch tests and to coordinate recovery operations.

a. Method of Approach

1 Jan 1969 - 30 June 1970: Activity during this period will
be primarily working groups maintaining close liaison until the
test site is activated. When the test site is activated for
flight tests, two communication engineer positions will be required.
These engineers will accomplish the initial hardware orientation
and familiarization to facilitate a smooth transition to operational
use. Early requirements for circuits and terminals in contractor
plants and the test site are expected both prior and during the
flight test period. These contractor communication needs will continue through the entire project period whenever secure communications
are required to support payload designs and operational applications.

FY 1971: The development of an operational capability will
commence with the procurement of staff communications equipment.
Additional supporting circuits are anticipated to both the launch
and recovery sites from the ground control system should either or
both be remoted. The transmission and distribution requirements for
relay of payload data to Headquarters or other field terminals will
require teletype transmission and relay equipment. Six positions
are required to staff the communication positions needed on one
deployment. These positions are: 1 Communications Operations
Officer, 3 technical positions comprised of 2 Engineers and 1
Technician, and 2 Cryptographers.

FY 1972: A second team will be organized and maintained at
the domestic test site to augment the first team and provide a
deployment capability using the ORD funded ground control station.
Testing and operational evaluation work would cease at the domestic
site during the dual deployment. Six additional positions will be
required resulting in a total complement of twelve positions.

FY 1973, 1974 and 1975: No additional positions will be required above those indicated in FY 1973 for communications, assuming
staff and data transmission volumes do not increase. Equipment
funding will be required primarily for augmenting and modifying the
communications systems to accommodate new control and/or payload
devices.

TOP SECRET

HANDLE VIA BYEMAN
CONTROL SYSTEM

b. Coordination and Joint Planning

Coordination is now being effected with ORD for joint planning during the remaining development phase. Joint planning will be established as necessary with other components of CIA to insure proper communications support for this program.

c. Risks Involved

Communications operations are conducted in locations where loss of assets is considered an unlikely event. Support requirements are expected to remain within current communications technology and reliability factors.

d. Alternatives Considered

Four levels of effort were considered for the period FY 70 - 74

The first consideration was attainment of a full operational capability during FY 70.

The second was establishment of a lesser capability during FY 70. Both of these alternatives involved the procurement of sophisticated control and navigations and communications equipment to be funded during FY 69. The funding required was in excess of availability of FY 69 funds. Further, it was questionable that the systems could be developed sufficiently early to enable production during FY 70.

The third alternative considered establishing one mobile unit during FY 70 capable of operating at ranges up to [   ] This would still require the sophisticated relay systems and control equipment which may or may not be available within the time required.

The fourth alternative which is recommended and funding for which is indicated in the assets required section of this call, is to establish a capability during FY 71, to concentrate on training, testing, and development of operational employment concepts. The equipment would be used to control the AQUILINE vehicle and will enable its recovery. This approach further will allow for a steady development program and an orderly transition from development over the years covered by this call.

e. Resources Required (Manpower and Funds):

Summary of Positions and Funds

	FY 68	FY 69	FY 70	FY 71	FY 72	FY 73	FY 74	FY 75
Positions	--	--	--	6	12	12	12	12
Funds								
Pers. Svs.	--	--						
Other	--	--						
Total	--	--						
Leases	--	--						
Contract Support	--	--						
Satellite Terminal Interface --								
Support Commo Equip. 2 ea.	--							
Staff Circuit Terminals	--							
Total	--	--						

The following positions are required to support this activity:

	FY 71	FY 72	FY 73	FY 74	FY 75
Commo Ops	1	2	2	2	2
Technical	3	6	6	6	6
Cryptographer	2	4	4	4	4
Total	6	12	12	12	12

PERSONNEL DESCRIPTIONS

FY-70

ELECTRONIC ENGINEER (Two) (Unfunded)   GS-12

Two electronic engineers are required to study the theory and
techniques used in the ground control systems. Familiarization and
orientation will be required for the transition from R&D to Operational
use.

FY-71

COMMUNICATION OPERATIONS OFFICER (One)   GS-13

Responsible officer performing chief communications' duties
of initiating actions for establishing required circuits, maintains
cryptographic security, and supervises communication complement.

TECHNICAL POSITIONS

ELECTRONIC ENGINEER (Two)   GS-12

Responsible for installation, calibration, and supervise
maintenance of communications systems in ground control system.

ELECTRONIC SEPCIALIST (One)   GS-11

Perform systems test, maintenance, and repairs for all communications systems. Maintain and service all staff and auxiliary
communications equipment.

CRYPTOGRAPHERS (Four: 2 Field; 2 Base)   GS-08 & GS-09

Perform all duties required in processing staff communications
and operate cryptographic devices needed on the support circuits to
the remote launch and recovery sites.

FY-72, 73, 74, 75

All positions are duplicated.

TOP SECRET   HANDLE VIA BYEMAN
                                    CONTROL SYSTEM

☐ 3.3(b)(1)
3.5(c)

BYE 9317-70
Copy _9_ of 12
3 August 1970

MEMORANDUM FOR THE RECORD

SUBJECT: Trip Report B/G Harold F. Knowles to Edwards AFB
and Area 51, 18-24 July 1970

I. Purpose of Trip: Observe Carrier Operations (BLUE GULL VI)

II. Persons Contacted:

Edwards AFB:

Colonel Schamber
Other Base personnel

Kitty Hawk:

Carrier personnel

Area 51:

Other Base personnel

III. Sequence of Events:

Saturday, 18 July:

Departed Andrews AFB via OSA C-118. RON Laredo AFB,
Texas.

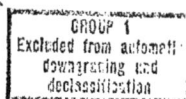

HANDLE VIA BYEMAN
CONTROL SYSTEM

S E C R E T

Sunday, 19 July:

Arrived Edwards AFB. Air Commodore Colin Coulthard, Air Attache, arrived as our guest for BLUE GULL. Dinner hosted by Colonel Schamber.

Monday, 20 July:

Briefings and tour of the Base. Observed preparations for carrier exercise.

Tuesday, 21 July:

Navy aircraft delivered A/C Coulthard, OSA observers, and me to Kitty Hawk by 0900. First U-2R pilots arrived soon afterward, completing four touch-and-go landings and one full stop (trap). As he departed, next pilot arrived, completing four touch-and-go's and two traps. The carrier operated just west of San Clemente Island, approximately 150 miles from Edwards. During the waiting period for the aircraft to make round trip home, refuel, and change to JACKSON crews, we lunched with carrier Executive and Operations officer. The JACKSON crews completed four touch-and-go's and two traps, each. They performed outstandingly, especially considering the additional pressure of maintaining their honor in front of A/C Coulthard. We immediately departed the Kitty Hawk for Edwards, via Navy aircraft, catapulted in fact. A/C Coulthard departed for Los Angeles to spend evening with JACKSONS before boarding airliner for Washington.

Wednesday, 22 July:

Detailed debriefings and critique of BLUE GULL VI.

Thursday, 23 July:

Departed for Area 51. Lunch with [   ] and [   ] Observed test firing of AQUILINE rail for launch speed. Discussed SAC use of Area with [   ] and

BYE 9317-70
Page 3

surveyed facilities extensively.   Cocktail party at "The Club"
and dinner at cafeteria.

Friday, 24 July:

Departed for Andrews AFB.

IV. Summary:

A/C Coulthard:

He was well hosted and enjoyed the opportunity to visit
Edwards and to take part in the operation. He was genuinely
pleased with the JACKSON contribution to the program, and
especially with their outstanding carrier performance - and
rightly so. He is a very knowledgeable and experienced airman
who is a definite asset to our program. I shall cultivate his
interest and friendship to the degree appropriate.

Edwards AFB:

Colonel Schamber's unit performed outstandingly. The one
problem he does have is to overcome the frustration caused by
insufficient operational action. The BLUE GULL exercise was
a shot in the arm. I took the opportunity to talk with the entire
unit, congratulate them, and urge them to stay on top. One minor
U-2R incident on the Kitty Hawk is worthy of note because it
demonstrates the inherent risks involved in spite of optimum
weather, expert crews, and ready aircraft. During a trap, the
pilot retards the throttle and waits for the hook to engage. If
it does not, or he thinks it has not, he advances the throttle
to regain airspeed for another try. If he waits too long, he may
end up in the sea. If the hook engages, advancing the throttle
merely extends his landing roll. Ordinarily this is no problem
for the Navy because their aircraft are designed for this operation.
The U-2R, however, has such a large wingspan that as the
landing roll is increased, more and more of the wing extends
over the angled deck. With the only landing gear being on the
fuselage, the U-2R can easily dip a wing during landing roll.

HANDLE VIA BYEMAN
CONTROL SYSTEM

S E C R E T

The "whiskers" hanging down from the wing tips help just as the "pogos" do during ground taxiing. However, if the aircraft is to the left of centerline during a longer roll, the "whisker" on the left wing tip hangs over the side of the ship and is useless. On the very first trap, the pilot encountered this situation and made contact with the ship's edge. The damage was slight (mere scratching and bending of non-control surfaces) but in the interest of safety we dispatched the pilot after only one trap. His proficiency was unquestioned. The incident was advantageous, however, because it reminded us of the inherent risks of this extraordinary operation. The Navy was greatly impressed and praised our efforts. I believe we can operate off carriers as long as we are so directed, but we must keep in mind the continuing possibility of losses heavier than usual.

Area 51:

Mr. [ ] should prove to be an outstanding member of the AQUILINE team. He briefed me during my previous visit to McDonnell-Douglas and convinced me at that time that he is a strong ally. After only two days at Area 51 he had a handle on everything. We are very fortunate. The rail testing was delayed one day for our benefit. It was successful. The catching net broke again, however, Mr. [ ], OSA AQUILINE Project Officer, is assigned there in an observer capacity to learn, plan, and be prepared to assume project responsibility when we enter the operational phase in January. I made it perfectly clear to everyone that AQUILINE responsibility presently rests with ORD; that Mr. [ ] will provide host services as requested, and that OSA personnel would not interfere. Everyone assured me that there would be no sovereignty problems.

After looking over the Base plans for SAC use and inspecting the present location of SAC equipment and the allocated SAC deployment space, I believe we need to modify our agreement with SAC. I have already initiated this action. The OXCART area is ideal for SAC deployment purposes and would unquestionably be used by them under wartime conditions. Some of their equipment was prepositioned in this area, I believe, in hopes of getting squatters rights because

HANDLE VIA BYEMAN
CONTROL SYSTEM

SECRET

BYE 9317-70
Page 5

we had denied SAC use of some parts of this area. We can
use this area for our continuing projects, e.g., [   ]
for AQUILINE, Hangar 8 for [   ] etc., without prejudicing
SAC's use. Likewise, SAC can rearrange their quantity and
location of prepositioned equipment to afford us the opportunity
to use the facility. I believe we can negotiate a better agreement
which will (1) provide better security to Area 51 by minimizing,
if not eliminating, periodic SAC visits for inspection; (2) provide
SAC a better operational facility in wartime; (3) minimize prepositioned equipment, much of which can and should be used
daily elsewhere, such as starting units, etc. The main SAC
considerations leading to the present agreement were alleged
to be (1) cost; (2) adequacy of facilities, and (3) maintenance
inspections of SAC equipment. If we accede to SAC's wishes
entirely, we could prejudice our security. I believe we can
satisfy them and ourselves if we offer them the best facilities
on a reasonable "hands off" basis.

C-118 Aircraft:

I believe it appropriate to comment on this aricraft, normally
used for cargo airlift with passenger capability. We took along
several of the OSA staff who have business at Edwards AFB and
Area 51 but not of sufficient importance to justify a commercial
airline ticket. By taking a larger contingent, we not only made
better use of the C-118 but gave these people an unprecedented
visit to these places. As a result, they and their counterparts
accomplished much more than can be done via telephone or cable.
Also, the sites were impressed that so many OSA staff members
would take the time to visit them personally. We had fifteen total
on board including the aircrew. I intend to use the C-118 similarly
in the future when appropriate.

HAROLD F. KNOWLES
Brigadier General, USAF
Director of Special Activities

HANDLE VIA BYEMAN
CONTROL SYSTEM

S E C R E T

D/SA/HFKnowles:fMcP
Distribution:
  #1 - D/SA
  #2 - DD/S&T
  #3 - DD/S&T
  #4 - D/M/OSA
  #5 - D/O/OSA
  #6 - D/R&D/OSA
  #7 - Compt/OSA
  #8 - C/SS/OSA
  #9 - C/AMS/OSA
  #10 - C/BFD/OSA
  #11 - D/SA Chrono
  #12 - RB/OSA

HANDLE VIA BYEMAN
CONTROL SYSTEM

S E C R E T

~~TOP SECRET~~

REFERRED TO OFFICE	RECEIVED			RELEASED		SEEN BY	
	SIGNATURE	DATE	TIME	DATE	TIME	NAME & OFFICE SYMBOL	DATE
C/AMS/OSA							

Distribution
AMA/OSA
DAT
JEF
DF
QT
EW
ESA
File   Destroy____
Tickler____   Other____

Handle Via Indicated Controls

BYEMAN

Access to this document will be restricted to those persons cleared for the specific projects;

....

....

WARNING

This document contains information affecting the national security of the United States within the meaning of the espionage laws U. S. Code Title 18, Sections 793 and 794. The law prohibits its transmission or the revelation of its contents in any manner to an unauthorized person, as well as its use in any manner prejudicial to the safety or interest of the United States or for the benefit of any foreign government to the detriment of the United States. It is to be seen only by personnel especially indoctrinated and authorized to receive information in the designated control channels. Its security must be maintained in accordance with regulations pertaining to BYEMAN Control System.

~~TOP SECRET~~

GROUP 1
Excluded from automatic
downgrading and declassification

www.ingramcontent.com/pod-product-compliance
Lightning Source LLC
Chambersburg PA
CBHW050409110426

42812CB00006BA/1837